No Fly Zones and International Security

This book discusses the practice of no fly zones in international affairs.

The first no fly zone was imposed over northern Iraq immediately after the first Gulf War, and since then they have become a regular recourse for policymakers confronted with humanitarian crises. They have come to be viewed as a feasible, essentially non-violent form of intervention that can be performed entirely from the air in a situation where some form of action is widely thought to be necessary, but the political will for a ground operation is insufficient. Nonetheless, even among policy makers there is limited understanding of the requirements, the shortcomings and the potentialities of no fly zones. This is the first comprehensive work on this topic, and examines the assumptions surrounding no fly zones by focusing on issues such as authority, cost, possibility of escalation and effectiveness. Looking back at 25 years of experience with no fly zones, the book's goal is to look at what historical lessons may be drawn and to make some predictions with regard to the politics and strategy of no fly zones in the future.

This book will be of much interest to students of air power, security studies, Middle Eastern Studies and IR in general.

Stephen Wrage is Professor of Political Science at the US Naval Academy. He has written widely on national security affairs and authored *Immaculate Warfare* (2004).

Scott Cooper is a retired lieutenant colonel and has flown hundreds of no fly zone enforcement missions, including the Bosnian and Iraqi no fly zones. He is the National Security Outreach Director at Human Rights First.

Military Strategy and Operational Art

The Routledge Series on Military Strategy and Operational Art analyzes and assesses the synergistic interrelationship between joint and combined military operations, national military strategy, grand strategy, and national political objectives in peacetime, as well as during periods of armed conflict. In doing so, the series highlights how various patterns of civil–military relations, as well as styles of political and military leadership influence the outcome of armed conflicts. In addition, the series highlights both the advantages and challenges associated with the joint and combined use of military forces involved in humanitarian relief, nation building, and peacekeeping operations, as well as across the spectrum of conflict extending from limited conflicts fought for limited political objectives to total war fought for unlimited objectives. Finally, the series highlights the complexity and challenges associated with insurgency and counter-insurgency operations, as well as conventional operations and operations involving the possible use of weapons of mass destruction.

Edited by Professor Howard M. Hensel, Air War College, USA

The Swedish Presence in Afghanistan
Security and Defence Transformation
Edited by Arita Holmberg and Jan Hallenberg

Culture and Defence in Brazil
An Inside Look at Brazil's Aerospace Strategies
Edited by Maria Filomena Fontes Ricco

The Future of US Warfare
Edited by Scott N. Romaniuk and Francis Grice

Limited War in South Asia
From Decolonization to Recent Times
Scott Gates and Kaushik Roy

No Fly Zones and International Security
Politics and Strategy
Stephen Wrage and Scott Cooper

For more information about this series, please visit: https://www.routledge.com/Military-Strategy-and-Operational-Art/book-series/MSOA

No Fly Zones and International Security
Politics and Strategy

Stephen Wrage and Scott Cooper

LONDON AND NEW YORK

First published 2019 by Routledge

2 Park Square, Milton Park, Abingdon, Oxon, OX14 4RN
605 Third Avenue, New York, NY 10017

Routledge is an imprint of the Taylor & Francis Group, an informa business

First issued in paperback 2020

Copyright © 2019 Stephen Wrage and Scott Cooper

The right of Stephen Wrage and Scott Cooper to be identified as authors of this work has been asserted by them in accordance with sections 77 and 78 of the Copyright, Designs and Patents Act 1988.

All rights reserved. No part of this book may be reprinted or reproduced or utilised in any form or by any electronic, mechanical, or other means, now known or hereafter invented, including photocopying and recording, or in any information storage or retrieval system, without permission in writing from the publishers.

Notice:
Product or corporate names may be trademarks or registered trademarks, and are used only for identification and explanation without intent to infringe.

British Library Cataloguing-in-Publication Data
A catalogue record for this book is available from the British Library

Library of Congress Cataloging-in-Publication Data
Names: Wrage, Stephen D., author. | Cooper, Scott A., author.
Title: No fly zones and international security : politics and strategy / Stephen Wrage and Scott Cooper.
Description: First edition. | London ; New York, NY : Routledge/Taylor & Francis Group, 2019. | Series: Military strategy and operational art | Includes bibliographical references and index.
Identifiers: LCCN 2018051768 (print) | LCCN 2018052503 (ebook) | ISBN 9781317087199 (Web PDF) | ISBN 9781317087182 (ePub) | ISBN 9781317087175 (Mobi) | ISBN 9781472452313 (hardback) | ISBN 9781315598383 (e-book)
Subjects: LCSH: No-fly zones. | Humanitarian intervention. | Security, International.
Classification: LCC JZ6368 (ebook) | LCC JZ6368 .W73 2019 (print) | DDC 327.1/17–dc23
LC record available at https://lccn.loc.gov/2018051768

ISBN: 978-1-4724-5231-3 (hbk)
ISBN: 978-0-367-73126-7 (pbk)

Typeset in Times New Roman
by Taylor & Francis Books

Contents

List of tables	vi
Acknowledgements	vii
List of abbreviations	viii
Military operations and no fly zones by order of starting date	ix
Preface	xi
1 About no fly zones	1
2 Iraq	38
3 Bosnia	65
4 Libya	100
5 The politics and prospects for no fly zones	125
Bibliography	153
Index	159

Tables

1.1	Aircraft used in a standard Operation Northern Watch package	15
2.1	Costs of Iraq no fly zone operations	58
3.1	Aircraft used in enforcing Deny Flight	74
4.1	Summary of the coalition forces	109

Acknowledgements

The authors would like to thank Doyle Hodges for his thoughtful, useful and insightful comments and guidance throughout the writing of the book, Mitt Regan for guidance to the literature on ethics of no fly zones, Gustav Meibauer of the London School of Economics for stimulating discussions and creative questions and Captain Sam Neill, US Coast Guard, (Ret.) and more recently of the Chairman of the Joint Chiefs of Staff's Commander's Action Group and the Office of the Chief of Staff of the Air Force for his thoughtful remarks on the strategic purposes of no fly zones.

We especially want to thank the persons who actually commanded no fly zones or were key staff and were tremendously generous with their time. They included

Major General Margaret "Maggie" Woodward, USAF (Ret.)
Lieutenant General Ralph J. "Dice" Jodice, Jr., USAF (Ret.)
General Michael E. Ryan, USAF (Ret.)
General Sir Hugh Michael "Mike" Rose, Royal Army (Ret.)
General Sir Rupert Anthony Smith, Royal Army (Ret.)
Admiral Leighton W. "Snuffy" Smith, USN (Ret.)
Vice Admiral Charles J. "Joe" Leidig, USN (Ret.)
General Anthony C. Zinni, USMC (Ret.)
Ambassador Ivo H. Daalder.

Abbreviations

AAA	anti-aircraft artillery
ATO	air tasking order
AWACS	airborne warning and Control System
CAOC	combined air operations center
CAP	combat air patrol
CAS	close air support
CDE	collateral damage estimate
CSAR	combat search and rescue
IADS	integrated air defense system
ISR	intelligence, surveillance and reconnaissance
KLA	Kosovo Liberation Army
KVM	Kosovo Verification Mission
MANPADS	man-portable air defense system
NATO	North Atlantic Treaty Organization
NFZ	no-fly zone
OAF	Operation Allied Force
OCA	Offensive Counter Air
ODF	Operation Deny Flight (also Operation Deliberate Force)
ONW	Operation Northern Watch
OOD	Operation Odyssey Dawn
OSW	Operation Southern Watch
OUP	Operation Unified Protector
POL	petroleum, oil & lubricants
ROE	rules of engagement
SAM	surface to air missile
SEADS	suppression of enemy air defense systems
UNPROFOR	UN Protective Force (in the former Yugoslavia)
UNSCOM	United Nations Special Commission on Iraq
UNSCR	United Nations Security Council Resolution

Military operations and no fly zones by order of starting date

Operation	Authorization	States involved	Location	Dates
Mole Cricket 19		Israel	Bekaa Valley	1982
Desert Storm	UNSCR 678	US & Coalition	Iraq	1990–1991
Haven	UNSCR 688	Britain	Northern Iraq	1991
Provide Comfort I	UNSCR 688	US & Coalition	Iraq & Turkey	1991
Provide Comfort II	UNSCR 688	US & Coalition	Iraq & Turkey	1991–1996
Southern Watch	UNSCR 688	US & Coalition	Southern Iraq	1992–2003
Sky Monitor	UNSCR 781	NATO	Bosnia	1992–1993
Deny Flight	UNSCR 816	NATO	Bosnia	1993–1995
Vigilant Warrior 1994	UNSCR 688	US & Coalition	Iraq	October 1994
Deliberate Force		US & Coalition	Bosnia	August 1995
Desert Strike		US & Coalition	Northern Iraq	1996
Northern Watch		US & Coalition	Northern Iraq	1997–2003
Desert Fox		US & Coalition	Iraq	December 1998
Allied Force	UNSCR 1199	US & NATO	Kosovo	1999
Iraqi Freedom		US & Coalition	Iraq	2003–2010
New Dawn		US & Coalition	Iraq	2010–2011
Unified Protector	UNSCR 1973	US & NATO	Libya	2011
Odyssey Dawn	UNSCR 1973	US	Libya	2011

Operation	Authorization	States involved	Location	Dates
Hartmattan		France	Libya	2011
Ellamy		UK	Libya	2011
Mobile		Canada	Libya	2011

*Operations Odyssey Dawn, Harmattan, Ellamy and Mobile were the US, French and Canadian designations respectively for their participation in Operation Unified Protector.

Preface

Even after a quarter century of experience and operations on three continents, no fly zones remain poorly understood. They are commonly called for – every humanitarian crisis since 1990 has brought demands that one be imposed – but what they can accomplish or even how they actually work has never been clearly stated anywhere. The literature on no fly zones is thin[1] and amounts to a few good studies produced by places like RAND and the Congressional Research Service, a half dozen scholarly papers and law review articles and a somewhat larger number of commentaries that have appeared on national security web sites.[2] To produce a more extensive and substantial study than any to date, the authors relied on interviews with senior officers who planned and directed no fly zones[3] and on the experience of one of the authors who flew in the enforcement of several no fly zones.[4]

All observations on the workings of no fly zones must be drawn from only three cases since no fly zones have been implemented in only three locations, Iraq, Bosnia and Libya, and in the case of Libya only very briefly. Even if the record of no fly zones is thin, however, it is largely positive. The first experience with them arose from a hasty, *ad hoc* measure instituted at the end of Operation Desert Storm in 1991, but that quick and improvisational response was extended and re-extended for over a decade and ultimately, 12 years later, morphed into a bombing campaign to shape the battlespace for the invasion of Iraq. (These events are described in Chapter 2.) No fly zones were imposed again over Bosnia in 1992 in a more complicated setting that exposed the great difficulty of coordinating two organizations, NATO, which was operating in the air, and the United Nations, which was operating on the ground. (That uneven sequence of events is explored in Chapter 3.) A third no fly zone was established over Libya in 2011, but almost from the first moment it escalated into a large air offensive rather than a no fly zone. Finally, no fly zones were called for many times over Darfur and over Syria but none was ever imposed. (For Darfur, Libya and Syria, see Chapter 4.)

All of these instances were responses to humanitarian atrocities, but there is no reason that in the future no fly zones will be applied only to such occasions. If, as appears likely, the third decade of the twenty-first century is destined to feature the US searching for ways to translate military power into political influence while avoiding committing large numbers of ground troops, no fly zones may again be turned to, and for other than humanitarian purposes (see Chapter 5.)

Operations Northern and Southern Watch in Iraq and Operation Deny Flight in Bosnia at least established that no fly zones can be relatively cheap, very low-risk measures that the US can easily undertake in cooperation with other powers. These operations never taxed the limits of American air power, they never raised serious resistance in the American public, they never proved to be slippery slopes to deeper invention and they never led to major loss of life. In fact, no American life has ever been lost to enemy action in the enforcement of a no fly zone. Far from being burdensome, intrusive or unpopular, no fly zones actually operated for months at a time with little or no notice being taken in the American press, and they were never difficult to terminate. They always came to a close with little debate over how to disengage, no fears of the consequences of departure and no calls for a "decent interval" to follow withdrawal. Precisely because they have proven useful but not terribly consequential, either for good or for ill, they have attracted no great opponents and no strong proponents. They have never proven particularly controversial.

On the other side of the ledger, no one could look at the record and say no fly zones offer a comprehensive response to a humanitarian emergency, or to any other situation. They certainly do not amount to a strategy; they are no more than a certain limited way to use force from the air.[5] Nonetheless, their limited nature, their low risk and low cost and the confidence decision makers have that they can keep them limited make them potentially attractive measures, especially when other measures carry more cost and more risk.

Experience has also shown that a no fly zone alone is not likely to be effective unless it is paired with other measures. Usually that means the commitment of ground forces, and even then, the ground forces must be adequate to the task. The failure to coordinate effective ground forces with a no fly zone resulted in the July 1995 Srebrenica massacre which took place while Operation Deny Flight carried on ineffectually overhead. The meager UN ground forces nearby and the distant aircraft thousands of feet overhead did no more than stand by while Serbian forces murdered more than 8,000 helpless Bosnians.

Even enthusiasts for the equivocal practice of "message sending" by military means ultimately find no fly zones unsatisfying since, ironically, the content of the message in time reveals itself to be "our commitment to this cause was inadequate to do more than send air patrols over the region."

In sum, what can be said for no fly zones? In the 1990s, in an era when the US was reluctant to involve itself in another humanitarian intervention like the one that ended badly in Somalia in 1993, no fly zones offered a way to act, albeit in a minimal way, without great cost or risk when pressure from popular opinion insistently called for some response, but the judgment of the civilian and military decision makers weighed against substantial intervention. No fly

Preface xiii

zones offered a limited, containable, cautious response when some response was required. When the pressure for intervention became irresistible, they offered, in short, a way not to do nothing.

Organization of the book

This opening chapter provides an overview of no fly zones and addresses matters of definition, outlines the varieties of no fly zones, lays out what they require and describes how they work and what they can do.

Chapter 2 looks in detail at the first pair of no fly zones, Provide Comfort/ Northern Watch and Southern Watch, which functioned over Iraq from the end of Operation Desert Storm until the beginning of Operation Iraqi Freedom.

Chapter 3 examines the many contrasts between the Iraq no fly zones and Sky Monitor and Deny Flight, no fly zones, which operated over Bosnia Herzegovina in the mid-1990s.

Chapter 4 assesses three instances in which the no fly zone option might have been applied but was not: Darfur, Libya and Syria.

Chapter 5 lays out the ethics, politics and prospects for no fly zones.

Notes

1 There is, to date, surprisingly little written on the subject of no fly zones. In fact, a google search on the phrase "no fly zones" in 2014 at the start of this project actually brought up among the first five hits an advertisement for screen doors.
2 For a list of sources on no fly zones, see Chapter 5.
3 The authors benefited greatly from interviews with the following persons: Major General Margaret Woodward, US Air Force, Lieutenant General Ralph Jodice, US Air Force, General Sir Hugh Michael Rose, British Army, General Sir Rupert Smith, British Army, Admiral Leighton Smith, US Navy, Vice Admiral Charles J. Leidig, US Navy, US Ambassador to NATO Ivo Daalder and General Anthony Zinni, US Marine Corps. Please see also the list of sources at the conclusion of this volume.
4 One of the authors, Lieutenant Colonel Scott Cooper, USMC (Ret.), served as a member of the aircrew of an electronic counter measures plane, the EA-6B Prowler, in the enforcement of Operations Northern Watch, Southern Watch and Deny Flight.
5 In writing this book, the authors have taken care to avoid the sloppy practice of op-ed writers who call no fly zones a strategy. A no fly zone is not a strategy. It is better described as an option, a tactic or a tool.

On the authors

The authors are a political scientist who has specialized in the formation of American foreign-policy and a retired Marine Lieutenant Colonel who flew in Northern Watch, Southern Watch, Allied Force and Deny Flight and who deployed five times to Iraq and twice to Afghanistan. The authors intend the book to be a combination of the theoretical and the practical, containing the lessons from both scholarship and experience.

This work contains the views of the authors only and does not represent the views of the Naval Academy, the Department of Defense, the Marine Corps or any other organization.

Dedication

The authors dedicate this book to Maggie McNamara and Alexandra Wrage.

1 About no fly zones

Matters of definition

What is a no fly zone?[1] In simplest terms, a no fly zone is an airspace from which the sovereign power has been excluded.[2] The target country's airspace has been seized, and its government has been denied the use of its air assets over its own land. The targeted power may have been barred or deterred, which is to say it may have been physically prevented from flying or it may have been persuaded not to fly by threats of punishment, but either way the airspace of a sovereign power has been usurped.[3]

Who seizes the airspace? In theory, a no fly zone can be imposed by any state on any state. In practice, the entity imposing a no fly zone has always been the United States, although the United States has never acted alone and has always been part of a coalition of some kind with international authorization of some sort. The countries that have been excluded from their own airspaces have in every case to date been dictatorships whose rulers have been in the midst of committing atrocities. This fact has put a favorable, humanitarian, law-enforcing cast on no fly zones, at least in the eyes of Americans and their coalition partners who have shared in enforcing them. In the future, other powers may very well impose no fly zones on other sorts of entities with other sorts of objectives and no fly zones may take on a different aspect and reputation. For example, China may be in the preliminary stages of imposing a no fly zone, or at least a "limited-fly zone" over parts of the western Pacific with its recently proclaimed "Air Defense Identification Zone."[4]

What is new about no fly zones? Of course, every state that could do so has always defended its airspace much the way it has defended its land and its nearby seas. In time of war, one state has always attempted to deprive its opponent of the use of its airspace just as it has sought to seize its territory or to block its ports. What is new about no fly zones and what makes them different from the traditional contest for air superiority and control is a coalition possessing superior air power banning flights into, out of, or over the territory of a power that has been engaging in humanitarian atrocities. This sort of no fly zone, imposed by a coalition, authorized by a multilateral organization and, to this point at least, aimed against gross violators of human rights, is

2   *About no fly zones*

the central focus of this book, but other sorts of no fly zones could and probably will exist. That possibility is discussed in Chapter 5.

No fly zones differ from prohibited zones. Within a single state, a sort of limited no fly zone may be established for security reasons, such as the no fly zone over the White House or over certain military bases.[5] For example, a no fly zone briefly was declared over the Republican National Convention in Cleveland in 2016, banning planes and drones from flying over the convention center, mostly for security reasons but perhaps also because the organizers feared the aircraft would be trailing political messages on banners. Such domestic no fly zones, better called "prohibited zones," lie outside the scope of this book. This book is concerned with the no fly zones created by one or several states over another sovereign state.[6]

No fly zones compared to naval blockades

A no fly zone is the aerial cousin of a naval blockade and the two practices are in many ways parallel. Naval blockades have been a factor in war since the time of Thucydides, no fly zones only since 1991, but exploring their characteristics may shed light on both.

Both consist of establishing an exclusion zone. Both involve patrols and impose the condition that if a vessel – ship or plane – ventures into the forbidden region, it will be subject to escort, attack, seizure or destruction. Both can be imposed simply by positioning forces in such a way as to pose the threat of violence, but neither may necessarily require violence unless the promise or threat of force is followed by an act of force, triggered by an act of resistance or other form of challenge by the target state.

While the state that imposes the no fly zone creates the situation, it is an act by *the target state* that will trigger the act of violence. Because of the terms dictated by the powers that impose them, no fly zones and naval blockades in some degree shift the responsibility for triggering specific acts of violence onto the target state. No fly zones are certainly aggressive acts in the sense that they violate sovereignty, and they depend on the potential for immediate or near-term violence, but they do not require that the imposing state commit acts of violence at the outset.[7] For this reason, they are usually the most measured and limited option available to policy makers along the spectrum of possible uses of force. If kinetic force must be used as part of the process of imposing a no fly zone, it is likely to be in response to what will appear to be a provocation by the targeted state, which is ironic since the imposition of the no fly zone is certainly a provocation in itself.

Both no fly zones and blockades typically include clear directives regarding what sorts of planes or ships may conduct what sorts of operations. For example, commercial traffic may be permitted when military missions are forbidden. Passenger planes or ships may be permitted when war planes and ships are banned from the space. In addition, clear rules of engagement typically are issued to the enforcing agents, but experience has shown that rules of engagement can be difficult to formulate in advance because of the many unforeseen circumstances and varying (and sometimes wavering) levels of commitment by the set of powers imposing the no fly zone.

Like a blockade, a no fly zone can be imposed separately from other acts of war and can be maintained for long periods. Experience shows that the powers that establish a no fly zone should be prepared to maintain it for a matter of months, years or even for the span of a decade, and the fact that no fly zones have been imposed for so long underlines the twin facts that they are neither very expensive to maintain nor very efficient in effecting change. Both a blockade and a no fly zone can in many cases be imposed without establishing a physical presence in the target state and both can usually be policed without bringing into danger the population of the target state and without subjecting the imposer's forces to more than moderate risk.[8] All this makes no fly zones very enticing to the policy makers in democracies like the United States, Britain and other countries with advanced air capabilities, political accountability and low tolerance for casualties.

No fly zones compared to ground occupations

While an occupying army is a perpetual insult and imposition on a population whose state has been invaded, a naval blockade or a no fly zone may be imposed by ships and planes that, because they are offshore or at high altitude, are rarely observed by the public. Robert Pape has demonstrated the provocativeness of ground occupations; In *Dying to Win* [9] he marshals evidence that suicide bombings are carried out almost always by persons in occupied lands and aimed at driving out the occupiers. No fly zones have never stimulated anything approaching such responses.

Over a decade and a half of American experience in Iraq and Afghanistan has shown how difficult it is to preserve ground-based troops from suicide attacks and from improvised explosive devices. The experience of the USS Princeton, a guided missile cruiser damaged by a mine in the Persian Gulf during Operation Desert Storm in February 1991, demonstrates that not only land forces but also naval vessels remain vulnerable to prepositioned explosive devices. Land troops and ships can be put at risk by passive devices like mines, but planes cannot be put at risk in the same way. Apart from marginally useful barrage balloons in World War II, prepositioned static devices have never been successful ways of putting planes at risk; nor, in the past, have unmanned ground-based weapons. Putting planes patrolling at altitude at risk has only been accomplished with actively aimed and fired anti-aircraft artillery or missiles. Such weapons systems use radar-targeting systems that give away the operator's approximate position and make the site vulnerable to a counterstrike with a high-speed, anti-radiation missile. That fundamental difference in patrolling from the air versus patrolling on the ground or patrolling at sea makes seizure of the air substantially less risky than seizure of the sea or the ground.

4 *About no fly zones*

Two no fly zones over Iraq operated for a dozen years with no loss of life due to enemy action and at such low cost and low profile that few Americans even remarked on their existence.[10] The record of media coverage of the no fly zone over Bosnia likewise suggests that from the point of view of the population of the imposing country, no fly zones may prove so easily sustainable and so completely uneventful as to pass practically unnoticed.

Instances of no fly zones

No fly zones have been imposed and sustained on only two occasions and on each occasion it was against a dictator abusing his people: the first was imposed on Saddam Hussein in the aftermath of Operation Desert Storm in 1991. The second was levied against Slobodan Milosevic over Bosnia and Herzegovina during his so-called "ethnic cleansing" operations in 1993. Operation Odyssey Dawn/Unified Protector, directed against Muammar Qaddafi in Libya in 2011 is often cited as a third no fly zone, but this is inaccurate. Odyssey Dawn/Unified Protector was an offensive air campaign that began with a brief interval of no fly zone enforcement. The United Nations authorized a no fly zone in UN Security Council Resolution 1973, and US Africa Command in concert with allied militaries implemented one labeled Odyssey Dawn, but within days NATO took over the operation, renamed it Operation Unified Protector, and used the fact that the Security Council had authorized "all necessary measures ... to protect civilians and civilian-populated areas ... excluding a foreign occupation force"[11] to convert the no fly zone into an air campaign that ended only with Qaddafi's death and regime change.

Iraq: Operations Provide Comfort/Northern Watch and Southern Watch

The first no fly zone was implemented over Iraq immediately after the end of Operation Desert Storm in 1991. At the signing of a ceasefire and surrender on 3 March, General Norman Schwarzkopf granted the request of an Iraqi general that the defeated military be allowed to use its helicopters for transportation, since many roads and bridges had been destroyed. On the spot and without consultation with Washington, Schwarzkopf declared that fixed-wing planes would remain grounded but that helicopters could fly. In this *ad hoc* way, without discussion or planning, the first no fly zone was established.

Almost at once Saddam began to use his helicopters, many of which were heavily armed, not for transport but to suppress uprisings among the Kurdish and Shi'ite minorities. President Bush had expressly called for those uprisings two weeks before, but in his desire to bring home the 500,000 troops deployed in Kuwait and Iraq, chose to ignore Saddam's brutal response. By contrast, the British responded to the crisis of the Kurds in northern Iraq by establishing Operation Haven, clearing Iraqi troops out of a safe space in northern Iraq and delivering food, tents, medicines and clothing to refugees located there. After a few weeks the British effort was supplemented by American, French and Turkish forces, the operation was renamed Provide Comfort, and the United States led the way in establishing a no fly zone to exclude Iraqi air power, both fixed-wing and rotary-wing, from the region. In that way the no fly zone that began with Schwarzkopf's proclamation was implemented and would remain in place for a dozen years.

Sixteen months later a second no fly zone named Southern Watch was established to protect Iraq's Shi'ite minority in the region of Basra. Northern Watch patrolled north of the 36th parallel; Southern Watch patrolled south of the 32nd parallel and later the 33rd. Northern Watch was enforced primarily out of Incirlik, Turkey. Southern Watch was enforced primarily out of Dhahran, Saudi Arabia until later, after the Khobar Towers attack, operations were relocated to Prince Sultan Air Base in a remote area near the center of the country.

Southern Watch was less effective at excluding Iraqi forces than Northern Watch, though in both cases, the Iraqis never utilized their air force to any tactical effect on the ground. It was more frequently challenged and evaded, and it required more enforcement. Northern Watch was enforced for 12 years with about 75,000 sorties. Southern Watch was enforced for a slightly shorter period with about 150,000 sorties. As the next chapter explains, a great difference between the two no fly zones was that the terrain to the north provided more protection to the Kurds, while the terrain to the south left the Shi'ites open to Iraqi ground attacks, though not from the air. In no fly zones, geography matters.

With regard to Northern and Southern Watch, several points about no fly zones in general are worth noting:

- Air defenses: Iraq's integrated air defense systems had already been destroyed in the weeks of air bombardment that preceded the ground invasion in 1991 so that crucial first step in implementing a no fly zone – the suppression of the target country's air defenses – had already been accomplished.
- Multilateral authorization: United Nations authorization for multilateral action against Iraq had been secured the previous November in the form of UN Security Council Resolution 678. Thus another crucial step in the creation of a no fly zone – multilateral authorization – was already in place.
- Nearby air base: As part of its participation in Operation Desert Storm, Turkey had provided access to its air base at Incirlik,[12] so a nearby operating base for Operation Northern Watch had already been secured. A no fly zone can be enforced from a distance by planes launched from carriers or from distant air bases, but such a remotely enforced no fly zone requires that pilots and aircraft spend many hours in the air and take many in-flight refuelings.

6 *About no fly zones*

- Resistance from policy makers: The creation of a no fly zone always raises the prospect of further involvement in a conflict and so raises concerns about entanglement and mission creep, but the ad hoc and sudden way the no fly zone in Iraq was created at the ceasefire ceremony preempted resistance.
- Geographic advantage: The Kurds enjoyed a natural sanctuary in the mountains, once Saddam had been deprived of his air assets. The Shi'ites enjoyed no such sanctuary, and Operation Southern Watch did little to protect them. While primarily justified as a measure for their protection, Operation Southern Watch functioned largely as a way to monitor, challenge and pressure Saddam Hussein.
- Prepositioned assets: Years later, in December 1998, when Saddam interfered with and resisted the UN-mandated weapons inspections under Richard Butler, the planes and personnel were already in place and US Central Command's General Anthony Zinni could easily execute four days of bombing of weapons research centers, supply depots, the barracks and command headquarters of Saddam's Republican Guard and even one of Saddam's palaces.
- Intelligence, surveillance and reconnaissance: Operation Northern Watch and Operation Southern Watch were rich opportunities for making detailed inventories, studies and maps of Saddam's defensive and offensive assets. Many of those assets were destroyed as part of enforcement actions for the no fly zones; most of the rest were eliminated in the attacks that shaped the battlespace as the no fly zones transformed into the offensive air campaign that launched Operation Iraqi Freedom.

Bosnia: Operations Sky Monitor and Deny Flight

The second no fly zone was imposed via a much more formal process than the first. In October 1992, the UN Security Council responded to violence following the break-up of Yugoslavia with a resolution that barred military flights in the air space over Bosnia-Herzegovina (UNSCR 781.) The UN did not authorize force to back up that prohibition however, and between October 1992 and April 1993, Operation Sky Monitor documented more than 500 violations by Bosnian Serb aircraft. In a second resolution in April 1993 (UNSC Resolution 816), the Security Council authorized NATO to implement Operation Deny Flight to use force to back up the unenforced no fly zone created seven months before. Both fixed-wing and rotary-wing flights were banned.

In contrast to the no fly zones over Iraq that were organized and carried out by a single and unified command, the operations in Bosnia were conducted by two, the United Nations and NATO, who acted in less than complete concert. On the ground in Bosnia were the forces of UNPROFOR, the United Nations Protection Force. In the air were the planes of NATO's Operation Deny Flight. The hope (and it was more a hope than a strategy) was that aircraft from Deny Flight would provide presence, strikes, and close air support to assure the safety of the UN ground forces. As events developed over a span of three years, Deny Flight only irregularly enhanced the security of UNPROFOR. Instead, on several occasions UNPROFOR troops were seized and threatened with death by Bosnian Serb forces if the strikes by Deny Flight were not lifted. In one instance UN soldiers were chained to artillery that NATO aircraft had been tasked to destroy. The series of no fly zones in Bosnia had its successes, however. Operation Deliberate Force in August and September 1995 almost certainly provided leverage that brought Milosevic to participate in the negotiations that led to the Dayton Accords. In over 50,000 missions, two NATO planes were shot down and two suffered mechanical failures but no aircrew were lost in any of these incidents. Four Bosnian Serb aircraft were destroyed early in the no fly zone enforcement.

Libya: Operation Odyssey Dawn

The third no fly zone, which was directed against the air assets of Libya's Muammar Qaddafi, began at the initiative of powers in the region working through the Gulf Cooperation Council and the Arab League. The United Nations picked up on their lead and produced UNSCR 1973 on 17 March 2011. For about a month prior to that, Qaddafi had been using jets and helicopter gunships to indiscriminately bomb, strafe and send missiles into areas in and around the city of Benghazi where rebel forces were strongest. The resolution specifically called for a no fly zone to ground Qaddafi's air force but also generally endorsed "all necessary means" to protect civilians.

Qaddafi had been flagrantly brutal in the way he used force not just from the air but on the ground as well, so this authorization to defend noncombatants was viewed by the intervening coalition as wide-ranging permission to destroy not only all of his air defenses, planes and helicopters, but also his ground forces, vehicles, artillery, armored transport and other assets. Air strikes originating in Italy, Greece, France and carrier forces in the Mediterranean destroyed Libya's surface-to-air missiles and antiaircraft artillery within hours and within three days all aspects of Libya's military had been brought under heavy attack. By the end of the third day, Qaddafi's own palace compound in Tripoli had been devastated.

Given its aggressive character, it is wrong to characterize Odyssey Dawn as a simple no fly zone operation. It might be more accurately described as the prelude to a comprehensive air campaign. Although Operation Odyssey Dawn officially terminated within two weeks, the program of airstrikes named Operation Unified Protector continued for eight months and terminated only with Qaddafi's death in October 2011.

By that point over 25,000 air missions had been flown, about 10,000 of them strike sorties. The operation cost no lives among the enforcers and likely saved thousands of Libyans from Qaddafi's brutalities. For several years after its conclusion in late 2011, it was held up as a model for the kind of intervention that might constrain Assad of Syria and save Syrian lives, but the violent anarchy that followed Qaddafi's death cast the intervention in a much less favorable light.

Varieties of no fly zones

Passive sky monitors or violent seizures of airspace

Experience with no fly zones has been quite limited, but even in the few occasions on which they have been used they have ranged in form from passive and unobtrusive sky monitoring operations at the pacific end of the spectrum to the violent seizure and sustained occupation and exploitation of a country's airspace at the warlike end. In between there are many possible variations aimed at limiting different kinds of aircraft, promising different kinds of enforcement measures and destroying different types and quantities of the target's assets and air defenses.

Formal or informal

No fly zones may be formal or informal. They may begin with a declaration by a coalition of states imposing a flight ban on certain kinds of aircraft in certain geographic areas on certain dates, or they may start as *de facto* no fly zones imposed by a single state by means of an unannounced use of force. Russia, for example, may be said to have imposed a *de facto* no fly zone over eastern Ukraine simply by supplying pro-Russian separatists with anti-aircraft weapons. A Russian surface-to-air missile was used to destroy Malaysian Airlines Flight 17 on 17 July 2014, killing 298 innocents, and commercial airlines have avoided that airspace since then. Nor has the government of Ukraine freely used the airspace over the Donbass region.

No fly zones may apply only to military aircraft, only to commercial aircraft or to both. Only fixed-wing aircraft may be controlled or rotary-wing aircraft may be ruled out as well, though the practical difficulties of implementing a no fly zone for helicopters are greater than for fixed-wing.

Air defense systems evaded, suppressed or destroyed

No fly zones may begin with the suppression of the enemy air defense systems or with their complete destruction, or they may be implemented with the enemy's air defenses left intact. In the no fly zones over Iraq, the air defense systems had already been destroyed in Operation Desert Storm. In the no fly zone over Libya, the air defense systems were destroyed on the first day. In the no fly zone over Bosnia, however, they never were destroyed because the Serbs might have retaliated against UN ground troops in the area and because the mobile surface-to-air missile systems of the Serbs were difficult to locate in mountainous terrain covered by dense vegetation. The pilots over Bosnia flying enforcement missions stayed above the range of anti-aircraft artillery and carefully threaded their way between the envelopes of known surface-to-air missile systems.

Enforced constantly or intermittently

No fly zones may be enforced constantly or intermittently. Deny Flight, the no fly zone over Serbia, required constant air patrolling and subjected pilots to greater risk than Odyssey Dawn, the no fly zone over Libya which, after the initial destruction of Qaddafi's air assets and air defense system, required little enforcement and involved limited risk. The enforcement in Iraq was never constant, and the timing was also subject to the approval of Turkey and Saudi Arabia, who controlled the use of their own air space for the transit of no fly zone aircraft.

Punitive measures immediate or delayed

The enforcement of a no fly zone may be pursued by means of immediate responses to violations or by measures executed at a time and place of the imposing powers' choosing. Pursuing the second course of action obviously greatly reduces the burden of no fly zone enforcement. As noted above, a no fly zone need not be enforced 24 hours per day and seven days per week. Operation Northern Watch, for example, was for the majority of its existence enforced only 17 days out of every month, (Turkey allowed coalition forces use of their air base at Incirlik from which enforcement missions were flown only at that tempo, and that proved sufficient.) If, as was sometimes the case, Iraqi forces entered the air space in the banned zone, the coalition made note of the act and in some cases later destroyed a missile launch platform or other asset on the ground in reprisal.

No fly zones that involve sanctuaries

Some no fly zones have involved sanctuaries protected from the air. This proved feasible in Iraq where a sanctuary in the north for the Kurds was created and protected by a large deployment of troops.[13] The "safe zones" in Bosnia concurrent with Operation Deny Flight proved impossible to protect with the small numbers of ground forces in the area.

No fly zones have shown a tendency to morph with time from passive observation to active enforcement and from relatively restrictive policies to fairly permissive and more punitive ones. The no fly zones in Iraq and Bosnia moved from passive to active and from surveillance to coercion; the no fly zone over Libya evolved much more rapidly. By the third day in Libya it had ceased to be a no fly zone at all and had become essentially indistinguishable from an all-out offensive air campaign.

Combat air patrol vs offensive counter air no fly zones

Karl Mueller, author of the best study to date of no fly zones,[14] identifies two models for no fly zone enforcement, the combat air patrol or CAP model and the offensive counter air or OCA model. The no fly zones over Iraq and over Bosnia followed the combat air patrol model while the no fly zone over Libya followed the offensive counter air model, he explains.

Under the combat air patrol model, the no fly zone is enforced by patrols that intercept, identify, then record, chase away or shoot down violating planes, depending on the rules of engagement. Planes under the combat air patrol model may also, again depending on the rules of engagement, attack enemy air defenses, particularly if they activate their radar targeting systems, or evade them by flying outside the envelopes of their missile systems or by flying at altitudes beyond their reach. This model of combat-air-patrol-based no fly zone requires more constant patrolling.[15]

The no fly zone over Libya, Mueller explains, followed the offensive counter air model and began with massive attacks on aircraft, air bases, air defense systems, fuel supplies, maintenance facilities, pilots' and crews' barracks and the roads leading to those facilities.

A no fly zone on the Iraq and Bosnia model represents a smaller initial investment of forces and involves much less initial destruction, but it may require essentially endless enforcement – what is sometimes called "the perpetual patrol problem." A no fly zone on the Libya model requires a massive initial effort but, assuming that effort is successful, should not require much maintenance enforcement.

The authors view this distinction as misleading, since they cannot see a substantial difference between an offensive counter air no fly zone and an outright air campaign against all air-related assets. To call Operation Odyssey Dawn/Unified Protector a no fly zone of any kind is to cloak an outright attack with the label of a restrained operation aimed at limiting a regime's ability to harm its own people.

Requirements for no fly zones

Imposing and enforcing a no fly zone is a demanding air operation, but it is also a routine one that consists of repeatedly performing a predictable flying regimen which is likely to be considerably less taxing than an equal number of unique sorties.

Authorization

Before military operations in a formal no fly zone can begin, diplomatic authorization must be secured and that may be the most difficult and certainly the most time-consuming element of launching a no fly zone. All of the no fly zones to date have been authorized by the United Nations, or by a multinational institution like NATO or the Arab League.

Such authorization takes diplomatic resources and effort and considerable time to secure. United Nations authorization was never obtainable before 1989 when the collapse of the Soviet Union meant the end of its regular veto over operations championed by the United States or its NATO allies, and the window of collaboration probably has closed with the return of more oppositional relations between the US and both Russia and China over the past decade.

Resources, diplomatic and military

Even the most passive and limited of no fly zones, Operation Sky Monitor (Bosnia, 1992–1993), required considerable military resources plus substantial diplomatic resources in order to secure authorization from the UN, the cooperation from NATO and the contribution of operating bases by Hungary, Greece and Italy. In an innovation that no doubt required considerable diplomatic effort to arrange, Hungary became the first former Warsaw Pact country to support a NATO operation when it deployed its MiG's to escort NATO's E-3s. These resources are smaller than those required for almost any other kind of military operation, but they are not inconsiderable.

Agreement from the UN must be preceded by agreement among the members of the coalition seeking to impose the no fly zone. This means that diplomats must conduct a dual negotiation process first to achieve a consensus among participants in the planned no fly zone, and second to secure the authorization of the UN Security Council, which is likely to include a number of states that are not among the enforcing coalition. All of this work must result in a UN resolution, and a resolution from that body is never achieved except at the end of a tortuous process. For these reasons, no fly zones authorized by the UN are practically certain to require prodigious diplomatic efforts.

Once authorization is secured, implementing a no fly zone requires that its terms be clearly determined and communicated. Where, when, what areas and what types of flights are prohibited must all be defined and announced. The consequences of a violation must also be communicated in advance. This must be done with great attention to detail to foresee and forestall the predictable probing and testing for loopholes, gaps, exceptions, oversights and possible misunderstandings. Specific provisions must be made for helicopters (whose brief flights are extremely difficult to detect and suppress, in part because helicopters can operate independently of air fields) for commercial flights and for private aviation. Identification procedures must be established in detail. If error were made and an unoffending aircraft was downed improperly, the legitimacy and viability of the operation could be ruined.

Logistics

By the time the terms of the no fly zone have been determined and communicated, the logistics of the operation must be established. Lines of supply and agreements with one or several host countries must be in place. It is preferable to base operations in two or more participating host countries to provide options and flexibility when there are changes in the weather: physical, political or diplomatic.

Absent a cooperating ally in the region to provide a base from which to launch and land aircraft, no fly zones can be imposed from aircraft carriers with support from an air bridge of refueling tankers. Aircraft participating in no fly zones have been launched from as far away as Missouri, which is the case of the B-2 stealth bomber that participated in the Kosovo air campaign as well as the Libyan operation, but such an operation is vastly more costly and taxing on air crews, especially when one bears in mind that no fly zones can go on for months and years. Turkey assisted in the enforcement of Operation Northern Watch and made the airfield at Incirlik available. Italy and other NATO allies collaborated in Operation Deny Flight and many allies took part in Operation Odyssey Dawn.

A no fly zone also requires a secure place to house air crews and pilots. Although no American lives have ever been lost in patrolling a no fly zone, the enforcement of Operation Southern Watch included an incident in some respects reminiscent of the Beirut Marine barracks bombing of 1983. Housing for US Air Force personnel supporting Southern Watch was provided at the Khobar Towers in Saudi Arabia near Dhahran. In June 1996 the housing complex was damaged by a truck bomb, and 19 American servicemen were killed. Thereafter the Americans were moved to Prince Sultan Air Base, a more remote and better fortified site in the desert 75 miles southeast of Riyadh.

Adaptation to geography

Some geographical settings and environments are more conducive to a no fly zone than others. A no fly zone is made more feasible by proximity to friendly bases, clear air, moderate weather, level, open terrain and empty, unpopulated spaces. Iraq and Libya offered these conditions; the Balkans did not. Mountainous terrain, hidden missile sites and populated areas to be avoided made enforcement of Operation Deny Flight more difficult than Northern or Southern Watch or Odyssey Dawn/Unified Protector.

Preparation for enforcement of a no fly zone includes mapping the terrain, charting enemy air defense systems and attempting to locate and track each mobile surface-to-air missile system. At the start of the enforcement a crucial choice must be made: whether to suppress, evade or destroy the enemy air defenses. Suppression can be carried out by striking at missile systems if they operate their targeting radar, and is most often only a temporary endeavor to prevent those systems from shooting down an aircraft while operating within their envelopes. Evasion can be accomplished by staying above a certain altitude or avoiding the envelopes of known surface-to-air systems. Destruction of enemy air systems can be achieved either by a brief and concentrated campaign, as in Libya in 2011, or a slow and thorough hunting down and taking out of missile systems, as in Iraq in 1991.

In operation Deny Flight, the Bosnian Serb air defenses were a persistent threat to the coalition aircraft, and the rules of engagement were severely restrictive. Pilots were ordered not to attack the air defenses and were permitted only to respond immediately to an attack by destroying the specific system that targeted them. This risky and difficult arrangement was dictated by concerns that more aggressive rules of engagement might put in danger United Nations troops operating on the ground and within reach of Bosnian Serb forces. In Iraq, the rules of engagement over time became more permissive, allowing pilots to respond to being targeted or fired at by targeting not just the threatening missile system but other parts of the air defense network, including early warning radars within a reasonable time frame, usually ten minutes to a half hour after the incident. In Libya the rules of engagement were more permissive still, such that the coalition executed a comprehensive, pre-emptive campaign to eliminate the Libyan air defense threat.[16]

Enforcement and patrolling

Actual enforcement missions may be more or less complex depending on the kind of no fly zone to be imposed, but even the most limited no fly zone requires dozens of aircraft and the crews to fly and support them. If an unenforced, part-time or intermittent air monitor operation is all that the situation demands, a single E-3 Sentry[17], the familiar AWACS[18] with the rotating radar dome, might be sufficient to perform the surveillance, but it would have to be supported by another fighter aircraft that would provide escort for the AWACS. In the unenforced Operation Sky Monitor over the Federal Republic of Yugoslavia in 1992, for example, two orbits were flown, one over the Adriatic and one over Hungary, and were maintained 24 hours a day. Although the E-3s stayed outside the airspace of the target country, they had to be accompanied by fighter escorts. These aircraft in turn had to be supported with CSAR (combat search and rescue) planes and helicopters in case a mishap or enemy action resulted in a downed plane. The E-3s were capable of extended flight without refuelling, but their escorts were not, so tanker planes were also necessary. In the end, no less than 11 NATO countries contributed aircraft to that quite limited operation, and since the aim of Sky Monitor was to create an arms embargo, it had to be accompanied by a separate naval operation called Sea Monitor.

In Operation Northern Watch, patrols were not extremely demanding on pilots, although they did impose many flight hours. Patrols for most of the 12-year operation occurred on only 17 days per month, a restriction imposed by the host country, Turkey. Pilots and crews seldom felt at risk, either in the air or on the ground, and they lived in secure quarters in reasonable comfort. They did endure extended and frequent deployments away from their home bases.

During a typical mission, E-3s provided surveillance in real time to detect apparent violators. Intelligence officers aboard and on the ground carried out analysis and interpretation to determine if the aircraft detected were likely to be violators. Communications intelligence and signals intelligence specialists eavesdropped on enemy air force and air defense forces and offered more information to authorities on the ground, who provided or withheld authorization to strike the aircraft. This stage in the process grew complex in the case of Deny Flight (see Chapter 3), when dual key authorizations were required. If a strike was authorized, it was typically carried out by one of the fighter/attack aircraft and the E-3 followed up with assessment of the strike. Few downings of violators were necessary. Although the no fly zones were tested, they were not repeatedly probed.

Once patrols were in progress, the main commitment a no fly zone required was attention and endurance, both on the part of the military personnel and the diplomats. No fly zones require that the coalition imposing them remain coherent, and in the case of Operation Deny Flight, there was a great deal of dispute over rules of engagement and target lists. Missions permitted by NATO were opposed by UN authorities. Some missions were flown by American aircraft only because aircraft from other participating countries were not allowed by their governments to carry them out. European officials at times exercised veto power over target lists and military commanders were repeatedly denied permissions they sought. (For more on these matters, see Chapter 3 on Bosnia.)

How a no fly zone works

Operation Northern Watch is used here to demonstrate the operation of a typical no fly zone. Although it was a comparatively stripped-down version of one, its outlines are representative of all no fly zones to date.[19]

Equipment and personnel

Operation Northern Watch comprised 45 planes and 1,400 military personnel. The operation was run out of Incirlik air base in Turkey and was sustained for 12 years. For most of that time it flew no more than 17 days and never more than 50 hours of enforcement per month due to restrictions on the operation that were imposed by the host government, Turkey. Nonetheless, its operations and its requirements were very like Operation Southern Watch and Operation Deny Flight.

For most of its existence, the enforcement of Operation Northern Watch consisted of a single, repeated operation in which a force package would

About no fly zones 15

launch from Incirlik Air Base in Turkey, proceed roughly 400 miles eastward across Turkey, then enter Iraq for a two to three hour enforcement period. No fly zones can be more costly and difficult to enforce if the operation must be carried out with carrier-based aircraft or from bases more distant than Incirlik was from Iraq.

This standard Operation Northern Watch "package" typically consisted of the following aircraft with the associated missions and roles.

Costs

From 1991–1995, Operation Northern Watch cost an average of $155 million annually while Operation Southern Watch, flown out of Saudi Arabia, cost an

Table 1.1 Aircraft used in a standard Operation Northern Watch package

# A/C	A/C Type	Mission	Notes
4	F-15C	defensive counter air	fighters armed with missiles to shoot down no fly zone violators
4–6	F-15E/F-16CG	air interdiction	fighters armed with bombs and air-to-ground missiles to strike ground targets
4	F-16CJ	suppression of enemy air defenses	fighters armed with sensors and anti-radiation missiles to strike enemy surface-to-air radar systems
2	EA-6B	suppression of enemy air defenses	armed with sensors, jammers, and anti-radiation missiles to strike enemy surface-to-air radar systems
3	Tornado/Jaguar	reconnaissance	armed with pods equipped with videotape and sensors to gain intelligence on enemy ground systems
1	E-3D	airborne warning and control	AWACS aircraft that provides accurate, real-time air picture of the battlespace
1	EP-3/RC-135	electronic reconnaissance	reconnaissance aircraft that provides near real time on-scene intelligence collection
6–7	KC-135/vC-10	air refueling	air-to-air refueling aircraft
1	KC-130	air refueling	air-to-air refueling of combat search and rescue helicopters
2	HH-60	combat search and rescue	helicopters tasked with rescuing downed pilots in the event a plane goes down.

average of $303 million annually. Southern Watch cost more in part because the Saudis permitted a higher tempo of operations.[20]

By contrast, the land war in Iraq from the invasion in 2003 through 2014 cost $815 billion,[21] which means that the land war cost about 150 times more than the two Iraq no fly zones combined on an annual basis. This figure, based on data from the Congressional Research Service, is far too low according to Linda Bilmes and Joe Stiglitz who calculated that the invasion of Iraq resulted in what they called "the three trillion dollar war."[22] Their calculations included such matters as the long-term cost for care and treatment for the thousands wounded but also, quite speculatively, the cost of the disruption to the nation's economy, the increase in the cost of oil and many other factors. Since the no fly zones produced no American fatalities and no wounded, and since they had no discernible impact on factors like the price of oil, no fly zones may be many times cheaper relative to land operations than the Congressional Research Service figures suggest.

Challenges in imposing Operation Northern Watch

The first great challenge in imposing any no fly zone is keeping the area of the no fly zone under observation. Until the E-3 Sentry Airborne Early Warning and Control aircraft was developed in 1977, the task of observation was almost impossible unless ground radars were placed and supported all around the borders of the space to be controlled. Mountainous and remote terrain, as in the former Yugoslavia, might have been impossible to observe without airborne radar.

A second challenge is positively identifying an aircraft apparently violating a no fly zone, since a no fly zone that downed innocent aircraft would be politically unsupportable. The Vincennes incident in 1988, when an American naval ship mistakenly destroyed a civilian Iranian airliner, Iran Air Flight 655, shows that gross identification errors can be made. The process of what US military doctrine calls "combat identification" typically begins with a radar return (a reflected radar signal) detected by an AWACS aircraft, a fighter, a ground-based radar or a ship off the coast of a no fly zone. The radar return or track is then "interrogated" using IFF (identification friend or foe) signals to classify the track as civilian or military, friendly or hostile. The interrogating system sends a pulse that is received by the tracked aircraft's transponder. A friendly aircraft will return an encrypted response that positively identifies the aircraft.

An aircraft may also be identified by PPLI (precise participant location and identification), which is part of the Link-16 tactical data exchange network. If an aircraft is in the network, it constantly transmits its encrypted location data to others in the network.

Identification procedures continue until the radar return is positively identified as friendly. Further means, many of them classified but collectively known as NCTR (non-cooperative target recognition) methods, use acoustic and thermal radiation, radio emissions, and various radar techniques to compare the signature of the tracked aircraft to known signatures. Inverse synthetic aperture radar imaging and jet engine modulation can also be used.

The target is categorized once an unambiguous NCTR result is achieved, but in the event that the process is inconclusive, often a visual identification is attempted by sending an enforcing aircraft close enough to get a good look at the target.

After observation and identification, a third challenge is the decision to engage. Rules of engagement must be outlined in great detail in advance so that decisions to use force to enforce the no fly zone can be arrived at within minutes of discovering a violation. Positive identification must be established with a high level of certainty, as ambiguity can lead to catastrophe. Warnings typically follow observation and identification, then enforcement.

One example of enforcement dates from 28 February 1994 during Operation Deny Flight. Six Bosnian Serb J-21 Jastreb and two J-22 Oraos aircraft took off from Udbina air base in Croatia. At 6:35 AM a NATO AWACS detected the unidentified contacts south of Banja Luka. It sent IFF signals which did not elicit the encrypted response that would emanate from a friendly aircraft. Two American F-16s were directed to the area, intercepted the aircraft and established positive visual identification. In accordance with established rules of engagement, the F-16s issued "land or exit the no fly zone or be engaged" warnings. The warnings were ignored, and the Bosnian Serb aircraft actually delivered their bombs over their target, the Brastvo military factory at Nov Travnik in Bosnia. The Combined Air Operations Center cleared the F-16s to engage the Bosnian Serb aircraft, this message being relayed via radio from the Air Operations Center to the AWACS and then to the F-16 pilots, and the first missile was fired at 6:45 AM, less than ten minutes after the Bosnia Serb aircraft were detected. Four of the six Bosnian Serb jets were destroyed.

No fly zones and the maturation of air power

No fly zones are one outcome of a century-long search for ways to exert force from the air, and moreover to do so with increasing effect but at the same time at decreasing risk and expense. They are one of the more recent innovations in a long string of designs and methods to leverage air power to exert influence yet at the same time to avoid having to put troops in harm's way. Such attempts began less than 20 years after the Wright brothers flew at Kitty Hawk.

Air policing

In 1920, for example, in the region then called Mesopotamia and now Iraq and Jordan, the British colonial rulers sought to use air power to exercise control while keeping troops out of the reach of local forces. Winston

18 *About no fly zones*

Churchill, who was then Secretary of State for War and Air, devised an air policing scheme that would permit the removal of most of the 25,000 British and 80,000 Indian troops stationed there.

On 22 March 1920, Churchill told the House of Commons that Britain's colonial possessions in Mesopotamia could be policed by planes armed with that he called "gas bombs." The pilots and air crews would be supported by 4,000 British and 10,000 Indian troops (reduced from 25,000 and 80,000), most of them deployed to defend the air bases. The goals of his early air policing scheme overlapped with the goals of no fly zones today: to project power into an area and create an air presence there, to keep troops out of the reach of the enemy, to do so cheaply and at little risk and to accomplish all this by exploiting the advantages that come with an asymmetry between the technological capabilities of the controllers and of the controlled.

Churchill's dreams of air policing were not fulfilled due to the unreliability of the aircraft of his time, their vulnerability to ground fire, the inaccuracy and ineffectiveness of their munitions, the uncertainty of their navigation and the limits of the command's communications and sources of intelligence and targeting information. Improvements in all those fields were what ultimately made no fly zones feasible, though the process would take seven decades.

Improved navigation, reconnaissance and targeting

A little more than two decades after Churchill's experiment in Mesopotamia, the continuing severe limitations of air power were captured by a joke made by the American B-17 crews flying missions over Germany. They boasted, ironically, that they could hit any city, "so long as it was big enough." John Keegan suggests that the performance of bombers early in World War II actually was so poor and the missions were so dangerous that the losses among the air crews were greater than the losses they were able to inflict in the cities they targeted.[23] As the war progressed, the missions became more lethal, even if they remained terribly risky. Massive raids, plus innovations like the Norden bombsight, meant that, by the war's end, city bombing had taken at least 300,000 German lives.[24] Now, with vastly better navigation, reconnaissance and targeting, American pilots can hit any city, or any building in that city, or any floor in that building, or any window on that floor. These changes mark the transformative maturation of American air power that has made no fly zones possible.

From the 1940s through the 1970s, war planners had to anticipate huge casualties and adapted the only way they could – by producing more pilots to fill the ranks of the lost and building more airframes to replenish the squadrons of the destroyed. In World War II an astonishing 300,000 planes were built,[25] and in Vietnam a frightening 2,561 planes were lost.[26]

Although the Vietnam War was costly, it also drove innovations that were crucial in developing American air power, ultimately making no fly zones possible. Out of that decade came the RC-135 Rivet Joint aircraft to intercept communications, (1961), the EA-6B Prowler to jam enemy radars (1966) and high-speed anti-radar missiles that could destroy anti-aircraft artillery and surface-to-air missile sites by homing on their targeting systems.

Increasingly accurate offensive weapons decreased the cost of airpower dramatically. One reason so many planes were lost in World War II, Korea and Vietnam was that it might take dozens of attacks to destroy a single target like a bridge. Pilots had to brave anti-aircraft artillery, surface-to-air missiles and anti-air patrols as they flew mission after mission at the same objective. The enemy could concentrate its defenses and improve its tactics, as American forces repeatedly exposed their aircraft, pilots and crews. During the 1960s, laser-guided bombs were developed that vastly improved the accuracy and effectiveness of munitions, decreasing their circular error probability[27] from about 450 feet for bombs guided only by gravity to about 25 feet for bombs guided by lasers.[28] Also developed in or immediately after the Vietnam War were aiming systems using radar, thermal sensors and electro-optical sensors, plus night-vision equipment, which had been under development since the 1950s, making all-weather and night-time operations more feasible. Stealth capability arrived in the form of the F117A prototype in 1977, and in the 1980s further improvements produced optical and infrared sensors covering a wide range of the electromagnetic spectrum, targeting pods containing synthetic aperture radars, as well as a range of means to detect targets on the ground at a distance by sensing movement and emissions of many kinds.

Of all the technological advances, the most central is the Boeing E-3 Sentry[29], known as AWACS, introduced in 1977 and equipped with its signature rotating radar dome which allows extensive monitoring of broad areas. The E-3, built on the frame of a Boeing 707, can stay on station for extended periods, can stand off at a distance from the area being monitored, can communicate without time lag with other planes and with ground control centers and can provide commanders with a single, comprehensive vision of a no fly zone. The AWACS is the keystone element of the force imposing a no fly zone.

Improved skills and training

Although only a small portion of the planes lost in Vietnam were lost in air-to-air combat, the Navy improved its aerial combat capacities and developed skills useful in no fly zone enforcement by creating the Top Gun school in 1969. The Air Force and Marine Corps followed suit in establishing weapons schools as all three services worked to provide more thorough and more realistic training for pilots.

One of the lessons from the Vietnam war and from subsequent experience in Grenada was that coordination between the services was crucial. No fly zones have been joint operations between the Navy, Marine Corps and Air Force, and "jointness" was considerably enhanced as a result of the Goldwater-Nichols Act of 1986 which mandated more joint cooperation among the services.

All of these innovations and improvements, and particularly the ones involving improved mapping and surveillance, real time intelligence, signals jamming, weapons accuracy and night, all-weather and joint operations, raised the possibility of suppressing the enemy's air defenses, then sweeping the sky of the enemy's aircraft. This is not quite the same as establishing and sustaining a no fly zone, but it is much like creating one briefly. It was the Israelis who first used the innovations listed above to entirely deprive another power of the use of its air assets and its own air space and so provided the first "proof of concept" of a no fly zone, even if it operated only for a few days.

Operation Mole Cricket 19

In 1982 in air operations against Syria over the Bekaa Valley, the Israelis deployed intelligence-gathering and command-and-control aircraft, remotely piloted decoy and surveillance aircraft, fighters with anti-radiation missiles, ground-launched battlefield missiles and artillery and fighters with air-to-air missiles to destroy 17 out of 19 surface-to-air missile sites in about 90 minutes.[30] Then, over the next few days, they shot down 85 Syrian aircraft while losing only two Israeli aircraft to enemy ground fire and none to air-to-air engagements.[31]

The US followed the Israeli example in 1991 in the air campaign that began Operation Desert Storm. In the opening two hours Iraqi air defenses were suppressed and aircraft dispersed or destroyed. Air supremacy[32] was achieved and sustained throughout the following 40 days of the air campaign and the 100 hours of the land campaign. This was not accomplished without losses: over those 40 days, 23 aircraft were hit and 25 airmen were killed, 14 of them in a single incident when an AC-130 gunship was shot down.[33]

Despite the loss of life and aircraft, the coalition air forces demonstrated that it was possible quickly to seize, control and occupy the airspace of another power. The air over Iraq was comprehensively monitored and controlled and all Iraqi air operations were shut down for an extended period. The maturation of air power had yielded all the elements of a no fly zone, and once all the technical capacities necessary to impose and sustain a no fly zone had been demonstrated, it was a matter of days before the first was initiated.

What a no fly zone can do – tactics

Clearly the primary role of a no fly zone is to prevent an adversary from using air assets, and no fly zones are by no means perfect instruments even for that limited and specific function. Nonetheless, no fly zones do offer opportunities to achieve a number of other ends as well, including the following.

- Organize an international response to a crisis, particularly a humanitarian crisis like Darfur: no fly zones have in all past cases been established only with authorization from an international organization like the United Nations. The process of securing that authorization can provide a useful context within which the efforts of concerned powers can be coordinated. Securing such authorization has in past cases stimulated debate (not always productive) in the General Assembly and Security Council, in the capitals of NATO countries and among and between the militaries that would participate in varying ways and degrees, among numerous non-governmental organizations, in the news media and among other elements of civil society.
- Overcome resistance to act among military and civilian bureaucracies: bureaucratic inertia, reinforced by a fear of mission creep, often defeats efforts to respond to a humanitarian crisis. Because no fly zones are low risk, low cost and low profile, they can serve as a kind of gentle "gateway intervention" which may prove acceptable to decision makers.
- Establish a military presence in or near an area of concern: creating a no fly zone is a relatively non-intrusive way to introduce air assets to a region, along with the command and control, intelligence and surveillance capabilities that come with them, and to do so under multilateral, multinational auspices.
- Pre-position military assets in a region where further response may be required: Northern and Southern Watch, the no fly zones established over Iraq, afforded General Anthony Zinni the assets with which to strike swiftly and without observable preparations when Saddam resisted and harassed inspectors from UNSCOM, the UN Special Commission on Iraq. (See Operation Desert Fox, Chapter 2.)
- Keep a close watch on a changing situation like the one in the former Yugoslavia in 1992–93: the regular overflights of Operation Sky Monitor and Operation Deny Flight collected real-time information on the volatile situation there and kept UN and NATO attention focused on the conflict.
- Comprehensively map and study a future battlefield: the thousands of sorties to enforce Operations Northern and Southern Watch provided detailed and current information on terrain, defenses and troop positions in the run-up to Operation Iraqi Freedom.
- Shape the battle space in advance of an invasion: the hundreds of strikes to suppress Iraqi air defenses over the course of 12 years of Iraqi no fly zone enforcement left the airspace clear for coalition air operations in Operation Iraqi Freedom and also provided great opportunities for detailed mapping and excellent intelligence with respect to responses to probing, aircraft profiles and the like.

It should be restated that a no fly zone alone cannot keep people safe in a so-called safe zone. Unless a no fly zone is accompanied and reinforced by other forces present in sufficient numbers and possessing the proper authorizations both to defend themselves and to project force, the people in sanctuaries will be left gravely at risk.

What a no fly zone can do – strategy

Two days before General Schwarzkopf created the first no fly zone, President George HW Bush, flush with triumph in the first Gulf War, celebrated at a gathering of legislators at the White House. It was not just the victory over Saddam that he was proud of. Rather, he saw fit to celebrate victory over what he saw as a longstanding American problem. "It's a proud day for America," he exclaimed. "And, by God, we've kicked the Vietnam Syndrome once and for all."[34]

"The Vietnam Syndrome" was shorthand for the reluctance to send American forces into action abroad due to the fear that they would become entangled and ultimately bogged down in a quagmire.[35] President Bush was congratulating himself by declaring that his decisive action in Iraq had put an end to a tentativeness that had hung over Americans since some time in the late 1960s or early 1970s when extricating US forces from Vietnam had proved difficult. The fear has been raised in policy discussions so many times over four decades that today even the single word "quagmire" is enough to evoke the entire discussion.

Ironically, even as he spoke another potential quagmire appeared to be forming. The president and his staff were working urgently to bring home all of the 500,000 troops he had sent to Kuwait and Iraq, but they were finding it difficult to do so because Saddam was attacking both the Kurdish and the Shi'ite minorities in his country.[36] To stop the attacks, Bush would need to interpose troops between Saddam's forces and his victims, which might mean marching them into a quagmire, yet to ignore the attacks and keep on withdrawing troops would likely stain the victory just achieved. Like Nixon in Vietnam, Bush could either extend a fight he wanted to close out or he could declare victory and withdraw. Neither option had worked well for Nixon, and in fact those unattractive choices had been the source of the Vietnam Syndrome in the first place.

It was too soon for Bush to congratulate himself on kicking the Vietnam Syndrome. Less than a year and a half later, in the final month of his presidency, he sent US troops into Somalia, touching off another Vietnam Syndrome debate which featured all the familiar terms of "achievable objective," "quagmire," "mission creep," "sufficient forces" and "exit strategy." The intervention ended badly in under a year at the Battle of Mogadishu.

In the case of Iraq in 1991, an ally offered President Bush a third option when the British stepped forward to protect the Kurds. (The Shi'ites were left to Saddam's mercies.[37]) As described in the next chapter, the British took the lead in working through NATO to organize Operation Haven to block the Iraqi forces. British, Dutch, Australian and American troops were deployed in April 1991 first to push Iraqi troops back, then to provide shelter, food and fuel to over a million Kurdish refugees. American Marines played a significant but brief role in the effort. The Iraqi troops offered no violent resistance and were withdrawn by October of that year. Operation Haven developed into Operation Provide Comfort, and had as part of its mandate a no fly zone, which in 1997 was renamed Operation Northern Watch.

This response to the Kurds' emergency, which was the first such humanitarian emergency after no fly zones were proven technically feasible, shows an interesting pattern: 1) a defenseless minority comes under attack; 2) faced with a potentially entangling situation, US policy makers are reluctant to deploy ground forces but 3) they are willing to provide air assets to defend and support the ground forces of other countries and 4) the US air support transforms from air patrols and delivery of supplies into a long-standing no fly zone operation. In short, when a humanitarian situation emerges, the US offers its air assets but turns to others to take the lead on ground operations. These US assets provide air cover for the duration of the intervention, then create a sustained American air presence long afterwards.

That pattern, repeated in Bosnia and in Libya, captures much of the strategic function of no fly zones. US policy makers, while reluctant to act in more decisive and extensive ways, may find in a no fly zone a low-key option that carries little risk of lost lives, high costs or continuing entanglements.

These no fly zones are not likely to be particularly effective at protecting the victims of the dictators, absent the ground troops provided by others. Without the intervention on the ground, the air assets provided in 1991 would have done as little to help the Kurds as they did to help the Shi-ites, which was essentially nothing. But the air operations in support of Operation Haven and later Operation Provide Comfort, which morphed into the no fly zones established over Iraq, constituted a response to the humanitarian emergency which, by sticking to air operations and outsourcing the work on the ground to allies and NGOs, finessed the concerns that made the Vietnam Syndrome a factor.

Moreover, those no fly zones and the ones over Bosnia and Libya proved so low-key that after a short time they went largely unnoticed by the public. This made extricating American forces much less complicated than extrication from a ground intervention would have been. Producing no casualties and costing relatively little, they operated largely out of sight of the American people and so out of mind as well, yet they kept an American presence in Iraq and in Bosnia and maintained an infrastructure that could support a swift air escalation. So General Anthony Zinni found when in December 1998, when he quickly launched Operation Desert Fox to compel Saddam to let UN weapons inspectors do their work, and so General Wesley Clark found in March 1999, when he pressured Milosevic to cease his predations on the Kosovars in Operation Allied Force.

Of course these same objectives, to minimize risks, casualties and costs, had been driving policy making for decades. With that in mind, it is worth looking back 50 years to the late 1960s to place no fly zones in the context of their predecessors.

24 *About no fly zones*

The 1960s featured two developments important to the history of no fly zones. First, the many newly developed technical capabilities described in the previous section were coming into operation in that decade; second, a new priority was being given to humanitarian interventions as well as to other operations where a concerned and mobilized public could demand action even when the situations did not include major threats to American lives, territory or security interests.

In these types of crises, many people were brutalized and killed under conditions in which the US could effectively intervene. In Biafra between 1967 to 1970, for example, in what was in many respects the seminal humanitarian crisis, helpless Ibos were slowly and agonizingly starved by the federal military government of Nigeria to compel them to abandon a bid for independence. Just as the war in Vietnam was the first televised war, the humanitarian crisis in Biafra was the first televised humanitarian crisis. Up to two million people were purposely starved to death as cameras from the West recorded their slow deaths.

Biafra presented no compelling US national interest in the sense that no or few American lives were at risk, and the strategic significance of Biafra to the US was slight. It did present a compelling human ethical obligation, however. In the eyes of many progressive editors, ministers, commentators and political figures, Biafra was not a matter of responding to a threat but rather of rising to an obligation. The ethical proposition was simple and had a common sense appeal to many Americans: the US was like a man standing at the end of a pier holding a life ring while helpless people struggled and drowned in the water at his feet. Didn't he have an obligation to throw the life ring?

The reply from military planners, for whom caution is a professional virtue, was plain: not if throwing the life ring actually meant sending the Marines. 1967, the year the Biafran crisis began, was also the year the Vietnam Syndrome took hold on the same military planners' minds. In the case of Biafra, the planners arrived at a policy response that presaged Operations Provide Comfort, Northern Watch, Deny Flight and Odyssey Dawn/Unified Protector in several important respects.

In the case of Biafra, various voices would have had the US military create safe zones, construct aid corridors, impose cease fires, interpose armed forces and make military threats of sufficient severity and credibility that they would compel the government in Lagos to relent and to cede oil-rich territory to a rebel republic. (The situation had some early echoes of Syria in 2015.) Notwithstanding these voices, the official US response for many months was to uphold the sovereignty of the murderous regime and to refuse to act.

After about two years of delay, the US at last offered a partial military response by reaching back into its repertoire of known and rehearsed operations. It essentially recreated on a limited scale the Berlin airlift of 20 years before. Eight of the same planes used in the Berlin airlift, Boeing KC-97 Stratofreighters, were deployed, flying in and out of a small airfield in Biafra.[38] The aid flights were far from sufficient to address the vast suffering and starvation, but at a time of great pressure to do something, they offered at least a way not to do nothing.

As in Bosnia and Libya, the US intervened only from the air and left the work on the ground to others. The US avoided deploying American troops to Nigeria by relying heavily on British, Spanish and French forces plus non-governmental organizations such as Oxfam and Médecins Sans Frontières. This was the first iteration of what would be an irregularly but repeatedly employed pattern for US interventions.

Although the US role in Biafra relief was not very effective and was widely and severely criticized, it had these practical virtues from a military planner's point of view: no ground troops were deployed, no uniformed Americans were hurt or killed, no commitments were made from which the US would later have difficulty extricating itself, no quagmire yawned and no one could say that the US had done nothing.

Twenty years would pass after Biafra before all the capabilities and requirements of a no fly zone would be in place. During those two decades there were occasions when no fly zones might have been useful, if they had been feasible. The US would have liked to impose a no fly zone over North Vietnam but lacked the capacity to do so. Lacking a better way to intervene, the US interposed a Marine amphibious unit between hostile factions in Beirut and saw 241 of them killed on 23 October 1983 when their barracks were blown up. It can be argued that if the option had existed, Beirut might have been handled on the same pattern that Bosnia was handled ten years later with American forces in the air only and forces from other countries and organizations on the ground. (58 French peacekeepers died in the same attack.) The catastrophe in Beirut sharpened and deepened doubt and opposition to ground deployments to handle humanitarian crises and factional struggles and gave rise to the Weinberger principles which raised obstacles to future such deployments.

The Grenada intervention, hurriedly launched on 25 October 1983, just 48 hours after the Beirut disaster, showed how difficult and dangerous combined operations can be, particularly when they are hastily staged. Grenada obviously was no occasion for a no fly zone but the events there, like the events in Beirut, deepened the reluctance to expose American troops to uncontrolled dangers.[39]

The Somalia intervention in December 1992 deepened that reluctance still further. The civil disorder that produced Mohamed Farrah Aidid and his clan might have been handled in a fashion less like a ground occupation and more like the ways Saddam Hussein and Slobodan Milosevic were handled in the 1990s. In the Somalia case, the US could have provided air support and food shipments while troops from other countries provided a ground force. Pakistani troops with tanks and Malaysian troops with armored personnel carriers were present when the American forces arrived. By October 1993 when the Battle of Mogadishu/Black Hawk Down incident occurred, the US had substantially taken over the situation.

An intervention without a US ground presence would likely have had much less potential to deliver effective humanitarian relief, but it would not have been subject to the same risks. No fly zone operations have never presented the temptations of mission creep and no fly zone enforcers have never been part of violent confrontations other than very brief, one-sided ones. No enforcers of no fly zones have been killed.[40]

The non-intervention in Rwanda is the case where the US is most often castigated for its failure to act. Samantha Power documents the resistance to any form of action in her September 2001 *Atlantic Monthly* article, "Bystanders to Genocide" and shows the way Somalia and Rwanda motivated the American national security bureaucracy under the guidance of Richard Clarke to produce Presidential Decision Directive 25

> which listed sixteen factors that policymakers needed to consider when deciding whether to support peacekeeping activities: seven factors if the United States was to vote in the UN Security Council on peace operations carried out by non-American soldiers, six additional and more stringent factors if U.S. forces were to participate in UN peacekeeping missions, and three final factors if U.S. troops were likely to engage in actual combat. In the words of Representative David Obey, of Wisconsin, the restrictive checklist tried to satisfy the American desire for 'zero degree of involvement, and zero degree of risk, and zero degree of pain and confusion.'[41]

The Rwanda genocide surprisingly offered an instance in which an air-only, no-ground-troops intervention might have saved lives. Rather than attempt to seize and occupy the air space of Rwanda, it might have been possible to seize the air waves. In that mountainous country, radio was important as one of the few means of communication between members of the Hutu Power forces and its militia, the Interahamwe. An American signals-jamming airplane, a specially equipped Hercules C-130J named a Commando Solo aircraft could have jammed the transmissions the Interahamwe were using to direct genocidal teams to concentrations of victims and even to broadcast the real-time location of persons on their kill lists. Citing fears of entanglement and doubts of effectiveness, the Pentagon strongly opposed such a measure.

The intervention in Haiti in 1994–1995, Operation Uphold Democracy, designed to compel the departure of a military dictator, Raoul Cedras, and install the elected leader, Jean-Bertrand Aristide, could not have been accomplished without ground forces. Nor could the deplorable situation in Haiti be ignored since desperate people were fleeing to Florida's shores and washing up on its beaches. The operation showcased what a ground intervention would look like if it were carried out with the primary objective and most stringent requirement that zero casualties be permitted, as if it were, like a no fly zone, a way not to do nothing.

The US troops in Operation Uphold Democracy performed an unresisted or "permissive entry"; they were sequestered away from the population and quartered at a distance from the capital in an industrial park; they were allowed to go out only in convoys; they wore such complete body armor that they were called "Ninja turtles" by the natives and they departed with the mission marginally accomplished after six months. As one of the officers in the 10th Mountain Division declared, the prime US mission in Haiti was "force protection, force protection, force protection."[42]

The intervention in Yugoslavia featured the pattern traceable back to Biafra. Americans operated only from the air and at altitudes and in locations that minimized risk and suffered no losses. United Nations troops operated on the ground at greater risk and cost.[43] Operation Sky Monitor, Operation Deny Flight and Operation Allied Force are discussed in Chapter 3.

The intervention in Libya in 2011, Operation Odyssey Dawn, followed the same pattern of a no fly zone which was designed not so much to keep *their* boots on the ground (Qaddafi's very limited air power was suppressed in the first few hours of the operation) as to keep American boots off of it. The operation is described in Chapter 4.

The terror attacks of September 11, 2001 changed the setting in which American interventions were framed. The humanitarian interventions of the 1990s were overshadowed by the counter-terror interventions of the next two decades. Operation Enduring Freedom in Afghanistan, Operation Iraqi Freedom in Iraq and most recently Operation Inherent Resolve against ISIS featured invasions and occupations as well as operations from the air, but under President Obama policy makers showed the familiar overwhelming preference for options shaped by caution and casualty avoidance.

As Linda Robinson of RAND [44] observed in February 2017,

> The number of United States troops killed in combat has plunged in the last five years, as President Barack Obama brought home more than 200,000 troops. In 2010, more than 500 service members were killed in action. Since the beginning of 2016, 18 have died. But 12 of them were elite trainers and commandos serving with the Army Special Forces or the Navy SEALs. Special operations troops make up about 5 percent of the military.

Just as no fly zones in the 1990s offered a low-risk, low-cost option where Americans operated from the air and outsourced the work on the ground, so special operations tactics have served in recent years. Special operators combined with air strikes performed in significant part by weaponized drones have lowered the cost of the use of force.

> "We've moved out of the major combat operations business," said Linda Robinson, a counterterrorism expert at the RAND Corporation. In recent years, she said, the military has effectively outsourced rank-and-file

infantry duties to local forces in places like Afghanistan, Iraq and Syria, leaving only a cadre of highly skilled Americans to train troops and take out high-value targets.[45]

In summation, no fly zones as policy options offer a minimal way to intervene. They are minimally costly and risky, but, absent cooperating ground troops, minimally effective. When used in combination with ground troops, they can produce for the US an easily sustainable presence that can monitor post-conflict compliance with the terms of a ceasefire and be adapted to coerce a figure like Saddam, Milosevic or Qaddafi to abide by those terms. They can be escalated into air campaigns, as they were in all three cases.

No fly zones have constituted a response to pressure, though usually a seriously incomplete response, to intervene in a crisis situation that has captured the attention and concern of the American public. They have amounted to a response to the pressure to intervene as much as a response to the crisis situation itself. They have been a way to respond to the American public more than to the people in the country where the violence and suffering is occurring. No fly zones have served, to say it once again, as a way not to do nothing.

The ethics of no fly zones

No fly zones generally are taken *a priori* to be ethically superior to other uses of force. That may be because enforcing a no fly zone seldom involves the taking of civilian lives and may not require the taking of any lives at all. Therefore, the argument seems to go, moral examination is unnecessary and such an inquiry amounts to an inappropriate exercise in moral perfectionism.

Moreover, no fly zones have in every case been imposed as responses to humanitarian atrocities, so perhaps they have been given a pass on the notion that they are so beneficial in their consequences, or at least so superior to the conditions they are meant to address, that they should not be faulted even if they are not ethically perfect.

Yet even if they have taken few lives and they have been responses to atrocities, no fly zones are undeniable violations of sovereignty and should be assessed as carefully as any other such violation. They should be examined as carefully as sieges and blockades, for example. As argued in the discussion of definitions at the beginning of this chapter, no fly zones are essentially aerial occupations and must be treated as what they are: violations or seizures of another country's sovereign air space.

Michael Walzer leads the way in lightly treating the ethics of no fly zones. In the preface to the latest edition of *Just and Unjust Wars*, he sets apart what he calls "measures short of war," such as precision air strikes, CIA operations and no fly zones. He does not exempt them from moral examination, but he does suggest that they should be placed in a different category from "actual warfare," saying "it is common sense to recognize that they are very different from war" because they lack "the unpredictable and often catastrophic consequences" that can follow on larger scale uses of force like invasions and bombing campaigns.

For these "measures short of war" Walzer proposes a separate framework for moral analysis which he calls "*jus ad vim*" or just coercion.[46] Other scholars[47] have argued that Walzer's new label is superfluous, but nonetheless his influential judgment may be a reason why little ethical scrutiny is applied to no fly zones. After all, he would maintain, they are not "actual warfare."

Walzer does not appear to take into account that no fly zones often begin with very substantial acts of violence to suppress the air defense systems of the target state. The no fly zones over Iraq began with the destruction of Saddam's air defenses in Operation Desert Storm. The air defenses of the Bosnian Serbs were never destroyed, only evaded, in Operation Deny Flight, in part because they were mobile and hard to discover in the mountainous terrain of the Balkans and in part because destroying them might have brought retaliations against UN troops deployed as peacekeepers. The air defenses of Qaddafi, by contrast, were quickly located in the open spaces of Libya and thoroughly silenced in the opening hours of Operation Odyssey Dawn.

While the standards of *jus ad vim* are not laid out in detail by Walzer, the familiar tests of *jus ad bellum* are well known. Once applied, they prove to yield a number of insights, particularly into the paradoxes that surround no fly zones.

Proper authority

No fly zones to date can hardly be faulted on the grounds of improper authority. The authority in all three cases was never a single state but rather was always in international organization like the 40-nation anti-Saddam coalition, the United Nations, NATO or the Arab League. Chapter 42 of the UN Charter authorizes the Security Council to impose "demonstrations, blockades and other operations by air, sea, or land forces of members of the United Nations" and a Security Council resolution represents the gold standard among authorizations. Multilateral actions are more acceptable than unilateral actions when the sovereignty of a target state is to be compromised. With UN Security Council authorization and multilateral enforcement, the three no fly zones fully met the standard of proper authority.

Paradoxically, the most effective humanitarian interventions have been carried out by the least fully authorized forces. UN forces have had the advantage of exceptional legitimacy, but they have required rescue by less legitimate forces. As James Kurth argued in *Orbis* in 2006, "The successful humanitarian interventions of the 1990s happened outside the jurisdiction of the UN. US and NATO forces successfully intervened in both Bosnia and Kosovo; Australian forces successfully intervened in East Timor in 1999; British forces successfully intervened in Sierra Leone after rescuing UN forces; and US forces stopped albeit briefly human rights abuses in Haiti in 1994."[48]

Proper intent

The test of proper intent typically demands that the use of force aims to establish a more just peace or to stop grave violations of human rights and to fulfill the Responsibility to Protect proclaimed by the United Nations in 2005. Since the no fly zones of the past have been responses to humanitarian atrocities, they have all shared that claim to proper intent and just cause – to stop the violations and to deliver the innocent from harm. In fact, however, no fly zones, unless they are accompanied by other much more forceful and extensive measures that go far beyond no fly zones, do little to stop atrocities and protect the innocent from harm.

Operation Provide Comfort was part of an effort that impeded Saddam's attacks on Kurds and Operation Southern Watch complicated his attacks on the Arabs of the marshlands of the Tigris and Euphrates. These no fly zones were effective, however, because they had been preceded by Operation Desert Storm in which Saddam's military capabilities were severely curtailed and because they were accompanied, in the case of Provide Comfort/Northern Watch, by the continued presence of coalition forces which were part of the initial operation. By contrast, the less well supported no fly zone over Bosnia, Operation Deny Flight, was inadequate to protect the victims of Milosevic. Operation Odyssey Dawn/Unified Protector may be said to have been effective in intercepting and blunting the efforts of Qaddafi's troops against innocents in Benghazi, but it was not the no fly zone but rather the offensive air campaign that accompanied it that actually prevented the planned slaughter.

Matters of intent present a just war test which is not easily satisfied in the cases of these three no fly zones. If the actual intent in each case were to protect the innocent, ground forces would have been sent at once. Instead, minimal sets of measures entirely from the air were deployed. The intent, one may conclude, was neither to fulfill a responsibility to protect the innocent, nor to drive the conflict to a swift, decisive and lasting conclusion. Instead, the intention was much more limited and equivocal. It can best be described as an intent "not to do nothing."

Probability of success

Just war theory also demands a reasonable likelihood of success, a test which serves in part to assure force is not used in a quixotic manner. A clear, plausible and achievable objective must be designated in advance. But only if one defines the objective of a no fly zone in a uselessly narrow and circular way can one affirm that these three no fly zones were successful. "Did the measures taken stop the enemy from using his air assets?" Yes, to a great degree they did. But if one poses the more appropriate definition of success, the one required for just intent, "Did the measures taken end the abuse and killing of innocents?," one must admit they did not. Saddam brutally ruled for over a decade under two no fly zones. War in the former Yugoslavia continued for more than a half a decade after Deny Flight was imposed. The massacre of 7,000 helpless persons at Srebrenica took place while Operation Deny Flight was in place. Only in Libya, where the no fly zone was accompanied with much greater commitments of force, was success measured in the form of the removal of the regime and the end of the abuses committed by the regime. Even there, the end of the abusive regime did not mean the end of violence. Indeed, according to Alan Kuperman[49] and others, the intervention very likely has increased the suffering of innocents.

When no fly zones are justified as acts of humanitarian intervention, success in a humanitarian intervention should by definition mean the innocent, the helpless and the vulnerable were protected. With this definition of success, in all three cases the no fly zones did not begin with a reasonable expectation of success or justify such an expectation.

Last resort

Just war theory requires that force be used as a last resort, after all less violent means have been exhausted. One may naturally frame this test by classifying a no fly zone as one of those measures short of war that must be exhausted before more force is employed, and if one does that then in all three historical instances no fly zones fell well within the canon.

If, however, one classifies no fly zones as acts of war, as violations of sovereignty and acts of aggression (as this study encourages one to do), then in none of the three cases had all means short of war been exhausted. In fact, no fly zones were in all three cases more like opening devices than last resorts. They were in those cases, as they are in most no fly zone debates, the preferred go-to option, the initial use of force for anyone arguing the need to intervene. When no fly zones are implemented without first suppressing enemy air defenses, as was the case in Bosnia, the last resort test matters less than when no fly zones are preceded by destruction of enemy air defenses, as was the case in Libya and Iraq. In all three cases, all other options had appeared distinctly less palatable than a no fly zone: more costly, more risky and more likely to require deeper involvement, and this fact alone, quite independent of whether no fly zones would likely be effective responses, recommended them to policy makers.

The last resort test captures particularly clearly what is paradoxical about no fly zones. It illuminates the fact that they are first recourse methods so that other potentially riskier and costlier recourses may be avoided, that they are a way to appear to have addressed a problem and that they are a way to evade more substantial commitment.

Proportionality

A final test prescribed by just war theory involves proportionality: "Is the good done by this measure proportionate to and likely to be less than the damage this measure is designed to prevent?" Because the three no fly zones did so little damage to other than military targets and because the regimes they targeted were committing atrocities, all three historical no fly zones may be said to meet this standard easily.

However, the proportionality test has an inverse sense that is equally cogent in moral terms: "Was the force used *adequate* to the cause to be accomplished?" Since the violations of human rights the no fly zones were meant to address were urgent and severe, were the measures taken to address them adequate to their gravity? In this inverse sense, the three no fly zones do not pass the proportionality test since in each case the force employed clearly was *inadequate* to end the abuses they were meant to terminate.

In sum, then, the traditional tests posed by just war theory bring equivocal and ironic responses. Perhaps the ethics of no fly zones are little discussed precisely because they are so complex, paradoxical and unsatisfying.

Notes

1 First, as Karl Mueller points out in a 2013 RAND report, (www.rand.org/pubs/research_reports/RR423.html), it is an awkward expression. It is pidgin English at best, both ungrammatical and graceless. Moreover, it tends to spawn equally awkward variations such as "No-Drive Zone" and "No-Sail Zone." The alternative expression, "No-Flight Zone," may be slightly more grammatical, but it is also more difficult to pronounce. Having considered and rejected the still more awkward "air exclusion zone" or "air interdiction zone," the authors will stick with "no fly zone."

2 The official military doctrine of the United States treats no fly zones as a variety of "exclusion zone." To quote from Joint Publication 3–0, *Joint Operations: Exclusion Zones*. A sanctioning body establishes an exclusion zone to prohibit specified activities in a specific geographic area. Exclusion zones usually are imposed due to breaches of international standards of human rights or flagrant violations of international law regarding the conduct of states. Situations that may warrant such action include the persecution of the civil population by a government and efforts to deter an attempt by a hostile nation to acquire territory by force. Exclusion zones can be established in the air (no fly zones), sea (maritime), or on land (no-drive zones). An exclusion zone's purpose may be to persuade nations or groups to modify their behavior to meet the desires of the sanctioning body or face continued imposition of sanctions or threat or use of force. Such measures usually are imposed by the UN or another international body of which the United States is a member, although they may be imposed unilaterally by the United States (e.g., Operation SOUTHERN WATCH in Iraq, initiated in August 1992, and Operation DENY FLIGHT in Bosnia, from March 1993 to December 1995). Joint Publication 3–0, Joint Operations, 11 August 2011, Chapter V, pages 13–14.

3 A more formal definition appears in Michael N. Schmitt, "Clipped Wings: Effective and Legal No fly Zone Rules of Engagement" *Loyola of Los Angeles International and Comparative Law Review*, Vol. 20, 1998, pp. 727–789. "A no fly zone

is a de facto aerial occupation of sovereign airspace in which, absent consent of the entity authorizing the occupation, only aircraft of the enforcement forces may fly."
4 Hodges, Doyle, "ADIZ'd and Confused: Challenges for the PLAAF, PLAN and PLANAF in Maintaining China's Declared East China Sea Air Defense Identification Zone," unpublished paper, Princeton University, 14 January 2014.
5 A 20-nautical-mile-wide no fly zone is imposed by the Federal Aviation Authority around a US president's destination wherever the president travels. A standing flight restriction surrounds the White House in Washington, DC; others currently are established around Bedminster, New Jersey, whenever President Trump visits his golf-club property there. At such times, a circular area with a 10-mile radius is designated a "national security airspace" and is subject to a TFR or "temporary flight restriction." Under a TFR, entry is denied to "general aviation aircraft," which includes private planes and any plane that has not undergone Transportation Security Administration inspections of all passengers. Such planes cannot pass through the TFR at any altitude below 18,000 feet, which is above the ceiling of most private aircraft. www.nbaa.org/ops/airspace/alerts/notams/temporary-flight-restrictions.php#presidential.
6 A no fly zone might conceivably be created to ground the air assets of a non-sovereign entity, although this has not happened to date, probably because groups large enough to possess significant air assets typically also possess and exercise sovereignty over some territory. A time may come when a no fly zone is imposed on a non-state actor that has deployed drones for intelligence gathering or for weapons delivery. Such a no fly zone or no-drone zone would likely be prohibitively difficult to enforce.
7 In two out of three instances to date (Operation Northern and Southern Watch over Iraq and Operation Odyssey Dawn/Unified Protector over Libya) the imposition of a no fly zone has been preceded or accompanied by attacks on the air defense systems of the target country. In the third case, Operation Deny Flight over Bosnia, the surface-to-air missiles held by the Bosnian Serbs were difficult to locate and strikes against them might have been answered by attacks on UN ground forces in the region.
8 Michael O'Hanlon says "Some believe that only a high-technology stand-off warfare force can make the U.S. military usable in a domestic political context, given Americans' aversion to suffering casualties." *Technological Change and the Future of Warfare* (Washington: Brookings Institution Press, 2000) p. 7. No fly zones represent an example of just the sort of high-technology stand-off warfare that O'Hanlon refers to. To date they have proven reliably casualty-free.
9 Pape, Robert, *Dying to Win: The Strategic Logic of Suicide Terrorism*, New York: Random House, 2005.
10 Media searches for the phrase "no fly zone" in the mid-1990s (when two no fly zones were in progress) bring few hits, even in papers like *The New York Times* with substantial international coverage. In more local papers the phrase rarely or never appears.
11 www.nato.int/nato_static/assets/pdf/pdf_2011_03/20110927_110311-UNSCR-1973.pdf.
12 Later Turkish pilots joined in enforcement missions as part of Operation Northern Watch.
13 In Operation Haven, which turned into Operation Provide Comfort and finally into Operation Northern Watch, about 20,000 troops were deployed between early May and mid-July 1991 to push back Iraqi troops, create a haven inside Iraq and deliver security, shelter, food and medicine to about 450,000 Kurdish refugees. After the troops were withdrawn, the air aspects of the operation continued uninterrupted until 2003. Geographic factors aided in creating and maintaining separation between Iraqi troops and Kurdish civilians.

34 *About no fly zones*

14 Mueller, Karl P., "Denying Flight: Strategic Options for Employing No-Fly Zones." Santa Monica, CA: RAND Corporation, 2013. www.rand.org/pubs/research_reports/RR423.html.
15 More than 75,000 sorties were flown in the enforcement of Northern Watch over the 12 years between 1991 when it was established and 2003 when it concluded with the beginning of the second invasion of Iraq.
16 Mueller, Karl P., "Denying Flight: Strategic Options for Employing No-Fly Zones." Santa Monica, CA: RAND Corporation, 2013, pp. 6–27.
17 The E3 is built on a Boeing 707 airframe with advanced sensor and avionics packages and flown by the US Air Force. The E2 is a carrier-capable propeller driven plane flown by the Navy and capable of carrier operations.
18 AWACS is an acronym for airborne warning and control system.
19 A more elaborate no fly zone might ban more kinds of flights (commercial as well as military, helicopter as well as fixed-wing) or might ban more than one side in a conflict from flying. A more aggressive no fly zone might begin with the suppression or destruction of air defense systems. In the case of the Iraqi no fly zones, those systems had already been destroyed or degraded in Operation Desert Storm.
20 Serafino, Nina, "Peacekeeping and Related Stability Operations: Issues of U.S. Military Involvement," CRS Report RL33557, 24 January 2007, p. 21. www.dtic.mil/dtic/tr/fulltext/u2/a479080.pdf.
21 Belasco, Amy, "The Cost of Iraq, Afghanistan, and Other Global War on Terror Operations Since 9/11," CRS Report RL33110, 8 December 2014, p. 6.
22 Bilmes, Linda and Stiglitz, Joe, *The Three Trillion Dollar War*, New York: Norton, 2008.
23 Keegan, John, *The Second World War*, New York: Viking, 1989, p. 420.
24 "The number of men lost in air action was 79,265 Americans and 79,281 British. More than 18,000 American and 22,000 British planes were lost or damaged beyond repair." *United States Strategic Bombing Surveys*, reprinted by Air University Press, 1987, p 6. https://web.archive.org/web/20080528051903/http://aupress.au.af.mil/Books/USSBS/USSBS.pdf. Accessed 27 June 2017.
25 Craven, W.F. and Cate, J.L. (eds.) *The Army Air Forces In World War II*. Vol. I: Prewar Plans and Preparations, pp, 106–107.
26 This was in addition to 3,587 helicopters.
27 The CEP or circular error probability is the radius of the circle within which half of the munitions predictably will fall.
28 Boot, Max, "From Saigon to Desert Storm: How the US Military Reinvented Itself after Vietnam," *American Heritage*, November 2006, Vol. 57, No. 6.
29 The Boeing E-3, used by the Air Force, has a counterpart in the Northrup Grumman E-2 which is used by the Navy. The E-2 provides much the same functions as the E-3 and is carrier-capable.
30 Lambeth, Ben, *The Transformation of American Air Power*, New York: Cornell University Press, 2000. This was a dramatic departure from the results eight years earlier in the 1974 Yom Kippur War when Israel lost at least 102 aircraft.
31 The surface-to-air missiles destroyed were Soviet-made SA-6s. It is important to note that in the air battle over the Bekaa Valley, the Syrians did not follow fundamental good defensive practices. Although the SA-6 is a mobile system, the Syrians had dug them in and left them unmoved for many months, which meant the Israelis had mapped and had practiced mock strikes on their precise locations. Nor had the Syrian operators practiced good radar emission control, which allowed the Israelis to record the unchanging frequencies the operators used and so first to jam, then to target the missile sites. The Syrians' poor practices made it possible for the Israelis to prepare and rehearse their operation, which was labeled Operation Mole Cricket 19, and the repeated rehearsals actually desensitized the Syrian and PLO forces who had reacted quickly to several early rehearsals but

remained passive at the opening of the actual attacks. The indiscipline of the Syrian operators cannot be counted on in future confrontations, but some of the advantages the Israelis gained may be available to enforcers of no fly zones because the repetitive mechanics of no fly zone enforcement tend to allow the kind of information gathering and rehearsal the Israelis practiced, unless the enemy is exceptionally active and attentive in their countermeasures. For a study of Operation Mole Cricket 19, see Clary, David E., "The Bekaa Valley: A Case Study," Thesis submitted to the Air War College. www.dtic.mil/dtic/tr/fulltext/u2/a192545.pdf (accessed 27 June 2017.)

32 The term air superiority describes a condition in which a power may use its air assets without *prohibitive* interference by its opponent. Air supremacy or air dominance refers to that further degree of control under which the power uses its air assets without *effective* interference in its operations. Operating without effective interference amounts to operating with impunity and at will.

33 Air Force Historical Research Agency, *USAF Manned Combat Aircraft Losses 1990–2002*, www.dtic.mil/dtic/tr/fulltext/u2/a434084.pdf.

34 The closing words of remarks to the American Legislative Exchange Council 1 March 1991, "It's a proud day for America. And, by God, we've kicked the Vietnam syndrome once and for all." www.presidency.ucsb.edu/ws/?pid=19351.

35 Halberstam, David, *The Making of a Quagmire: America and Vietnam during the Kennedy Era*, Lanham, MD: Rowman and Littlefield, 2008.

36 The situation was made more difficult by the fact that Bush himself had called on the Kurds to rise. On 15 February 1991, during the air campaign that initiated Operation Desert Storm, President Bush spoke to the Iraqi people over Voice of America, saying "There is another way for the bloodshed to stop: and that is, for the Iraqi military and the Iraqi people to take matters into their own hands and force Saddam Hussein, the dictator, to step aside and then comply with the United Nations' resolutions and rejoin the family of peace-loving nations." He repeated this appeal on several occasions. http://transcripts.cnn.com/TRANSCRIPTS/0101/05/cp.00.html. Accessed 17 July 2017.

37 The geography west of Basra where the Shi'ites were located made creating an enclave much more difficult than in the mountains to the north where the Kurds had fled. Nor did the Shi'ites have supporters among NATO powers to the degree the Kurds did.

38 From an NSC paper by the Interdepartmental Group for Africa, 10 February 1969: "the role of the U.S.: Except for our deep concern regarding humanitarian relief, we have regarded the civil war as primarily a Nigerian and African problem. We have: (a) continued to recognize the FMG [Federal Military Government]; (b) imposed an arms embargo on both sides; (c) contributed to the international relief effort ($30 million publicly and privately, approximately 60 percent of the total, plus eight Stratofreighter aircraft); and (d) voiced political support for a negotiated settlement in the context of one Nigeria with workable safeguards for Ibo protection. We have looked to (1) the OAU, the British and the Commonwealth Secretariat to take the lead in peace-making, with active encouragement from us both publicly and privately, and (2) the ICRC (together with the religious voluntary agencies in Biafra) and the OAU to take the lead in the negotiation and operation of relief arrangements, with our active moral, diplomatic and material support." Office of the Historian, US Department of State, Paper Prepared by the NSC Interdepartmental Group for Africa, Washington, 10 February 1969. https://history.state.gov/historicaldocuments/frus1969-76ve05p1/d35 (accessed 28 December 2017.)

39 See the analysis of Operation Urgent Fury in Luttwak, Edward, *The Pentagon and the Art of War*, New York: Simon & Schuster, 1985.

40 The Somalia intervention occurred just about the time no fly zones became technically feasible. It was also the time that they became geopolitically possible. No

fly zones have in all cases required multilateral authorizations, typically through the United Nations. The dissolution of the Soviet Union in 1991 removed, for some years at least, the expected Soviet veto and made UN Security Council resolutions for such purposes attainable.

41 Power, Samantha, "Bystanders to Genocide," *The Atlantic Monthly*, September 2001. www.theatlantic.com/magazine/archive/2001/09/bystanders-to-genocide/304571/.
42 Shacochis, Bob, *The Immaculate Invasion*, New York: Grove Press, 2010.
43 The UN Protection Force in the former Yugoslavia, UNPROFOR, consisted of troops from over 40 nations and suffered 167 deaths. "Former Yugoslavia UNPROFOR Profile," Department of Public Information, United Nations, 31 August 1996. https://peacekeeping.un.org/en. Accessed 2 December 2017.
44 New York Times article by Dave Philipps, 4 February 2017, titled "Special Operations Troops Top Casualty List as U.S. Relies More on Elite Forces," www.nytimes.com/2017/02/04/us/navy-seal-william-ryan-owens-dead-yemen.html.
45 www.nytimes.com/2017/02/04/us/navy-seal-william-ryan-owens-dead-yemen.html?rref=collection%2Fsectioncollection%2Fus&action=click&contentCollection=us&region=rank&module=package&version=highlights&contentPlacement=6&pgtype=sectionfront&_r=0.
46 Since *jus ad bellum* can be translated "the right to war," this phrase might also be translated "the right to force."
47 Brunstetter, Daniel and Braun, Megan, "Recalibrating Our Understanding of the Moral Use of Force" *Ethics and International Affairs*, Vol. 27, No. 1, February 2013. www.ethicsandinternationalaffairs.org/2013/from-jus-ad-bellum-to-jus-ad-vim-recalibrating-our-understanding-of-the-moral-use-of-force/.
48 Kurth, James, "Humanitarian Intervention After Iraq: Legal Ideals versus Military Realities," *Orbis*, Vol. 50, No. 1, 87–101.
49 Kuperman, Alan, "A Model Humanitarian Intervention? Reassessing NATO's Libya Campaign," *International Security*, Vol 38, No. 1, 105–136.

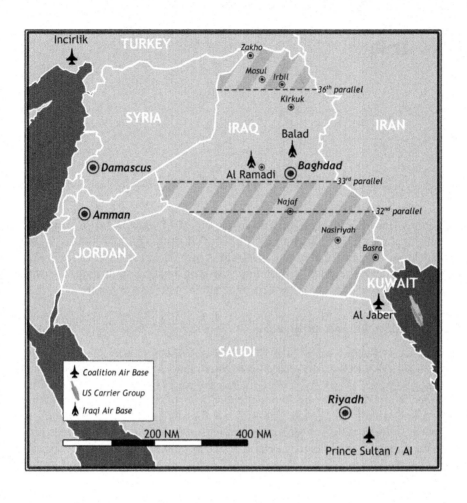

2 Iraq

Saddam Hussein's invasion of Kuwait in August of 1990 ended in a military rout. Operation Desert Storm was a 38-day air campaign followed by a 100-hour ground offensive that left the Iraqi Army decimated. On 27 February 1991, President George HW Bush addressed the nation, announcing, "Kuwait is liberated. Iraq's army is defeated. Our military objectives are met."[1]

Establishing the first no fly zone

Three days after the speech, the UN Security Council passed Resolution 686, which set the terms for the ceasefire negotiations. It noted the coalition's suspension of the offensive combat operations and laid out the actions Iraq needed to take to permit the definitive end to the hostilities, including accepting liability under international law for any loss, damage or injury in Kuwait, releasing all Kuwaiti or foreign nationals detained in Iraq, returning all Kuwaiti property seized, ceasing hostile actions including missile attacks and flights of combat aircraft, arranging for the release of all prisoners of war and remains of any deceased personnel, providing information on Iraqi land mines and booby traps as well as any chemical and biological weapons, and finally designating military commanders to meet with the coalition military commanders.[2]

The next day ceasefire negotiations took place at Safwan air field in Iraq. General Norman Schwarzkopf, the Commander in Chief of Central Command and overall commander of Operation Desert Storm, dictated the terms of the ceasefire – the release of prisoners of war, the identification of coalition soldiers missing in action, the return of bodily remains, the disclosure of minefields, the release of civilian Kuwaitis taken to Iraq against their will and the drawing of the ceasefire lines.[3] At the end of the discussion, General Schwarzkopf asked if there were any other matters to discuss. Iraqi Lieutenant General Sultan Hashim Ahmad, leader of the Iraq delegation, spoke up, "We have one point .... You know the situation of our roads and bridges and communications .... We would like to fly helicopters to carry officials of our government in areas where roads and bridges are out. This has nothing to do with the front line. This is inside Iraq."[4]

Schwarzkopf agreed, noting in his memoir: "It appeared to be a legitimate request. And given that the Iraqis had agreed to all our requests, I didn't feel like it was unreasonable to grant one of theirs . . . . So we will let the helicopters fly. That is a very important point and I want to make sure it's recorded, that military helicopters can fly over Iraq. Not fighters, not bombers."[5]

Over the course of the next month, the UN Security Council worked on a subsequent resolution, eventually passing Resolution 687 on 3 April 1991. It laid out the comprehensive terms with which Iraq was to comply, none of which envisioned a military or observation force in Iraq. It did allow for a United Nations Iraq-Kuwait Observation Mission that would be deployed along the demilitarized zone that was established 10 kilometers into Iraq and 5 kilometers into Kuwait. Its concluding paragraph, however, unremarked upon at the time, gave the justification and authority for what became the no fly zones. That paragraph stated that the UN Security Council would "take such further steps as may be required for the implementation of the present resolution and to secure peace and security in the region."[6]

The no fly zones in Iraq lasted from 1991–2003. They are unquestionably the most successful no fly zone operations in history. Not a single coalition aircraft was lost to enemy fire, and the coalition successfully contained and restrained the Iraqi armed forces throughout those years.

Iraq was the first attempt in history to impose no fly zones, and the two zones created in Iraq are the most straightforward and most easily applied to date. First, they were instituted after the Iraqi military was soundly defeated. Before the war Iraq possessed over 900 combat aircraft including modern French Mirage and Russian MiG fighters.[7] By the war's end those forces had been destroyed or dispersed. Second, there was no need to roll back Iraqi air defenses. They had already been severely damaged. Third, the no fly zones were imposed in Iraq, a location where the geography makes it one of the easier places to make war, especially war from the air. The desert offers great advantages to those in the air, making it difficult for those on the ground to conceal and camouflage their equipment, and the fact that most military equipment, especially air defense systems, is apart and away from urban areas makes it easier to locate and strike without doing unintended damage or killing. Fourth, the command structure was unitary, and the world was unified in its opposition to Saddam Hussein and its desire to contain him in the aftermath of his invasion of Kuwait.

Initially created as a way to stop President Saddam Hussein from flying his fixed-wing aircraft, the no fly zones evolved over the course of their enforcement, mutating and adapting to serve the increasingly wider goals of constraining Saddam from injuring his own people, then of containing his recovering forces and his ambitions and restraining his returning power to intimidate both his own people and other states. Iraq is a study in the practicality of no fly zones, how they can be a scalable and valuable use of force, how they can adapt to new circumstances, and ultimately, how they are especially useful to prevent or to contain, how they have some value to coerce and how they are often a much longer term commitment than any initially envision.

The no fly zones changed over the course of a dozen years. Initially serving to protect the Kurds and Shia, they became a tool to target and to monitor Iraq's military and its pursuit of weapons of mass destruction. They grew into a coercive tool to try to convince Saddam to comply with mandated United Nations inspections of his weapons of mass destruction program, and they eventually, after the September 11 attacks and the Bush administration's decision to retaliate against Iraq, served as a pre-invasion systematic rollback of the Iraqi air defenses. In the latter years of the no fly zones but before 911, many questioned their efficacy and believed they were too risky and costly with no end in sight. They were, however, effective in containing Saddam Hussein at a much lower cost than the invasion of Iraq, though they were unable to bring about any fundamental changes to the regime. This demonstrates some of the limits of no fly zones. Undoubtedly Kurdish and Shia lives were saved – in fact the northern no fly zone allowed the Kurds a freedom of action and independence to begin a path toward self-governance – but there were severe limits to what could be accomplished beyond preventing Saddam from turning his military on his people.

The northern and southern no fly zones were two separate but related campaigns. The first was imposed in April 1991 and the second was imposed in August 1992. The story of their development and execution reflects the unique circumstances and nature of the operation in Iraq, as well as the favorable geography for such operations. The no fly zones were supported by most of the world's leaders, were feasible, moderately costly, minimally risky, possessed little chance of escalation and were politically useful as tools of containment and limited coercion.

Northern no fly zone

Operations Provide Comfort I and II

After Operation Desert Storm was complete, the Bush administration was eager to pass the situation back to the Iraqis. On 13 March, ten days after the Safwan meeting, President Bush stated "I think it would be better if everybody stayed out and let the Iraqi people decide what they want to do."[8] White House Press Secretary Marlin Fitzwater reaffirmed this position 13 days later stating, "We're not going to take a position (in Iraq's postwar situation)."[9] Given these statements of American intent, and perceiving Saddam's position of weakness at war's end, the Shias in the south and the Kurds in the north were motivated to act. They expected that President Saddam Hussein, responsible for the systematic and brutal repression they had endured, was vulnerable. At this juncture, President Bush implicitly offered strong encouragement for an uprising but extended no promises of practical assistance.

Earlier he had been far more explicit and encouraging. Hoping to incite a swift military coup, he made a statement on Voice of America on 15 February, during the air campaign. He called on "the Iraqi military and the Iraqi people to take matters into their own hands and force Saddam Hussein, the dictator, to step aside and then comply with the United Nations' resolutions and rejoin the family of peace-loving nations."[10] He made a similar appeal on 1 March, two days before the ceasefire, encouraging the Iraqi people to put Saddam aside.

Kurds in the north and Shia in the south rose up immediately. The pattern of rebellions in each city and township was very consistent during the first week of March. Masses would gather in the streets to denounce Saddam Hussein. They would seize the mayor's office, the Baath party headquarters, and the secret police building, but beyond these initial steps, they were disorganized and showed no unified capacity to carry their efforts further. Nor did they possess the weapons and means to fight the military and police forces who remained loyal to Saddam.

The same divisions that prompted rebellion also made its success less likely because they meant that Saddam faced a divided opposition. Kurds comprised approximately 17 percent of the population; Shia Arabs comprised another 60 percent and the ruling Sunni Arabs comprised approximately 20 percent. The Sunni Arabs dominated the Kurds and Shia, and fear of losing their dominance was a critical factor in their response to the rebellions.

Saddam initially tried to coopt the Shia and Kurdish leaders by offering them posts in the central government, but they rejected his proposals. Saddam and his forces then regrouped and went on an offensive against the rebellious minorities. Saddam's forces were helped by several factors, the first of which was that the most loyal of Saddam's forces, the elite Republican Guard, had been damaged but by no means destroyed in the war to liberate Kuwait. Crucially, the ceasefire agreement of 3 March had allowed the Iraqi military to fly helicopters.

Saddam's Sunni forces responded brutally, flying helicopter gunships that fired indiscriminately on rebels and other civilians, firing artillery barrages into opposition areas, and rounding up thousands and arresting or executing them. When the US and its allies did not respond, the Iraqi army launched a major offensive into northern Iraq on 28 March. Finally, when Iraqi forces shelled the northern town of Dahuk, Jalal Talabani, the leader of the Patriotic Union of Kurdistan and Massoud Barzani, the leader of the Kurdistan Patriotic Union, publicly called on the departing coalition forces to stop the slaughter.

In his memoirs, Secretary of State James Baker reflected the reluctance of the administration to intervene:

We never embraced as a war aim or a political aim the replacement of the Iraqi regime. We did, however, hope and believe that Saddam Hussein would not survive in power after such a crushing defeat. Ironically, the uprisings in the north and south, instead of lessening his grip on power as we felt they would, contributed to it, as he skillfully argued to his army that these events required his continued leadership in order to preserve Iraq. When he managed to consolidate his power, Saddam scrambled our strategic calculations.[11]

Baker continues: "our political calculations were bolstered by an intense reluctance within the government to do anything that might result in the eventual reinvolvement of US military forces in Iraq."[12] And yet, as the humanitarian crisis escalated, the Bush administration was unable to avoid involvement.

As Saddam's forces brutalized the Kurds, the Kurds fled north where the world press captured their plight as they massed in the mountains of northern Iraq and Turkey. By 2 April, it is estimated that 800,000 Kurds had fled to Iran, 300,000 to southeastern Turkey and another 100,000 to an area along the Iraq/Turkey border. International relief agencies reported that 800 to 1,000 Kurds were dying each day. The humanitarian crisis sparked a global movement calling for some form of intervention. Pressure on the United States to act was increased by the fact that Turkey, a stalwart US ally throughout the previous months, was facing a crisis with which they could not contend.

Led by the United Kingdom and their new Prime Minister, John Major, and encouraged by France, the United Nations Security Council passed Resolution 688 on 5 April. This resolution condemned the repression of the Iraqi civilian population and demanded that Iraq "immediately end this repression and express[ed] the hope in the same context that an open dialogue will take place to ensure that the human and political rights of all Iraqi citizens are respected." It insisted that Iraq allow immediate access by international humanitarian organizations, and requested that the UN Secretary-General pursue humanitarian efforts in Iraq. Although experts have debated the legal basis for the humanitarian intervention efforts (UNSCR 688 did not authorize the use of force under Chapter VII of the UN Charter, nor did it mention a no fly zone), the Bush administration used this resolution as a basis for beginning Operation Provide Comfort, the massive United Kingdom and US-led military operation to defend the Kurds fleeing Iraq, to deliver humanitarian aid and eventually to resettle the Kurds back in Iraq. In order to carry out Operation Provide Comfort, a no fly zone was necessary.

Three days after the UN Security Council Resolution, Secretary of State James Baker visited the Kurdish refugees on the border with Iraq. Whatever reservations about the intervention he may have held, they were overcome during his visit to the mountains of the Turkish/Iraqi border on 8 April. He wrote that "my experience on that rugged hillside was not only the catalyst for a huge expansion of American and international relief to the Kurds that came to be known as Operation Provide Comfort: it also galvanized me into pressing for a new policy ... of establishing safe havens for the Kurds in northern Iraq—refugee camps secured by US forces."[13]

The operation was initially led by US Air Force Major General James Jamerson who recognized from the outset that it was to include much more than airdropping humanitarian supplies. The scope of the operation expanded greatly, and it became clear that a ground presence in Iraq would be necessary. Army Lieutenant General John Shalikashvili took command, with Major General Jamerson serving as the commander of the air component.

Two days after the passage of UNSCR 688, on 7 April, President Bush declared that no Iraqi aircraft of any kind would be allowed to fly north of the 36th parallel. This declaration was the beginning of what would be a nearly twelve-year enforcement of the northern Iraqi no fly zone.

This no fly zone was not something envisioned when the operation began. Air Force General Charles Wald, Deputy Commander for Operations of the 86th Tactical Fighter Wing, was sent to Incirlik along with General Jamerson in the early hours of the operation. Wald was an F-15 fighter pilot who saw that armed escorts would be needed to assure the safety of the slow, low flying C-130 cargo planes that would deliver the food and supplies into northern Iraq

The MC-130Es flew their first mission on 7 April when two aircraft dropped 2,000-pound bundles of blankets and troop rations.[14] General Wald was the lead planner for this. The overriding concern was the vulnerability of the slow-flying C-130 aircraft. If the Iraqis chose to oppose this effort, the C-130s would be an easy target for Iraqi fighters or surface-to-air missiles. Wald and his planners left nothing to chance, not knowing how the Iraqis would react. Flights of A-10 Warthogs preceded cargo planes conducting airdrop missions, looking for any Iraqi opposition. F-16 and F-15 fighters patrolled the skies to prevent any Iraqi aircraft from flying, with an E-3 AWACS constantly airborne to provide command and control as well as radar coverage of any air activity. Coalition aircraft provided close air support. Bombs were never dropped, and pilots termed these missions "motivational CAS," as low-flying fighters would "buzz" Iraqi unit positions that had not withdrawn.[15] In launching Operation Provide Comfort, General Wald pioneered the tactics for the first no fly zone and set the pattern for others to follow.

Despite the flurry of air activity, it was still not envisioned that a no fly zone would go beyond a humanitarian mission to become a tool of containment and coercion. The immediate task at hand was to deliver humanitarian assistance, and then encourage the Kurds to return to Iraq. The Turkish government had been a close ally in the war against Saddam, but they were not willing to accept the Kurdish refugees permanently.

The initial relief effort lasted from 7 April until 24 July. The Iraqis did not oppose the no fly zone at this early stage, nor did they oppose the ground operation in Iraq. Two joint task forces (JTFs) conducted the military effort on the ground. First was JTF "Alpha" led by Army Brigadier General Richard Potter, composed primarily of the 10th Special Forces (SF) Group. Their task was to alleviate the dying and suffering in Turkey. The second component, JTF "Bravo," led by Army Major General Jay Garner, was centered around the Marine Corps 24th Marine Expeditionary Unit, commanded by Colonel Jim Jones, and the 3d Battalion, 325th Infantry, commanded by Lieutenant Colonel John Abizaid.

It is noteworthy that each of these three officers of JTF Bravo rose to great prominence. General Garner would earn three stars and would be tapped to lead the post-war reconstruction efforts in Iraq in 2003. Colonel Jones would earn four stars and rise to become the Commandant of the Marine Corps, the Supreme Allied Commander in Europe, and then the National Security Advisor. Lieutenant Colonel Abizaid would also earn four stars and become the Commander of Central Command. Out of roughly 10,000 lieutenant colonels in the Army, only seven can achieve four star rank at any one time.[16] In addition, Lieutenant General John Shalikashvili earned a fourth star and became Chief of Staff of the Army, Supreme Allied Commander in Europe and Chairman of the Joint Chiefs of Staff.

This component pushed into Iraq, occupying the town of Zakho on the border with Turkey, and prepared it for incoming Kurds. They pushed further into Iraq, led by Abizaid's battalion. "Abizaid was fighting what he would later call a 'dynamic war of maneuver.' He was operating aggressively but generally without shooting to carve out a safe area for the Kurds by moving around Iraqi army outposts ... . U.S. Air Force warplanes circling overhead, ready to attack. Wary of having American troops behind them, with routes of retreat cut off by the planes overhead, the Iraqi forces would then fall back and yield control of territory."[17] The safeguard against attack, and the containment tool for the Iraqi military was coalition fighter jets, a model that would continue for 12 years.

Coalition ground military forces departed Iraq on 24 July, leaving the operation to the United Nations. Provide Comfort I officially ended, although the military coalition maintained a residual force in southeastern Turkey to keep the Iraqi military in check.

Operation Provide Comfort II began immediately thereafter with a different goal from its predecessor. Commanded by Major General Jamerson, Provide Comfort II had as its mission a "show of force" to deter any new Iraqi attacks on the Kurds. The coalition believed that a continued "virtual presence" of aircraft flying over the Kurdish areas would provide a sufficient deterrent to keep the Iraqi army from attacking the Kurds.

Few expected that this no fly zone would continue and evolve as it did. The history of events is instructive since it demonstrates in this case at least the ability of air power to contain a hostile force (the Iraqi Army) as well as to serve as a way to initiate action, which on occasion it did.

The coalition continued to fly over northern Iraq north of the 36th parallel throughout 1991 and 1992, largely without incident. During late 1992, however, the no fly zones took on a new aspect as Saddam made them occasions to dramatize his defiance to the Americans and their coalition, and the coalition in turn used them as opportunities to display their dominance. Saddam made a point of refusing to return Silkworm missiles his forces had taken from Kuwait and delaying in withdrawing from police posts on land that Iraq was to hand over to Kuwait. He also attempted to limit UN access to Iraq by cutting back on the number of flights he would allow to enter. Finally, on January 16, 1993, Saddam announced his intention to shoot down coalition aircraft over the no fly zones. His behavior and the coalition's response demonstrate no fly zones functioning as theater for competitive displays of power and will.

The Iraqis first began actually opposing the no fly zone in January 1993, firing antiaircraft artillery (AAA) at American F-111 fighters on 17 January 1993, just three days before the end of the administration of George HW Bush. The American fighters did not respond, but two days later, Iraqi AAA once again fired on American F-16s. Within an hour an F-4G attacked an air defense site that was targeting a French reconnaissance plane. That same day an American F-16 shot down an Iraqi MiG-23 that had violated the no fly zone in northern Iraq.

The next day American F-4Gs attacked a surface-to-air missile site that had targeted them, and F-16s attacked a AAA site that fired on them. There would be seven more incidents in 1993 (three more in January, one in February, two in April and one in August) when Iraqi air defenses targeted or fired on coalition aircraft. The aircraft responded by bombing air defense sites.

The Black Hawk friendly fire incident

After August 1993, Iraqi activity in the northern no fly zone stopped. The only significant event of 1994 was a friendly fire incident in which two US F-15s misidentified and shot down two US Army Black Hawk helicopters that were carrying members of the United Nations Provide Comfort coalition leadership. The incident is the only friendly fire incident in the history of American no fly zones and the only loss of life. (There have been no lives lost to enemy action.) Its occurrence reflects a unique confluence of events.

The Black Hawk helicopters began their flights from Diyarbakir, Turkey, 150 miles northwest of the Turkey-Iraq border. They proceeded into northern Iraq, picking up their passengers from the Provide Comfort military coordination center in Zakho, Iraq, just across the Turkish border. They then flew southeast toward Irbil, some 100 miles away, for scheduled meetings with Kurdish leaders. It was on this leg of their flight that they were targeted and shot down by the American F-15s.

How did this breakdown in coordination and communication occur? First, there was so little air activity in northern Iraq that the coalition rules of engagement permitted firing on both fixed wing and rotary wing aircraft. This would not have been the case in Bosnia, for instance, because the air traffic, especially the number of rotary wing flights, was so large as to be impossible to monitor and enforce.

Second, those involved made a number of mistakes. First, the F-15 pilots misidentified the Black Hawks as Russian made Mi-24 Hind helicopters during the visual identification pass (they flew within 1000 feet of the helicopters). Also, the IFF transponders (identification friend or foe) on the Black Hawks was not operating correctly. The controllers on the E-3 AWACS monitoring and controlling the airspace knew about the Black Hawk helicopters and had communicated with them, but the controllers failed to keep track of the Black Hawks after the helicopters departed Zakho and entered mountainous terrain, losing radar contact with them. Also, and most critically, the F-15 pilots were unaware that the Black Hawks would be flying in northern Iraq because the Black Hawk helicopter operations from Diyarbakir were not integrated with the no fly zone operations being flown out of Incirlik airbase. There were actually two air tasking orders published, one for Incirlik operations and one for Diyarbakir operations.

In the aftermath of the incident, the US Air Force implemented a number of specific actions to prevent the reoccurrence of such a tragedy, including a modification of the rules of engagement that restricted procedures for engaging Iraqi helicopters, inclusion of the Black Hawk flight times on the daily air tasking order, requirement for verbal confirmation of a positive IFF mode IV check for helicopters prior to entering Iraq, clarification of the responsibilities of the controllers on the AWACS aircraft, and painting white recognition stripes on the Black Hawk rotor blades to ease identification from the air.

As tragic as the friendly fire incident was, three years of experience in enforcing the northern Iraqi no fly zone had proven the operation to be remarkably effective. The Iraqi Air Force and Army were not operating in northern Iraq. The area had become a semi-autonomous zone that the Kurds dominated.

The rest of 1994 and 1995 were uneventful, with not a single incident occurring in the northern no fly zone. If the purpose of the no fly zone was to create a safe haven for the Kurds, then the operation must be considered an unambiguous success. That was not the declared or anticipated purpose of the no fly zone, but it became part of the de facto strategic policy toward Iraq, a policy that not only saved the Kurds a great deal of suffering but also helped keep alive a movement toward autonomy that has continued to the present day. This reality was not without complications, as the Kurds began to fight among themselves in 1996.

As the Kurds gained greater autonomy, in significant measure because of the protection provided by the no fly zone, the Patriotic Union of Kurdistan (PUK) and the Kurdistan Patriotic Union (KDP) fought each other. The PUK, led by Jalal Talabani, received support from Iran. The KDP, led by Massoud Barzani, faced with the prospect of fighting both Iran and the PUK, requested assistance from Saddam Hussein. Saddam saw an opportunity to retake northern Iraq and on 31 August 1996, 30,000 Iraqi troops attacked Irbil, a PUK held city that lay north of the 36th parallel.

In response, President Bill Clinton launched Operation Desert Strike on 3 September 1996. B-52 bombers supplemented by cruise missiles launched from navy ships attacked air defense missile sites in southern Iraq. Iraqi troops withdrew from northern Iraq, leaving the KDP in control of Irbil. The US, fearing an escalation by Iraqi forces, in turn evacuated over 6,000 pro-Western Kurds.

The dynamic of the northern no fly zone had fundamentally changed. Five and a half years into the operation, Provide Comfort continued to provide a blanket of security to the Kurds, but the feuding among the Kurds had complicated the situation, especially because Saddam's forces had intervened on behalf of one of the Kurdish parties, the KDP.

France withdrew from the coalition at the end of 1996, claiming that Provide Comfort no longer had a humanitarian mission. The Turkish Grand National Assembly approved a new, smaller operation, and the no fly zone enforcement changed its name from Operation Provide Comfort to Operation Northern Watch.

Northern no fly zone – Operation Northern Watch

The PUK-KDP conflict was further complicated by another Kurdish faction, the Kurdistan Worker's Party, or PKK, a militant organization that was fighting an armed struggle against Turkey for political rights and self-determination. In the intra-Kurdish conflict, the PKK sided with the PUK. In May of 1997 at the request of Massoud Barzani and the KDP, Turkey launched Operation Hammer, sending in over 30,000 troops to northern Iraq against the PKK.

The political dynamics of the situation were complicated. The entire northern no fly zone was executed from Turkish airbases, primarily Incirlik airbase, located in Adana near the Mediterranean coast and some 400 miles from Iraq. American and coalition forces flew with the permission of the Turkish government. From the beginning of Operation Northern Watch in January 1997 until the beginning of Operation Iraqi Freedom in March of 2003, the Turks limited the number of aircraft deployed to their air bases. They also limited the number of days each month in which the coalition could fly (never more than 18 days per month). It is important to note that these restrictions did not make it impossible to enforce the no fly zone. Northern Watch demonstrated that no fly zones can operate and accomplish their purpose with much less than full time surveillance and enforcement.

The contradictions in the situation were severe. Coalition aircraft were flying out of Turkey over northern Iraq to protect the Kurds from Iraqi forces, while at the same time, or during periods in which the coalition was not flying, the Turks were conducting an offensive against the PKK in northern Iraq and Turkey.

Nonetheless, the no fly zone continued, primarily because it was evolving into a new mission, which was seeking to coerce Saddam to comply with UNSCR 687, the resolution passed on 3 April 1991 that demanded that Iraq remove and destroy all chemical and biological weapons and ballistic missiles with a range greater than 150 km as well as abide by the Nuclear Non-Proliferation Treaty which stipulated that Iraq not seek to develop nuclear weapons. Previously the justification for the no fly zone had been UNSCR 688, which was the humanitarian mission to protect the Kurds. UNSCR 687 became the justification for the no fly zone and would also serve as the justification for subsequent bombings of Iraq and for the invasion in 2003.

The feuding among Kurdish parties and the Turkish conflict with the PKK largely resolved themselves over the course of 1997 and 1998. The Turks made progress in their military offensive against the PKK, eventually capturing their leader, Abdullah Ocalan in February of 1999. The KDP and PUK signed a formal peace treaty in September of 1998, known as the Washington Agreement. This accord, mediated by the US, resolved power and revenue sharing issues, denied the use of northern Iraq to the PKK and pledged the US to use military force to protect the Kurds from any aggression by Saddam Hussein. Through all this political activity, the northern no fly zone continued to operate. The no fly zone proved itself a flexible device, able to morph to fulfill changing roles and relatively easy to maintain over a good part of a decade. Throughout this time, the no fly zone did not attract substantial attention in the US populace. No fly zones, perhaps because they are not eventful or costly, would seem sometimes to fly under the radar of the American people.

Enforcing Northern Watch

The level of effort required to enforce the no fly zone was not insignificant, but it proved to be less than many would suppose. Aircraft were never airborne 24-hours a day, patrolling the skies of Iraq. In fact, as stated above, the Turkish government only permitted the coalition to fly 18 days each month, though there were periods of tension with Iraq in which they flew more frequently. The forces deployed to Incirlik consisted of a single F-15C squadron, an F-15E squadron, an F-16 squadron, an EA-6B Prowler squadron, a detachment of British Tornado or Jaguar aircraft for reconnaissance, three AWACS aircraft, a single RC-135 Rivet Joint aircraft, a half dozen tanker aircraft and a detachment of C-130 and Black Hawk helicopters for combat search and rescue. In total, it was just under 50 aircraft and 1,500 personnel.

On the days the coalition flew, the evolution began with the AWACS launching from Incirlik. The large Boeing 707 with a radar dish atop the fuselage would hold in the air near Incirlik and establish a data link with Turkish ground sites, a requirement of the Turks. Once that data link was established, the force would be cleared to launch.

Some 20 aircraft would line up in order on the taxiways. The synchronization of take-offs was critical to getting everyone airborne quickly so the package could transit together and enter Iraq together. If two aircraft take off together every 60 seconds, that would still mean over 10 minutes to get the package airborne. Generally the package would consist of four F-15C aircraft, armed with air-to-air missiles, whose sole mission was to be prepared to shoot down any Iraqi aircraft violating the no fly zone. Then there would be eight F-15E aircraft, armed not only with air-to-air missiles but also bombs to strike at air defense sites that might target coalition aircraft. Joining the F-15s would be six F-16CJ aircraft, also carrying air-to-air missiles as well as HARM (high-speed anti-radiation) missiles, an air-to-surface missile designed to home in on radar transmissions of surface-to-air missile systems. Then two EA-6B aircraft would follow, carrying HARM missiles along with jammers to suppress any radars that might target the aircraft. And finally, three Tornados or Jaguars followed carrying reconnaissance pods to take photos of Iraqi missile sites and military equipment.

The force would fly almost due east for an hour – 400 miles – and gather in the airspace immediately north of Iraq. The AWACS and Rivet Joint would take up their orbits while the fighters refueled on the tanker aircraft. The F-15Cs were normally the first to enter the airspace, initially to conduct a weather reconnaissance to ensure that any cloud coverage would not prevent the package from operating.

Then the entire package would follow, spending the next two to four hours patrolling the skies, dipping back north into Turkey to refuel every 45 minutes to an hour. For fighter aircraft, it was a relatively tight airspace – 80 miles from north to south and 235 miles from west to east. For aircraft traveling at seven miles per minute, that meant that a fighter pointed south could only maintain that direction for 10 minutes before turning back north in his circuit. For years, it was a quiet and uneventful, even mundane mission, 36 to 50 hours a month flying over Iraq, continuing to serve warning to Saddam that the US would not permit him to advance north. This quiet patrolling in the northern no fly zone continued without incident until immediately after Operation Desert Fox in December 1998, after which the no fly zone became an almost daily confrontation and exchange of fire, the Iraqis firing on coalition aircraft the coalition responding by bombing Iraqi air defense sites.

During the course of Operation Provide Comfort and Operation Northern Watch, the coalition flew about 78,000 sorties.

Southern no fly zone

Operation Southern Watch

The uprisings against Saddam Hussein in the south of Iraq in March 1991 in some respects resembled the Kurdish uprisings in the north but also differed in crucial ways. The Iraqi Army had been routed and many Shia soldiers had changed sides and joined the insurrection. When the Shia rebels asked for help from the Americans, they were rebuffed, in part because the Americans feared the insurgents were aligned with Iranian Islamists. There was less capacity to cooperate among the Shia than among the Kurds. Also, the flat, open geography south of the 32nd parallel initially made it hard for the insurgents to put themselves out of the reach of Saddam's forces though later, after their defeat, they retreated to marshy areas near Basra.

Saddam's forces counterattacked quickly, with the Republican Guard fighting against the Shia insurgents in Karbala. The diverse groups of Shia rebels did not support each other despite their shared desire for regime change. They had no common political or military program, no integrated leadership, very little coordination among them, and no American support. After the Shia forces were routed, Iraqi helicopter crews bombed, strafed and poured kerosene on the Shia refugees and set them on fire while American observation aircraft circled high overhead.

Within a week of the uprisings in the south, the Iraqi Army had brutally suppressed them. Thousands were killed, but although there were refugees, there was not an enormous refugee crisis as there was in the north.. Many of the Shia, including thousands of civilians, army deserters, and rebels, sought shelter in the remote Hawizeh Marshes that were adjacent to the Iranian border. Saddam's forces drained the marshes in reprisal.

There was an international effort to assist the Shia, but it was not effective. The United Nations announced on 10 July 1991 plans to open a humanitarian center at Lake Hammar in the south, but Iraqi forces did not allow UN relief workers into the country. Unlike the Kurdish crisis in the north, the international community did not follow through to assist those repressed by Saddam.

Little attention was paid to the plight of the Shia in southern Iraq until March-April 1992 when the Iraqi Army commenced an offensive against the refugees. The Iraqi forces used fixed-wing aircraft, and observers claimed that the Iraqi forces dumped toxic chemicals in the waters to try to drive out the Shia. In July the Iraqi government again attempted to drain the marshlands and to displace the Shia, burning down their homes, arresting thousands and moving them to detention camps.

This offensive finally generated enough political will among Western nations to cause them to act. On 11 August 1992, Britain, France and the United States voiced their collective opposition to Iraq's military campaign and pledged possible consequences. On 22 August President Bush announced a second no fly zone south of the 32nd parallel in order to protect the Shia from attacks by the Iraqi government. He justified this by referring to UNSCR 688 of 5 April 1991, the same resolution which was used to justify the northern no fly zone. This resolution condemned the suppression in Iraq but did not specifically authorize the use of force in Iraq. Thus began Operation Southern Watch.

The operation was under the direction of Joint Task Force-Southwest Asia, and the preponderance of the forces flew out of Saudi Arabia, though there were also assets that flew out of Kuwait, the United Arab Emirates, and from aircraft carriers based in the Persian Gulf. In total, the operation comprised approximately 70 aircraft. The southern no fly zone was a much vaster area to patrol, spanning nearly 250 miles from north to south and over 400 miles from west to east. Patrols would go from Basra in the far south almost to the southern suburbs of Baghdad and to the western Al Anbar province that housed many of Iraq's remaining fighter aircraft.

Iraqi forces initially complied with the no fly zone, but after the UN decided in November of 1992 to retain sanctions against Iraq, they began to challenge it. On 27 December 1992 an Iraqi MiG-25 Foxbat violated the no fly zone, flying south of the 32nd parallel. The MiG pilot locked his radar onto an American F-16 patrolling the no fly zone. The MiG was quickly shot down by the American F-16.

In response, Iraqi forces deployed surface-to-air missiles south of the 32nd parallel. The coalition ordered that Saddam move the missile batteries, but the order was ignored by the Iraqis and consequently, for approximately a week in January 1993, at the same time the northern no fly zone was being challenged by Saddam, coalition aircraft struck at the missile sites, and Navy Tomahawk missile strikes were conducted against a suspected nuclear weapons plant near Baghdad. The Iraqis de-escalated the crisis after President Clinton was inaugurated later in January, and events in the southern no fly zone continued without incident until June of 1993.

After Iraqi agents were suspected of trying to assassinate former President Bush during his visit to Kuwait, the Clinton administration responded with more cruise missile strikes. The rest of 1993 was quiet and uneventful, as were the first several months of 1994. In October of 1994 however, Saddam deployed two divisions of his Republic Guard to the Kuwaiti border, demanding that United Nations sanctions be lifted.

Operation Vigilant Warrior

The US responded to Saddam's actions with what would become known as Operation Vigilant Warrior, a deployment of American troops to the Persian Gulf region. Included in this deployment was an increase in the number of deployed air assets to over 170 aircraft. Concurrent with this deployment, the UN Security Council passed Resolution 949 on 15 October 1994, which demanded that Iraq withdraw its troops or face further measures. The day after UNSCR 949 was passed, Iraq began withdrawing its forces.

It is noteworthy that no air strikes were conducted during the crisis, but the presence of aircraft enforcing the southern no fly zone and the threat of air attacks were an important deterrent. As the crisis de-escalated, the US maintained a robust air presence, with over 120 aircraft deployed to the region, including A-10 Warthog ground attack aircraft in Kuwait.

1994 and 1995 were quiet periods in enforcing the southern no fly zone. 1996 was similarly quiet until 25 June 1996 when terrorists attacked the Khobar Towers military housing complex in Khobar, Saudi Arabia. The truck bomb destroyed an eight-story housing complex, killing 19 US air men, some of whom had been enforcing Operation Southern Watch. Although Iraq was not found to be responsible for the attack (the investigation concluded that Iran and Hezbollah were behind it), the US and coalition subsequently relocated the forces at Khobar and nearby Dhahran to the highly secure and remote Prince Sultan Air Base near Al-Kharj, Saudi Arabia.

Events in the southern no fly zone escalated again in September 1996 when, as noted above, Iraqi forces invaded northern Iraq on behalf of the KDP as the Kurds fought each other. In order to respond in the north, the US needed permission from the government of Turkey, which was unwilling to sponsor such action. The US instead launched 27 cruise missiles at targets in southern Iraq. The missiles were launched from US navy ships and B-52 bombers flying out of Guam. In addition, the southern no fly zone was extended 60 miles north from the 32nd parallel to the 33rd parallel.

As 1996 drew to a close, Northern and Southern Watch took on a new dynamic. Rather than serving as a means of protecting the Kurds and Shia, the no fly zones became an instrument of coercion as the coalition sought to gain Iraqi compliance in disarming their weapons of mass destruction (WMD) programs. The inspection regime created by the UN after the Gulf War was the United Nations Special Commission (UNSCOM), under the umbrella of UNSCR 687. The inspectors were to have unrestricted and unimpeded access to any site or facility in Iraq for the purpose of on-site inspection. Between 1991 and 1995, UNSCOM claimed to have uncovered a massive program to develop biological and nuclear weapons.

In the aftermath of Operation Iraqi Freedom, the Iraq Survey Group, a fact-finding mission sent to locate the weapons of mass destruction alleged to be possessed by Iraq, concluded that Saddam ended his nuclear program in 1991, that only a small number of old, abandoned chemical munitions could be discovered, that Saddam's regime abandoned its biological weapons program in 1995, and finally that Saddam desired to recreate Iraq's WMD capability in an incremental fashion, focusing on ballistic missile and tactical chemical warfare capabilities. Lastly, the Iraq Survey Group concluded that Saddam had deceived his own army as well as Western intelligence agencies into believing that he had WMD, believing that appearing to possess such weapons would deter his enemies from attacking Iraq or attempting to dislodge him.

In November of 1997, Saddam ejected the majority of the UNSCOM inspectors from Iraq. They returned shortly after intense negotiations at the United Nations, although their access was inhibited throughout the rest of 1997 and 1998. Finally, on 31 October 1998, Iraq announced that it was ceasing all interaction and cooperation with UNSCOM, and on 11 November 1998, UNSCOM left Iraq.

Throughout 1998 the foreign policy community was divided over America's Iraq policy. Many outside the administration were growing impatient with the strategy of containing Saddam and sought more decisive action. Republicans in academia and think tanks as well as members of Congress were critical, believing more should be done to compel Saddam to comply with the UN resolutions relating to his WMD program.

Representatives Benjamin Gilman (R-NY) and Christopher Cox (R-CA) introduced a bill known as the Iraq Liberation Act of 1998. It stated that Iraq had committed many and serious violations of international law, it had failed to comply with the requirements following the end of the 1991 Gulf War and it had further violated resolutions of the UN Security Council. It further declared that "it should be the policy of the United States to support efforts to remove the regime headed by Saddam Hussein from power In Iraq and to promote the emergence of a democratic government to replace that regime."[18] It went on to authorize the President to provide assistance to the Iraqi democratic opposition of up to $97 million, including military assistance. President Clinton signed the bill on 31 October 1998.

The Iraq Liberation Act showed the impatience of policymakers on both sides of the aisle and may highlight a weakness of no fly zones. They are not costly or risky or likely to excite opposition by being too demanding. They may, in fact, be so unobtrusive as to practically escape public notice. At the same time, however, they might cause frustration since they do so little to change a situation. In such circumstances, it is very likely that they will be underappreciated for their capacity to keep a situation stable. They are primarily instruments for stability and not for change. The two no fly zones in Iraq proved to be good instruments of containment but very poor instruments of coercion. They deterred much more effectively than they compelled Saddam Hussein. Absent a much more effective domestic opposition, they would not be good instruments for overthrowing the dictator. Subsequent events showed that a ground invasion followed by a long-term occupation could bring regime change, but not the establishment of a new regime.

The strongest voice of opposition to the Iraq Liberation Act was General Anthony Zinni, the commander of Central Command from 1997 to 2000. During Congressional testimony in October 1998, he dismissed the Iraq Liberation Act as a "Bay of Goats," referring to the failed 1961 Bay of Pigs operation in Cuba. At a Defense Writers Group interview after his testimony he stated, "I think a weakened, fragmented, chaotic Iraq, which could happen if this isn't done carefully, is more dangerous in the long run than a contained Saddam is now."[19]

Operation Desert Fox

Saddam's continued resistance and his stubborn refusal to allow the UN inspectors free access to questionable facilities brought affairs to a head. Air strikes had been threatened throughout 1998, and finally the UN inspectors left Iraq in frustration. Military planners at Central Command were tasked with providing options for a response. Chairman of the Joint Chiefs, Army General Hugh Shelton, directed General Anthony Zinni to plan 72 hours of air strikes, and to do it only with the forces that were already deployed to the theater. In other words, no other forces would be repositioned and deployed to conduct the air strikes.[20] The forces already in place to enforce the no fly zone, already supplied and manned and covered with a pre-existing UN authorization, would be repurposed to carry out the strikes. The bombing campaign, named Operation Desert Fox, demonstrated a no fly zone's flexibility and usefulness as prepositioned, pre-authorized resources already in region, well established, supplied, supported and oriented to the task and equipped with a pre-existing UN authorization. The long experience of running the no fly zones had generated superb intelligence and had produced well practiced forces.

The four-day bombing campaign began on 16 December 1998. Over the course of four days, nearly 200 US Air Force and US Navy carrier-based aircraft, as well as a dozen British aircraft, struck 97 targets, including air defense systems, command and control sites, suspected WMD industry and production sites, Republican Guard units and airfields. Among the more than 600 munitions were Tomahawk cruise missiles launched from US Navy ships as well as B-52 aircraft.

Significantly, Turkey did not allow aircraft to participate in Desert Fox. Aircraft that had been flying in Northern Watch stood down during the strikes of Desert Fox. There were, however, considerable forces available. Two aircraft carriers, the USS Enterprise and the USS Carl Vinson, were in the Persian Gulf, and both carrier air wings participated in the strikes. Two USAF F-16 squadrons flew from Al Jaber Air Base in Kuwait. EA-6B Prowler and F-15 Eagle aircraft flew from Prince Sultan Air Base in Saudi Arabia. B-1B aircraft flew from Thumrait Air Base in Oman. B-52 bombers flew from Diego Garcia. Support aircraft flew out of Al Dhafra Air Base in the United Arab Emirates as all as Sheikh Isa Air Base in Bahrain.

Not a single aircraft was lost during the four-day air campaign. The Iraqi air defense forces did not aggressively oppose the strikes, shooting their missiles without turning on their radar to guide the missiles and firing anti-aircraft artillery barrages haphazardly and without aiming. They would seem to have been deterred from using their weapons more effectively by the prospect of being interrupted in the firing sequence by a high-speed anti-radiation missile.

Desert Fox shows how a no fly zone can be an entree to further action, but not necessarily a slippery slope of escalation. The fact that sufficient forces were deployed and available is significant, as is the fact that the containment of Saddam continued after the 100-hour air campaign. No invasion of Iraq was necessary to deal with his behaviors.

Post Desert Fox no fly zone enforcement

A week and a half after Desert Fox, coalition forces once again began enforcing the no fly zones, both in the north out of Turkish air bases and in the south from carriers and air bases in Saudi Arabia and Kuwait. The first no fly zone efforts occurred on 28 December 1998 in northern Iraq. The pattern of quiet confrontation would change on that day and remain more contested for the remainder of the no fly zones. Iraqi air defense forces fired two SA-3 surface-to-air missiles at F-16s patrolling the northern no fly zone near Mosul, illuminating the aircraft with their radar. Coalition forces responded, dropping laser guided bombs on the missile site.

Two days later in the southern no fly zone, on 30 December 1999, Iraqi SA-6 surface-to-air sites fired six to eight missiles at American fighters. US F-16s responded by bombing the sites. A week later, on 5 January 1999, four Iraqi MiG-25 aircraft crossed into the southern no fly zone, initiating an air engagement in which American F-15 and F-14 aircraft fired missiles at the Iraqi MiGs, but the MiGs were able to evade and escape back to the north.

Saddam's strategy appeared to be aimed at cautious but continued confrontation. He sought to offer challenges without provoking crushing strikes, turning the no fly zones into theater where he could publicly act out his defiance. He offered a $14,000 reward for shooting down an American pilot.

What followed were almost daily challenges, an extended series of tests that showed the remarkable dominance of American air power. Over the course of four and a half years, coalition aircraft were regularly fired on by Iraqi air defenses and did not lose a single aircraft. This illustrates the unwillingness of Iraqi air defense operators, and perhaps Saddam himself, to truly provoke the American coalition. Rarely were any of the missiles fired guided by radar. Missile site operators had learned a hard lesson during Desert Storm, and that is if they used their radar systems for more than a few moments, then they would in all likelihood find the radar system targeted and destroyed by a coalition anti-radiation missile or precision guided bomb. This period also brought about a quiet debate, mostly among policy elites, about the utility and risk of no fly zones. As long as the enforcement of a no fly zone is deemed to provide strategic value without any risk and with limited costs, then the effort seems to be worth it. Remarkably, throughout this period the American populace appeared to be unaware that US aircraft were being fired on several times per week. The two no fly zones both offered the spectacle of an unusual use of force, one in which lives are unlikely to be lost, and the entire operation can be sustained for a matter of years with hundreds of hostile encounters, yet pass unnoticed.

Even if the public was unaware or indifferent as the almost daily confrontations continued, political and military leaders began to question the utility of the no fly zones. Coalition aircraft would fly into Iraq from the north and south, waiting for the Iraqi air defenses to initiate the action. The rules of engagement prohibited any coalition action until fired upon or targeted by Iraqi air defense radar systems. Iraqi air defenses would respond, and they would almost without exception be bombed.

Exact statistics are not available, but a press release by US Central Command reported that Iraq fired against allied aircraft on more than 1,050

56 *Iraq*

occasions from December 1998 to November 2001 in the southern no fly zone and had violated the southern no fly zone more than 160 times between December 1998 and November 2001. In the northern no fly zone, US European Command reported 143 incidents in 1999, 145 in 2000, 97 in 2001 and 32 during the first six months of 2002.[21]

One more massive air strike was conducted on 16 February 2001, when US and British aircraft struck five Iraqi air defense command and control installations, four of them located above the 33rd parallel. The primary goal of these strikes was to destroy a fiber optic network being installed by the Chinese that would have upgraded the Iraqi air defenses.

Throughout the period from Desert Fox until the invasion of Iraq in March 2003, the no fly zones served a different purpose than their original one. While the Kurds and Shia were not disturbed by Saddam's army or air force, the no fly zones grew to have a two-fold purpose: to coerce Saddam to allow UN inspectors into his country and to degrade Iraqi air defenses as the US planned to invade Iraq.

A year after Desert Fox, the UN created the United Nations Monitoring, Verification and Inspection Commission (UNMOVIC), passing UNSCR 1284 on 17 December 1999. It was envisioned as the follow-on organization to UNSCOM and was intended to carry on with the mandate to disarm Iraq of its WMDs and to operate a system of ongoing monitoring and verification to check Iraq's compliance. It would not conduct any inspections in Iraq until November 2002, when UNSCR 1441 was passed, which declared that Iraq was in material breach of previous resolutions that required its disarmament and that Iraq would be given "a final opportunity to comply with its disarmament obligations" and that the UN would "set up an enhanced inspection regime with the aim of bringing to full and verified completion the disarmament process."[22] Those inspections would be short-lived. Saddam continued to deny complete access. The US gave Iraq a deadline of 17 March 2003 to fully comply, and the inspectors withdrew from Iraq on 18 March 2003, a day before the invasion of Iraq.

Assessing the Iraqi no fly zones

At the end of 2002, support among senior policy makers for no fly zones appears to have been diminishing. There was an increasing concern about the risk involved, and had an aircraft been shot down, the calculus of the utility of the no fly zone would have changed markedly. Similarly, there was concern within the military about the long-term costs of flying aircraft at such an increased rate that the US would be unable to sustain such a tempo. Lastly, diplomats and statesmen were concerned about maintaining a coalition against Saddam Hussein as the embargo and other containment strategies seemed to be slowly degrading.

General Anthony Zinni remained a strong proponent of the no fly zones. As Tom Ricks recounts that Zinni's conclusion was that US policy on Iraq succeeded in the late nineties. "Containment worked. Look at Saddam—what did he have?" Zinni asked later. "He didn't threaten anyone in the region. He was contained. It was a pain in the ass, but he was contained. He had a deteriorated military. He wasn't a threat to the region." What's more, he said, it wasn't a particularly costly effort. "We contained, day-to-day, with fewer troops than go to work every day at the Pentagon."[23]

Zinni was in the minority at that time, but his analysis looks prescient many years later. When Zinni retired in September 2000 as the commander of Central Command, there were just over 23,000 troops in the region. A low-level war with Saddam was ongoing, the sanctions were leaking, and the coalition was not as unified as when it began. But as he stated, it was working, and at reasonable cost and risk, so much so that the no fly zone was not a topic in any of the presidential debates.

The no fly zones were of course only two of the tools used in a larger strategy of containment. Economic sanctions against Iraq, prepositioning ground forces in Kuwait as a deterrent, and intrusive inspections of Saddam's WMD program were also tools used in the execution of this strategy.

But containment is a status quo pursuit. It seeks to prevent one side from acting, or to prevent an enemy from expanding. As George Kennan declared in his famous "X" article, containment must be "long-term, patient but firm and vigilant."[24] Containment does not produce rapid change.

As the no fly zones entered their seventh and then eighth years, and as the daily clashes continued, the voices for a more aggressive strategy to depose Saddam were growing, as were the voices of those who questioned the effectiveness of the no fly zones. Two of the more respected voices in the foreign policy community wrote an op-ed in February 2001, stating

> Ten years after these zones were first established, Washington and London have little to show for this low-level war. Nor is it clear that maintaining the zones is important to our overall objective in the region—which is to make sure Hussein does not reconstitute his capability to produce weapons of mass destruction and to keep him firmly within a box so that Iraq's neighbors are secure and its internal minority populations are as safe as possible. [A]t a time when U.S. armed forces overseas may be overextended, the value of continuing this operation is questionable.[25]

Those who were bearing the brunt of the no fly zone operations, the US Air Force, were vocal in lamenting the toll it was taking. Tom Ricks quotes a tanker pilot, "We're running back-to-back marathons.... The airplanes may not be able to take it, and more importantly, the people may not. At some point you've got to say, I love my country, but I can't stay away from my family for eight years."[26]

There was also growing comment about the possibility of a pilot being shot down by the Iraqis and that the law of averages would eventually see a pilot

Table 2.1 Costs of Iraq no fly zone operations
Iraq No-fly Zone Operations Cost, FY 2005 Dollars[27] Millions of Dollars

Operation	FY91-FY95	FY96	FY97	FY98	FY99	FY00	FY01	FY02	Total of all years
Provide Comfort/Northern Watch	773.1	88.9	93.1	136.0	156.4	143.7	148.6	1,372.4	
Southern Watch	1,517.3	5,76.3	597.3	1,497.2	954.8	755.4	963.5		
Desert Strike/Intrinsic Action/Desert Spring		-	102.7	5.6	13.8	239.8	261.6		
Vigilant Warrior	257.7	-	-	-	-	-	-	-	
Desert Fox	-	-	-	-	92.9	-	-	-	
Totals	2,548.1	665.2	793.1	1,638.8	1,217.9	1,138.9	1,373.7	1,372.4	10,748.1

Estimated War Funding, Operation Iraqi Freedom[28] Millions of Dollars

FY03	FY04	FY05	FY06	FY07	FY08	FY09	FY10	Total
51,000	77,000	79,000	96,000	131,000	144,000	93,000	65,000	736,000

lost. The clear assumption in such commentary was that a single pilot lost would be an unacceptable cost. The sense of what was unacceptable had changed over the course of the past 30 years. In 11 days in December 1972, the US lost 14 B-52s during Operation Linebacker II over Vietnam. Each plane went down with a five-man crew for a loss of 70 persons – seven lives lost per day for the better part of two weeks. In 2001 it seemed unacceptable to lose a single pilot or aircraft.

As military planners and political leaders searched for something "beyond the no fly zones," an invasion of Iraq was put forward as the best option. With the benefit of hindsight, one can see the enormous costs involved, which should be compared to the costs of the no fly zones and the containment of Saddam.

Below is a table summarizing the cost of the no fly zones and the cost of the invasion of Iraq:

The cost in terms of dollars: over a span of twelve years the no fly zones over Iraq cost between ten and eleven billion dollars. Over a span of eight years the cost of the ground invasion of Iraq was around 740 billion dollars. This is a partial total since the war and the spending in Iraq has continued for six more years.

The cost in terms of lives: during the invasion and occupation of Iraq, 4,489 were killed, and over 32,000 were wounded among the coalition forces. For the dozen years of no fly zones, the losses to death and wounding by enemy action were zero. Casualties among the Iraqis since 2003 number well above 100,000. Iraqi casualties in the enforcement of Northern and Southern Watch were likely near zero.

Such a calculation can rightly be criticized for comparing incomparables. The invasion delivered regime change, something air power alone would not accomplish. And if, absent an invasion, the no fly zones had continued beyond 2003, the US and the coalition might still be depending on them to contain Saddam. One can imagine pilots being shot down, captured, held prisoner or killed. One can imagine the service chiefs going to Congress stating that they needed to reconstitute the force after flying fighters at three and four times the planned rate.

But if one does compare the no fly zones to the invasion and occupation, even such potential costs are nominal in comparison to the costs endured by the US and coalition and the costs inflicted on the Iraqis. The Iraqi no fly zones were conducted without the expense of inordinate treasure or blood, and they were maintained as part of a broad coalition that the US had only moderate difficulty in sustaining and keeping intact. Moreover, having such an armada constantly ready to act provided options, whether it was in opposing Saddam's deployment of forces to the Kuwaiti border in 1994 or in punishing Saddam's resistance to UN weapons inspectors in 1998's Operation Desert Fox.

When no fly zones were first considered in response to Saddam's attacks on the Kurds in 1991, the Bush administration was not only reluctant to intervene; it publicly opposed any action in Iraq even as the uprisings occurred.

Pressure from the British, the French and the Turks, reinforced by the world reaction to a grave humanitarian crisis, moved the Bush administration to intervene in northern Iraq, and it was not until another 17 months had passed that the Bush administration intervened in southern Iraq. Yet in retrospect, instituting a no fly zone to protect humanitarian aid deliveries did not prove difficult, costly or dangerous. Still, the same cycles of reluctance and delay emerged as policy makers sought responses to similar atrocities in Bosnia, Libya and Syria.

As the operations in Iraq proceeded, it appeared that air power could deny access, indeed almost control terrain, which previously was not something that was anticipated by even the staunchest air power advocates. There were a number of reasons why this was possible, some of which were unique to Iraq.

First, the Iraqi air defenses had been pummeled by the coalition during Desert Storm. After trying to oppose the coalition during the liberation of Kuwait, Iraqi air defense and air force pilots simply accepted that they could not survive against coalition fighters.

Second, the no fly zones were effective because the terrain in northern Iraq favors this kind of operation. The Zagros mountains of northern Iraq are so rugged as to prevent Saddam's ground forces from operating effectively, especially after they had been denied transport and supplies by air. Access is difficult, but also the lack of natural cover to hide forces makes them especially vulnerable to attack from the air. Most of the rest of northern Iraq is desert, which makes any movement of military forces susceptible to observation from the air.

Third, the operation also had unusually firm authorization from a coherent coalition which did not face high costs or high potential threats for participating. The authorizations from the United Nations may have been indefinite and incomplete, but they were sufficient to allow the US, Britain, France and Turkey to do what they were inclined to do. The coalition was also flexible and responsive to the concerns of its members. For example, because of Turkish objections the coalition's response to the Iraqi Army incursion into Kurdistan in 1996 was to conduct strikes in the southern no fly zone and not the north. It helped that Saddam was despised by nearly all of his neighbors (as were Slobodan Milosevic and Moammar Qaddafi in the two other no fly zone cases), and his defiance and threatening behavior helped maintain the coalition against him. In the end he overplayed his hand by hinting that he might have weapons of mass destruction and his false claims were used to end the no fly zones and institute the invasion and overthrow.

Could the no fly zones have continued to the present day, and continued to contain Saddam? They had been in place for 12 years by the time of the invasion, and they would have been in place for 14 more by the time of this writing. Although such longevity for a policy seems improbable, it is not clear why they could not have continued. Technological advances in the form of sensors and drones would only have made surveillance less difficult and less risky. In time the will to continue the sanctions that denied Saddam oil revenues might have failed and so undermined the coalition. Recourse to air strikes like those in 1994 and 1998 might in time have been ruled out as consensus faded. Still, it is hard to make the case that no fly zones, after working for 12 years, were on the brink of failure. It was impatience, not poor performance, that led to their termination and replacement with more violent and costly alternatives.

They were not on the brink of forcing out Saddam either, and that static and indeterminate state of affairs was not acceptable, especially to neoconservatives who saw in Saddam an opportunity to destroy a malefactor, plant a democracy, begin the transformation of the Middle East and improve the security of Israel. Nor was the situation tolerable to liberal internationalists who aimed both to end human rights abuses and to affirm the principles and establish the institutions that would raise the standard of behavior of actors like Saddam. No fly zones can't accomplish such ends and so tend to be less than completely satisfactory measures to neoconservatives and liberal internationalists. No fly zones in time may even come to seem to such analysts like obstacles to taking more effective steps.

To persons with more realist, limited ambitions, however, persons who aim to stabilize rather than to transform situations like the one in Iraq, no fly zones are more satisfactory options. Such realists have no difficulty accepting the fairly disappointing fact that in international affairs "problems" are seldom "solved." To their minds, figures like Saddam present "situations" to be "managed." Success is not a matter of transforming a complex region of contrasting cultures and competing interests. Rather it is a matter of somehow finding a way forward, "continuing to continue," of constraining the oppressors and sustaining the oppressed, and the two longstanding no fly zones in Iraq had by 2003 proved themselves quite useful for such applications.

Lessons learned from the Iraq no fly zones

The no fly zones in Iraq

- provided "proof of concept" of a no fly zone
- established that a no fly zone can be enforced with 50 planes backed by 1500 people at a rough cost of one billion dollars per year
- showed that two no fly zones could be enforced for a dozen years without loss of life to enemy action
- demonstrated that a no fly zone does not require 24/7 enforcement
- established that punishment for violations of a no fly zone does not have to be immediate. Punitive strikes at a time and place of the enforcer's choosing proved effective
- showed that geography matters and that the proximity of friendly air bases is not essential but cuts risks, effort and costs
- proved flexible, serving first as an impediment to Saddam's attacks on his own people, then as ways to monitor his compliance with post-defeat mandates, then as a means to compel him to admit UN weapons

inspectors, then as ways to performed reconnaissance before the 2003 invasion and in the end as means to shape the battlespace
- did not lead to mission creep
- did not raise resistance from allies or from the American public
- proved to be career-enhancing commands for John Shalikashvili, Jay Garner, James Jones and John Abizaid
- functioned as only one tool only in dealing with Saddam. They were accompanied and reinforced by economic sanctions, prepositioned ground forces in Kuwait and intrusive UN inspections.

Notes

1. Bush, George H.W. "Address on the End of the Gulf War," White House, Washington, DC. Web. 27 February 1991. http://millercenter.org/president/bush/speeches/speech-5530. Accessed 15 October 2015.
2. UN Security Council, 46th year. "Resolution 686," 3 March 1991. http://daccess-dds-ny.un.org/doc/RESOLUTION/GEN/NR0/596/22/IMG/NR059622.pdf?OpenElement. Accessed 17 October 2015.
3. Schwarzkopf, H. Norman, and Petre, Peter, *It Doesn't Take a Hero: General H. Norman Schwarzkopf, the Autobiography*, New York: Bantam, 1992. pp.. 564–565.
4. Schwarzkopf, p. 566.
5. Schwarzkopf, p. 566.
6. UN Security Council, 46th year. "Resolution 687," 3 April 1991. http://daccess-dds-ny.un.org/doc/RESOLUTION/GEN/NR0/596/23/IMG/NR059623.pdf?OpenElement. Accessed 17 October 2015.
7. "Iraqi Military Is Again a Formidable Force," *Associated Press*,8 September 1996.
8. Devroy, Ann, " 'Wait and See' on Iraq'," *The Washington Post*, 29 March, 1991, p. A-14.
9. Devroy, p. A-14.
10. Public Papers of the Presidents of the United States: George Bush, 1991, p. 149.
11. Baker, James Addison, and DeFrank, Thomas M., *The Politics of Diplomacy: Revolution, War, and Peace, 1989–1992*, New York: Putnam, 1995. p. 435.
12. Baker, p. 439.
13. Baker, p. 434.
14. Rudd, Gordon W., *Humanitarian Intervention: Assisting the Iraqi Kurds in Operation Provide Comfort, 1991*, Washington, DC: Department of the Army, 2004. pp. 39–40.
15. Author interview with General Charles Wald, 7 January 2015. CAS refers to "close air support."
16. Halloran, Richard, "Many Are Chosen, But Few Get to Wear Stars" *New York Times*, 16 October 1984. www.nytimes.com/1984/10/16/us/pentagon-many-are-chosen-but-few-get-to-wear-stars.html?_r=0. Accessed 15 December 2015.
17. Ricks, Thomas E., *Fiasco: The American Military Adventure in Iraq*,New York: Penguin, 2006. p. 9.
18. Iraq Liberation Act of 1998, Public Law no. 105–338.
19. Ricks, pp. 22–23.
20. "Interview with General Anthony Zinni," personal interview, 13 August 2015.
21. Loeb, Vernon, "No Fly Patrols Praised," *The Washington Post*, 26 July 26, p. A23.
22. UN Security Council, 57th year. "Resolution 1441," 9 October 1992. http://daccess-dds-ny.un.org/doc/UNDOC/GEN/N02/682/26/PDF/N0268226.pdf?OpenElement. Accessed 11 October 2015.

23 Ricks, p. 22.
24 Kennan, George. "The Sources of Soviet Conduct." *Foreign Affairs*, July 1947. www.foreignaffairs.com/articles/russian-federation/1947-07-01/sources-soviet-conduct.
25 Daalder, Ivo and O'Hanlon, Michael, "Overextended in Iraq." *Newsday* n.p., 18, February 2001. Accessed 12 October 2015.
26 Ricks, p. 45.
27 CRS Report RL33557, *Peacekeeping and Related Stability Operations: Issues of US Military Involvement*, Serafino, Nina M., 13 July 2006, p. CRS-20.
28 CRS Report RL33110, *The Cost of Iraq, Afghanistan, and Other Global War on Terror Operations Since 9/11*, Belasco, Amy, 8 December 2014, p. 15.

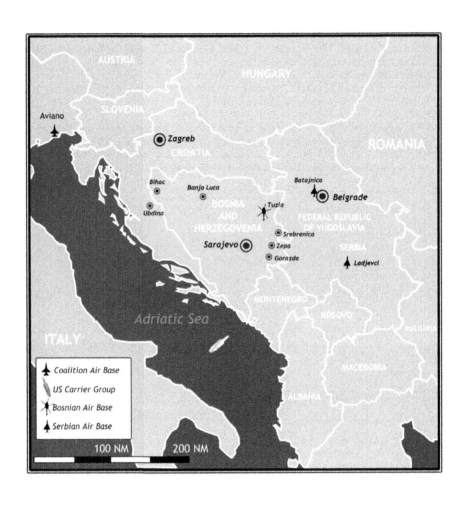

3 Bosnia

The breakup of Yugoslavia was one of the most violent and costly events subsequent to the end of the Cold War. From April 1992 until December 1995, Bosnia and Herzegovina were engulfed in violence as the forces of the Republic of Bosnia and Herzegovina, the forces of the Serbian Republika Srpska (the Bosnian Serb Army), and the forces of the Croatian Herzeg-Bosnia fought each other, claiming over 100,000 lives. The conflict could have been one more of the brutal chapters of violence where the international community chose not to involve itself, like the 800,000 killed in Congo's civil war at about the same time, or the 900,000 killed in Rwanda's civil war in 1994 or even the 400,000 killed in Afghanistan's civil war from 1988 to2001; however, this moment in history played out differently. Perhaps the end of the Cold War brought with it an optimism and a renewed hope in the United Nations. Perhaps decision makers came to believe that with modest effort and risk NATO or the United Nations could act to stop such catastrophic humanitarian crises from occurring. Perhaps the fear of the violence increasing the number of refugees flooding into neighboring countries caused those organizations to act. Probably for all these reasons, the UN and NATO did act, and creating a no fly zone was part of their response. They acted in the expectation that the violence could be quelled with only minimal effort, but the situation proved far more complicated. This second experience with no fly zones, which began slightly after the no fly zones in Iraq and extended through much of their duration, proved a great deal more complex and equivocal in its application and outcomes.

On the conflict in the former Yugoslavia

It is important to understand the conflict in order to follow the UN, NATO and American responses and strategies. It was not simply a war of Serbian aggression against the Bosnians and Croats; it was a multilateral war in which atrocities were committed by all sides. The alliances and parties to the conflict were a tangled web—Croats, Bosnian Muslims and Serbs fought against and were allied with each other at various points and places in the country. For instance, in Bihac in the northwest, Bosnian Muslims allied with Serbs and fought Bosnian government soldiers. In Mostar in the south, Croats fought

Bosnian Muslims. In north central Bosnia Serbs and Croats allied with each other to fight Muslims. In Croatia Krajina Serbs fought Croats. In eastern and northern Bosnian Serbs fought Bosnian Muslims.

Non-combatants were not spared. Often they were targeted. The Bosnian Serb Army killed over 10,000 civilians during the siege of Sarajevo from April 1993 to February 1996. The Croatian Defence Council killed some 2,000 civilians in the Lasva Valley from April 1993 to February 1994. The Bosnian Serb Army killed over 2,700 civilians in the Foca region of Bosnia from April 1993 to January 1994. The Markale marketplace in Sarajevo was shelled twice, first in February 1994 and then in August 1995, killing over 100. Serbian police and military forces killed over 3,000 civilians in the town of Visegrad during the spring of 1992. The Army of the Republic of Bosnia and Herzegovina murdered 13 civilians in the village of Grabovica in September 1993. Most infamously, the Bosnian Serb Army murdered over 8,000 Bosnian Muslim men and boys in July 1995 in Srebrenica.

The Bosnia conflict posed unprecedented challenges to NATO, and the alliance responded with hesitation and resistance, refusing most of all to commit ground troops to the conflict. It was not until the massacre at Srebrenica in mid-1995 that the alliance found the will to act effectively, and even then it would act only in the air. In making air power the central facet of American action, and in fact practically the only aspect because the US steadfastly refused to put boots on the ground, America did not run the same risks as the other countries who had peacekeepers in the former Yugoslavia. But as the US and others looked to air power, they expected to accomplish more than prohibit and prevent the warring parties from flying. They turned to air power to support peacekeepers and to coerce the Serbs to comply with NATO's demands for cessation of violence. They called all this action a "no fly zone" but in fact the Bosnia operation was far more extensive than the no fly zones in Iraq had been. The US and NATO looked to air power because they believed, or pretended to believe, that air power alone could provide the extra military force needed to protect six designated "safe areas," knowing that the UN ground forces in place were wholly inadequate to that task.

The hope was that NATO air forces and UN ground troops would operate in tandem and mutually reinforce each other. In fact, the UN ground forces actually weakened the impact of NATO air power. The peacekeepers were few in number, were deployed in widely separated locations, were unable to intercede effectively between the factions and were vulnerable to capture or killing. When air power was sent in to punish violations by the warring parties, the UN forces proved to be liabilities – prepositioned hostages ready to be taken and held as pawns or human shields. The Bosnia intervention began as a no fly zone but quickly developed into a case study in the limits of air power, a disappointing story of ill-suited tools applied to a large and urgent humanitarian task.

At the outset, the intervention was small and insufficient. It was never a plausible use of force commensurate to the aim of ending the violence and protecting the innocent, but it was wrapped in rhetoric describing it as the first measure in establishing a new world order in the post-Cold War era. While it is true that the UN operations in Bosnia were spared a Russian veto (something that would not happen outside of the decade of the 1990s), they were hardly the launching of a new era in cooperation.

President George HW Bush proclaimed a new world order in a speech on 11 September 1990, and he again evoked this ideal in a speech to the dual session of Congress on 6 March 1991. The collaboration witnessed at the United Nations may have been historic and momentous, but it did not prove to be very effective.

The UN and NATO efforts in Bosnia carry the science of air power and no fly zones further by introducing ground forces to the equation. In Iraq, air power operated largely without ground resources. In Bosnia, ground forces were expected to be a major asset and force multiplier, but because they were few in number and were deployed before the no fly zone was imposed, they functioned as a hindrance. The UN and NATO could not request and authorize the use of air power out of a fear that the warring factions, especially the Bosnian Serbs, would subsequently attack UN forces.

UN responses before the no fly zone

As the conflict expanded in 1991 and 1992, the United Nations Security Council passed several resolutions. UNSCR 713, passed on 25 September 1991, imposed an arms embargo on all parts of the former Yugoslavia. UNSCR 743 passed on 21 February 1992, established the United Nations Protection Force (UNPROFOR), a ground force tasked with providing aid to Sarajevo, escorting humanitarian aid, protecting six safe areas (after April 1993) and monitoring weapons exclusion zones. UNSCR 757, passed on 30 May 1992, imposed a wide range of measures that effectively severed economic links between the Federal Republic of Yugoslavia and the global economy.

These resolutions show the dynamic of the policy and military force options considered in Bosnia. Air power was not the first alternative considered by the United Nations. Sanctions and peacekeepers were sent before bombs were dropped from fighters. Nonetheless, while the Balkans spiraled toward chaos, the UN Secretary General persisted in seeing opportunities for peacekeeping. In June 1992 Secretary General Boutros Boutros-Ghali published "An Agenda for Peace: Preventive Diplomacy, Peacemaking and Peace-keeping," laying out an argument of immense ambition and optimism.

After an embargo was imposed in September 1991, the next step was to deploy ground troops. UNPROFOR, the United Nations Protection Force, arrived in Bosnia-Herzegovina in June 1992 with the mandate to protect the Sarajevo airport and to run a security corridor for aid convoys between the airport and the city. Their mission would expand to include the escort of humanitarian relief convoys, and then in 1993 with the passage of UN Security Council Resolutions 819, 824 and 836, the mandate to secure the UN-declared safe areas of Srebrenica, Tuzla, Gorazde, Zepa, Bihac and Sarajevo. Unfortunately, UNPROFOR never possessed sufficient military forces to carry out these missions. They never numbered more than 39,000 troops and were lightly armed. They spent most of their time muddling through as bystanders to the violence occurring around them and on several occasions they were treated like pawns and taken hostage when the stick of air power was used.

Operation Sky Monitor

The arrival of UNPROFOR did not suppress the violence. In fact it increased in the autumn of 1992, most notably the Croatian attack on the village of Prozor, where Bosnian Muslims were ethnically cleansed from the village. In response the Bosnian Army laid siege to the town of Gornji Vakuf. Bosnian Serb forces continued to use their aircraft against the Bosnian Muslims, and the Security Council passed Resolution 781 on 9 October 1992, which established a tentative no fly zone over Bosnia and Herzegovina. This tepid resolution called on member states to monitor noncompliance, directed the Secretary-General to report evidence of violations, called on member states to take all measures necessary to provide assistance to the United Nations Protection Force, and in the case of violations, pledged to consider urgently further measures necessary to enforce the ban.[1] The resolution authorized Operation Sky Monitor, a six-month NATO mission to observe but not enforce a no fly zone, the effectiveness of which, of course, was negligible. Operation Sky Monitor merely served as a compilation tool for tracking no fly zone violations. The rules of engagement under which Sky Monitor was implemented were particularly restrictive. Participating aircraft were only authorized to use force in self-defense, and they were expected to take evasive action if attacked and not to engage a hostile aircraft. From October 1992 until April 1993, NATO documented more than 500 violations of the no fly zone and never intervened in any way other than to record them.

Meanwhile, the war continued and violence escalated throughout the fall of 1992 and winter of 1993. The Serbs continued their siege of Sarajevo and heightened their aggressiveness throughout that time. On 8 January 1993 Serb troops stopped an UNPROFOR convoy, extracted the Deputy Prime Minister of Bosnia and Herzegovina and assassinated him. Serb authorities set up concentration camps while Croatian forces warred on Bosnian forces in parts of Herzegovina, attacking the village of Gornji Vakuf in January 1993 and expanding their offensive throughout the Lasva Valley in what would become known as the Lasva Valley ethnic cleansing campaign.

Operation Deny Flight

As winter turned into spring, on 31 March 1993 the United Nations passed Security Council Resolution 816, finally turning the no fly zone from an observer mission into an enforcement mission. Operation Sky Monitor gave way to Operation Deny Flight. In a significant further action six weeks later, UNSCR 836 of 4 June 1993 stated the roles expected of the ground forces of UNPROFOR: to "deter attacks against the safe areas, to monitor the cease-fire, to promote the withdrawal of military or paramilitary units other than those of the Government of the Republic of Bosnia and Herzegovina and to occupy some key points on the ground, in addition to participating in the delivery of humanitarian relief to the population."[2] The same resolution also stated that "member states, acting nationally or through regional organization or arrangements, may take, under the authority of the Security Council and subject to close coordination with the Secretary-General and UNPROFOR, all necessary measures, through the use of air power, in and around the safe areas...to support UNPROFOR in the performance of its mandate."[3] This language in UNSCR 836 greatly expanded the role of air power. Now NATO had a mission to provide close air support to UNPROFOR, and possibly a mission to conduct air strikes against violators of the Security Council resolutions.

This resolution also established what became known as the "dual key" arrangement for the use of air power. Approvals from both the UN and NATO were required in order for a pilot to conduct an air strike or an enforcement measure for the no fly zone. Initially this meant contact with the UN headquarters in New York City, but authority was eventually delegated to the UN special representative in Bosnia, Yasushi Akashi, and then in 1995, it was further delegated to the UNPROFOR commander in Bosnia. On the NATO side, the dual key resided with the Commander in Chief Allied Forces South. The command delays and difficulty in gaining UN approval would prove to be one of the bigger challenges to implementing a no fly zone or using air power in Bosnia. Critics of the dual key claimed that it was an unworkable system, generating tensions and frustrations. It also made evident that some countries, alliances and organizations were far more ready than others to take action in an extremely difficult and complex situation.

Within two weeks of the passage of USNCR 836 it became apparent that the expectation that air power would support UNPROFOR was unrealistic. In June 1993, UNSCR 844 was passed, increasing the number of troops in UNPROFOR by 7,600 more troops, less than a quarter of the 34,000 troops that the UNPROFOR commander, Lieutenant General Lars Eric Wahlgren, had said would be needed in order to implement the safe areas policy. The UN simply could not muster as many troops as were needed. Member states were unwilling to contribute that many, and the Americans refused to offer any ground troops at all. The resolution did, however, also reiterate the air power language of UNSCR 836. The logic seemed to be that UNPROFOR would be unable to defend the safe areas, and instead air power would be used to deter any attacks into them. Either this plan showed great confidence in the ability of air power to augment and support the UNPROFOR mission, or it simply showed desperation and wishful thinking. In the end, air power was unable to do much to support the UNPROFOR mission until the UNPROFOR forces redeployed to more defensible and less vulnerable positions.

The expectations attached to air power were all the more unrealistic because the violence occurring in Bosnia was primarily, almost exclusively, among ground forces. The warring factions were not using air forces to bomb or attack each other. Unlike Operations Northern Watch and Southern Watch in Iraq which were fundamentally about stopping the Iraqi Air Force from flying, Operation Deny Flight was expected to do much more than just stop a military from flying. NATO and the UN expected air power to be the great equalizer in the protection of safe zones.

Operation Deny Flight took some time to achieve success at keeping fixed-wing aircraft out of the air but did so in the end. Neither the Bosnian Muslims nor the Bosnian Croats possessed fixed-wing aircraft. The Krajina and Bosnian Serbs possessed 32 fixed wing planes, all of them ground attack aircraft, all of them based at either Banja Luka, in northern Bosnia, or Udbina, in eastern Croatia. Banja Luka's location in north central Bosnia made it nearly impossible for the Serbs to fly from that location if the no fly zone was being enforced. NATO aircraft could easily place a fighter combat air patrol directly over or near Banja Luka. Udbina, on the other hand, located in eastern Croatia, just across the border from Bihac in Bosnia, lay outside the geographical mandates of the no fly zone, and the Serbs did fly out of Udbina on a number of occasions, although with little effect in most cases.

The most well-known fixed-wing no fly zone violations occurred on 28 Feb 1994 near Banja Luka. Early in the morning a flight of six Serb Jastreb aircraft took off from Udbina to bomb Bosnian Muslim positions in Bosnia. US Air Force F-16 fighters and an AWACS surveillance aircraft detected the flight of Jastrebs and the lead F-16 pilot, Captain Gordon Wright, saw the Jastrebs attacking ground targets in the Bosnian town of Novi Travnik. He quickly received the order from the Combined Air Operations Center to shoot down the planes. He downed three of the Jastrebs, and a follow-on section of two F-16's downed a fourth Jastreb.[4]

The incident displayed the effectiveness of NATO's air forces. It was the only incident throughout the 970 days of the no fly zone in which fixed wing aircraft were shot down. The Serbs never again directly challenged the no fly zone, but after the February 1994 incident, they did so in many less direct ways. They gradually increased the presence of surface-to-air missiles and anti-aircraft artillery around Bihac, and on a few occasions they flew their fighters out of Udbina and into Bosnia on bombing missions, using the sanctuary of Croatian airspace to their full advantage. It became a cat and mouse game, with the Serbs timing their very short flights into Bosnia around the moments when NATO aircraft were refueling.

The game came to a head on 18 November 1994 when Serb jets from Udbina attacked the Bosnian Army's 5th Corps headquarters hear Bihac, and the next day a Serb jet crashed trying to attack an ammunition factory north of Bihac. In response NATO conducted air strikes against Udbina, striking the runway and taxiways on 21 November 1994. After this episode the Bosnian Serbs almost completely ceased their fixed-wing flight activities.

Preventing helicopters from flying was a different story. Most participants in the conflict flew helicopters – to resupply forces, to move troops, to evacuate casualties, and to move important commanders and diplomats. The mountainous terrain made the roads often treacherous to navigate, and helicopters were essential to all, including the United Nations forces.

The protocol for flying helicopters mandated that flights in Bosnia receive pre-takeoff approval from the United Nations flight coordination center in Zagreb, Croatia. This rarely occurred. Thus the NATO aircraft were frequently confronting unauthorized helicopters flying in Bosnian airspace, and NATO fighter pilots operated under extremely restrictive rules of engagement. A helicopter had to be witnessed committing a hostile act in order to be classified as a target to be engaged. Even if the rules of engagement had been more permissive, it was extremely difficult to restrict helicopter flights when all sides are flying. Most helicopters are used for transport, carrying supplies or people, and shooting down a helicopter is not like shooting down a fighter where only a pilot and perhaps one other aircrew will be aboard. On a helicopter there likely will be many noncombatants who may include medical personnel, diplomats, aid workers and civilians. Moreover, determining the nature of the violation of the rules, beyond the simple fact that flight rules are being violated, is nearly impossible. If a NATO fighter shot down a Bosnian Serb helicopter and the Bosnian Serbs claimed that the helicopter was filled with medical supplies and medical personnel tasked with providing care to their injured, the situation might be impossible to resolve conclusively.

It was decided that NATO fighters would intercept helicopters violating the no fly zone and instruct them to land, but then would depart. There was no further enforcement of the rules. It is like a highway patrolman waving down a speeding car on the highway, then speeding away himself. This quickly became a game. The helicopters would simply wait until the interceptor fighter departed, and then take off again and continue on its route. The reluctance to stop helicopters from flying is understandable, especially after the tragic incident in northern Iraq in April of 1994 when two US helicopters carrying UN personnel were misidentified and shot down by American F-15 pilots.

By most estimates, over 6,000 helicopter no fly zone violations occurred, which would seem to be a strong indictment of the effectiveness of the no fly zone. Defenders of the no fly zone might point out that the helicopter flights were not playing a violent role in the events in Bosnia. Helicopters were rarely if ever used to attack forces on the ground. Rather, they were used to transport people and supplies, and because they were used by all sides in this role, it became prohibitively difficult to enforce a no fly zone against helicopters.

In other situations, where helicopters are being used in an attack role, shooting them down could be important and effective. That was the case in Iraq in 1991 and in Syria after the Arab Spring and subsequent civil war. Attack helicopters differ from transport helicopters in that they have a smaller airframe, usually carrying only two pilots and a load of weapons (the one exception being the Mi-24 Hind, which is an attack helicopter that can also carry up to eight troops). If attack helicopters are striking targets on the ground, or, for instance, dropping barrel bombs, this activity can be observed. Once such activity is confirmed, those helicopters can be targeted and shot down. This was not, however, the case in Bosnia, where there was no certain record of helicopters conducting attacks.

NATO conducted the no fly zone enforcement with minimal risk and minimal cost, which of course was part of the logic and the appeal of the option. The Bosnian Serbs challenged the no fly zone more and more throughout 1994 and 1995 by reinforcing their air defense assets in northwest Bosnia, especially around Bihac, but their efforts had little effect. Only three aircraft were lost to enemy fire during the entire no fly zone enforcement. A British Sea Harrier was shot down in April 1994 by a shoulder launched surface-to-air missile. An American F-16C was shot down in June 1995 by an SA-6 radar guided missile. Finally, a French Mirage 2000D was shot down in August 1995 by a shoulder fired surface-to-air missile.

Had NATO and the UN limited their expectations strictly to the enforcement of a no fly zone, there would be little debate about the success of Operation Deny Flight. There is little difficulty in stopping warring factions from making fixed-wing flights. That does not mean, however, that Operation Deny Flight made a significant contribution to controlling Serb aggression or bringing about peace. Overall, the Bosnian Serb fighter aircraft had little effect on the battlefield, so excluding them from the conflict had little impact. Helicopters, while frequently flown, played little role in the violence and killing beyond transporting and supplying the troops that were engaged in the fighting. The no fly zone should be listed alongside economic sanctions and diplomacy as a weak and insufficient effort to resolve the conflict. But commanders, diplomats, and policymakers instead understandably but mistakenly tried to get more impact from air power, even though they continued to call the expanded operation a "no fly zone."

Operational requirements of Deny Flight

The level of effort required to enforce the no fly zone was significant, but far less than is broadly believed. In total, NATO flew over 100,000 sorties over the course of 970 days of almost continuous operations. Nearly 4,500 personnel from 12 NATO countries were continuously deployed, and over 250 aircraft were dedicated to the operation. A snapshot of deployed forces from September 1995 is illustrative (Table 5.1).[5]

The air armada in the above table may appear to be a significant investment of assets and people, but contrasting the 4500 troops assigned to Deny Flight to the 39,000 troops assigned to UNPROFOR show that the no fly zone required an eighth as many persons. Moreover, 320 UNPROFOR soldiers were killed during operations in Bosnia. None were killed flying in the no fly zone enforcement.

From June 1993 until August 1995, NATO and the UN struggled to cooperate and to find a balance between mission accomplishment and force protection, between peacekeeping and peace enforcement, between easing the suffering of the Bosnian people and facilitating negotiations in Geneva, between humanitarian assistance and enforcement of safe areas. The no fly zone was a limited part of that inadequate effort.

Experimentation with enforcement

It is worth looking in some detail at the record of experimentation with no fly zone enforcement, coercive air strikes and close air support missions as NATO sought ways to fulfill its UN mandate. NATO began enforcing the no fly zone in April 1993, and UNSCR 836 expanding the no fly zone mandate to close air support for UNPROFOR was passed in June. The UN military leadership transitioned that summer as well. French General Jean Cot took over as the overall UNPROFOR Commander in Zagreb in July, and Belgian General Francis Briquemont took over the Bosnia-Herzegovina UNPROFOR command the same month. The next six months, until the February 1994 Banja Luka shoot-down incident, was a period of intense discussions and negotiations between NATO and the UN regarding what military actions should be taken. It included threatened air strikes and severe frustration on the part of UNPROFOR commanders who were undermanned and incapable of implementing the safe areas policy they were tasked with carrying out. They felt their forces were constantly threatened with casualties as the warring factions continued to fight each other.

As Generals Cot and Briquemont assumed their new commands in the summer of 1993, the Bosnian Serb Army continued its assault on Sarajevo. By July the Bosnian Serbs threatened to take Mount Igman, a mountain plateau southwest of Sarajevo which was the lone route by which Bosnian troops and supplies were able to pass into Sarajevo. It also provided the only passage from Sarajevo to the safe area of Gorazde. If the Bosnian Serbs controlled Mount Igman, they would control all road routes into and out of Sarajevo.

NATO responded by threatening air strikes. In a statement on 2 Aug 1993, the North Atlantic Council issued the following statement: "The Alliance has now decided to make immediate preparations for undertaking, in the event

Table 3.1 Aircraft used in enforcing Deny Flight

Country	Air Base	Type of Aircraft (Mission Role)	# Aircraft
France	Istrana, Italy	Mirage F-1CR (Recon)	5
	Cervia, Italy	Mirage 2000C (NFZ)	6
	Istrana, Italy	Jaguar (CAS)	6
	Cervia, Italy	Mirage 2000K/D (CAS)	6
	Aircraft carrier	Super Étendard (CAS)	6
	Istrana, Italy	Mirage F-1CT (CAS)	3
	Istres, France	C-135 (Air-to-air refueling)	1
	Avord, France	E-3F AWACS (Airborne command and control)	1
Germany	Piacenza, Italy	Tornado (UN Rapid Reaction Force)	14
Italy	Ghedi, Italy	PA-200 Tornado (CAS)	8
Netherlands	Villafranca, Italy	F-16A Falcon (NFZ)	6
	Villafranca, Italy	F-16A Falcon (CAS)	7
	Villafranca, Italy	F-16R Falcon (Recon)	5
Spain	Vicenza, Italy	CASA 212 (Support)	1
	Aviano, Italy	EF-18 Hornet (CAS/NFZ)	8
	Aviano, Italy	KC-130 Hercules (Air-to-air refueling)	2
Turkey	Ghedi, Italy	F-16C Falcon (NFZ)	16
United Kingdom	Gioia del Colle, Italy	F-3 Tornado (NFZ)	6
	Gioia del Colle	GR-7 Harrier (CAS)	10
	Gioia del Colle	GR-7 Harrier (Recon)	2
	Aircraft carrier	Sea Harrier (CAS/NFZ)	6
	Palermo, Sicily	K-1 Tristar L-1011 (Air-to-air refueling)	2
	Aviano, Italy	E-3D AWACS (Airborne command and control)	2
United States	Aviano, Italy	F-15E Strike Eagle (CAS)	8
	Aviano, Italy	F/A-18D Hornet (CAS/NFZ)	12
	Aviano, Italy	F-16C Hornet (CAS/NFZ)	12
	Aviano, Italy	F-16C/D Hornet (CAS/NFZ)	8
	Aviano, Italy	O/A-10 Warthog (CAS)	12
	Aviano, Italy	EC-130 ABCCC (Airborne battlefield command and control)	3
	Aviano, Italy	EC-130 Compass Call (Electronic warfare)	3

Country	Air Base	Type of Aircraft (Mission Role)	# Aircraft
	Brindisi, Italy	AC-130 Spectre (CAS)	4
	Pisa, Italy and Istres, France	KC-135 Stratotanker (Air-to-air refueling)	12
	Aviano, Italy	EA-6B Prowler (Electronic Warfare)	10
	Aviano, Italy	EF-111A Raven (Electronic Warfare)	6
	Aircraft carrier	F/A-18C Hornet (NFZ)	12
	Aircraft carrier	F/A-18C Hornet (CAS)	6
	Genoa, Italy	KC-10 Extender (Air-to-air refueling)	5
	Capodichino, Italy	C-21 (Transportation)	2
	Geilenkirchen, Germany	E-3A AWACS (Airborne command and control)	8

that the strangulation of Sarajevo and other areas continues, including wide-scale interference with humanitarian assistance, stronger measures including air strikes against those responsible, Bosnian Serbs and others, in Bosnia-Herzegovina."[6]

The Serbs did in fact capture part of the Mount Igman road on 4 Aug, but they eventually withdrew, by most counts because of the threatened air strikes. Mount Igman was declared a demilitarized zone, and UNPROFOR units were stationed on Mount Igman in order to ensure the road was used only for humanitarian goods.

Despite the success of these threatened coercive air strikes, General Briquemont disagreed with this strategy. As an infantryman, he strongly believed that the role and utility of air power lay solely in its capacity to support ground forces. He also believed that such air strikes against the Bosnian Serbs would jeopardize the UN's impartiality in Bosnia.[7] Finally, he was uncomfortable with the vulnerability of his UNPROFOR troops, undermanned as they were and thus relying on the threat of air strikes to protect them.[8] After the Mount Igman episode he refused to countenance any further threats of air strikes. General Briquemont's priority was the safety of his troops, and he did not believe he could rely on NATO air support to back up the UNPROFOR troops without putting the troops at risk of Serb reprisals. The remaining time of his command was marked by UNPROFOR passivity. General Briquemont sought to avoid any provocation of the Bosnian Serb Army and refused to put his troops at risk to enforce the safe areas. His assessment of the vulnerability of UNPROFOR troops would prove to be prescient.

General Briquemont relinquished his command in January 1994 to British army officer Lieutenant General Sir Michael Rose. Less than two weeks after General Rose assumed command, on 5 February 1994, a 120 mm mortar shell landed in the center of the Markale marketplace in Sarajevo, killing 68 people and wounding 144. Although it was initially unclear who launched the mortars, it was soon concluded that the Bosnian Serb Army was responsible. UN Secretary General Boutros-Ghali asked NATO to authorize air strikes against Bosnian Serb artillery and mortar positions around Sarajevo.[9] NATO threatened air strikes but never conducted them. The crisis was de-escalated when General Rose mediated an agreement between the Bosnian government and the Bosnian Serbs that established a heavy weapons 20-kilometer exclusion zone around Sarajevo. The Serbs acquiesced and removed their weapons prior to the 21 February 1994 ultimatum deadline.

Only a week later, on the last day of February, the Jastreb shoot-down incident occurred near Banja Luka. At that point the no fly zone appeared effective, and the threatened air strikes seemed to be working as well. The Bosnian Serbs were not flying their fixed wing aircraft and the two separate threats of air strikes had relieved the siege of Sarajevo. But these were short-lived successes, as events in Gorazde were to prove.

The Serbian assault on the UN-designated "safe area" in Gorazde in April 1994 exposed the limits of air power in support of a lightly armed and undermanned force like UNPROFOR. In early April 1994, the Bosnian Serb Army under General Ratko Mladic attacked the safe area. UNPROFOR forces in Gorazde were far from adequate to stop the Bosnian Serb offensive. A week into the offensive a Serb artillery shell killed a British UNPROFOR soldier. NATO responded with air strikes. First, two F-16's dropped bombs on a Serb mobile command post on 10 April 1994. The next day a NATO F/A-18 strafed Serb military vehicles.

In response General Mladic surrounded the 150 UNPROFOR soldiers in Gorazde, effectively taking them hostage. He threatened to kill them if NATO did not stop its bombings. Bosnian Serb president Radovan Karadzic publicly declared that his forces would shoot down NATO aircraft. NATO continued to seek to influence events with its fighter aircraft, making high speed low altitude passes, but they never dropped any ordnance. This met with no success, and at the same time the Bosnian Serb Army aggressively opposed these actions. A French Étendard was hit by a Serb infrared missile on 15 April 1994. The pilot was able to land safely back on the carrier Clemenceau, but the aircraft sustained damage. A British Sea Harrier was shot down by an infrared missile the next day. The pilot safely ejected and joined his Special Forces compatriots in Gorazde.

The standoff was resolved when Russian envoy Vitaly Churkin arranged for the suspension of threatened NATO air strikes in exchange for Bosnian Serb pledges to release the UNPROFOR hostages. This established a pattern of Bosnian Serb responses to NATO air strikes.[10] The Bosnian Serbs would interfere with humanitarian aid deliveries; they would withdraw from negotiations with the UN; they would take UNPROFOR soldiers hostage; and they would aggressively fire against NATO aircraft.[11] Absent larger deployments of troops plus more aggressive rules of engagement for aircraft –

precisely the measure the countries that were contributing forces and assets wanted to avoid – these Serbian tactics were likely to be successful.

After Gorazde

Gorazde changed the calculus of UNPROFOR. Lieutenant General Sir Michael Rose chose to focus more narrowly on the humanitarian and peacekeeping aspects of his mission and to avoid confrontations, specifically any attempts at coercion. He recognized that he did not have sufficient forces to do more than that, and like General Briquemont before him, he refrained from placing his forces at extra risk. In his efforts to minimize risk, he attempted to remain impartial and neutral, arguing that UNPROFOR necessarily operated with the consent of the warring factions (though occasionally that consent could be extracted or at least encouraged through the threat of punitive air strikes from NATO.) UNPROFOR did not, however, have the military capability to impose the UN's will on the situation. Having the consent of the warring factions, he maintained, is in the nature of peacekeeping, a point that Rose would state on numerous occasions during his tenure as UNPROFOR commander.

Subsequently, General Rose has argued strenuously that policy makers and military commanders must distinguish between warfighting and peacekeeping. Peacekeeping entails many restrictions, chief among them the requirement to be an honest broker among the warring parties. He believed that NATO developed an agenda of its own, a warfighting agenda, which included as one of its goals the leveling of the playing field. This necessarily meant NATO was siding with the Bosnian Muslims and against the Bosnian Serbs, a circumstance that placed Rose's UNPROFOR troops in a precarious position and also violated one of the objective principles of peacekeeping.[12]

Rose was not a complete skeptic about the usefulness of air power, although his point of view was the quintessential perspective of an infantryman who believed that air power should always serve as a supporting element to the ground commander. After the Gorazde events in April 1994, the next time NATO conducted air strikes was in August, and the outcome illustrates Rose's point. On 5 August 1994, Bosnian Serb forces injured a Ukrainian peacekeeper during a raid to the west of Sarajevo. General Rose requested air strikes. He also intervened as the responsible commander and designated a different target than the one proposed by NATO air commanders. Rose's target was an abandoned and unusable armored fighting vehicle. Throughout the approval process for the attack and during the execution of the attack, General Rose maintained communication with the president of the Bosnian Serb Assembly, even providing warning to the Bosnian Serbs. Just after the air strike Rose negotiated the return of military equipment the Bosnian Serbs had captured during the raid that injured the Ukrainian peacekeeper.

The NATO air commander during this incident was Admiral Leighton "Snuffy" Smith, an A-7 Corsair pilot who had three carrier tours flying over

78 *Bosnia*

Vietnam, and a strong personality. Admiral Smith was frustrated by General Rose's actions during this episode, rightly believing that Rose put NATO aircrews unnecessarily at increased risk by choosing such an insignificant target and announcing in advance that it would be struck. He also believed that striking such a target diminished the effect of the air strikes. Rose, on the other hand, believed, also rightly, that NATO aircrews were far less exposed than his peacekeepers on the ground. He also judged that by giving the Serbs warning he was limiting collateral damage and keeping the door open to further negotiations with the Serbs, which was critical to the UNPROFOR mission.

Operation Antelope

The conflicting perspectives of General Rose and Admiral Smith on how to use air power were exacerbated during the summer of 1994. General Rose proposed a scheme wherein NATO would respond to the unauthorized removal of heavy weapons from UN cantonment areas by conducting air strikes against the exact piece of equipment. Labeled Operation Antelope, Rose envisioned punishing the perpetrator immediately and also directly tying the enforcement action to the prohibited act committed. Unfortunately, the execution of the plan would have required an exceptional effort with significant risk. A UN helicopter would have to track the equipment as the violating force moved it, which inevitably meant that the helicopter would be vulnerable to ground fire. Then, according to the scheme, NATO aircraft carrying out the strike would launch. This would require a significant force – refueling tankers, suppression of air defense aircraft, combat search and rescue aircraft, and the striking aircraft.[13]

Operation Antelope was never carried out, but it is worth considering today especially with the technological advances since 1994. Unmanned systems such as the MQ-1 Predator and MQ-9 Reaper, today provide near persistent surveillance. A Predator has an endurance of 24 hours, and a Reaper has an endurance of 14 hours. Both can carry weapons, such as GPS-guided bombs or Hellfire missiles. The operations that have been conducted in Afghanistan, Pakistan, Iraq and Yemen are similar to the concept of operations drawn up for Operation Antelope. The unmanned systems remain over an area of interest for long periods, sometimes days or weeks, and once relevant activity is detected, the drones continue to monitor the activity, even if that means tracking a vehicle as it moves. One can imagine a completely different conversation in 1994 had these capabilities existed at the time.

The conflict between General Rose and Admiral Smith came to a head on 22 September 1994. NATO was planning another air strike after French peacekeepers near Sarajevo came under fire from Bosnian Serb forces, with two French soldiers sustaining injuries. General Rose was traveling to the UK and his deputy, French General André Soubirou, was in charge. Together with Admiral Smith's staff, they had chosen an ammunition depot near Pale as the target. Rose intervened from the UK, changing the target to a T-55 tank that was located in the Sarajevo exclusion zone. Rose also warned the Serbs. He wrote in his memoir, "Admiral Leighton Smith had ordered that no warning be given to the Serbs prior to the attack in order to avoid giving them time to alert their air defense system, putting NATO pilots at greater risk. I told my chief of staff in Sarajevo, Brinkman, to ignore that order."[14] The strike was eventually conducted on the T-55 tank, after several delays as NATO air commanders tried to ensure that non-US aircraft conducted the strike. This exchange between Rose and Smith illustrates the tensions that use of air power provoked between ground commanders and air commanders, between British officers and American officers and between restrained peacekeepers and forceful "peacemakers."

Bosnian Serbs challenge the no fly zone

The Bosnian Serbs began to challenge the no fly zone more aggressively in the fall of 1994. They built up their air defenses in the northwest part of Bosnia, near Bihac, as well as around Sarajevo. In July NATO suspended humanitarian airlift missions into Sarajevo after two C-141 cargo aircraft sustained hits from small arms fire as they landed in Sarajevo. In August NATO suspended airdrops into the Muslim enclave of Bihac because of the Serb air defense build-up and the frequent targeting of aircraft by the engagement radars of their missile systems. General Rose sent a letter to Bosnian Serb Army commander General Ratko Mladic, expressing his concern over the aggressive actions of the Serbian air defense forces and stating that the activation of target tracking radar modes would be considered acts of aggression. He also warned General Mladic of NATO's prerogative to respond to such actions.

The Bosnian Serbs escalated their flouting of the no fly zone in November by sending aircraft into Bosnia to support the Bosnian Serb Army offensive against the Bosnian Muslim forces. Because the airfield at Udbina was such a short distance to Bihac (approximately 25 nautical miles) Bosnian Serb pilots could time their flights into Bosnia when NATO aircraft were refueling or otherwise out of position to respond, and they were in Bosnian airspace for only a few minutes. Events finally came to a head on 18 November 1994 when Serb jets from Udbina dropped napalm and cluster bombs on a Bosnian army headquarters near Bihac, and then the following day a Serb aircraft crashed into an apartment building in Cazin while making a bombing run.

NATO decided to act, but with great restraint. General de Lapresle, the overall UNPROFOR commander, insisted that the targets be limited to the runway at Udbina and Serb air defense systems. NATO aircraft would not target Serb aircraft nor any buildings or maintenance facilities at Udbina. This was far less than what Admiral Smith desired. In the end, a compromise was reached in which Admiral Smith was permitted to target the air defense systems that would threaten the NATO aircraft, but the strikes would be limited enough to avoid what General de Lapresle and General Rose feared most: Serb reprisals, especially the taking of UN peacekeepers as hostages.

The attacks were conducted on 21 November 1994, but as was feared and expected, the Serbs responded by taking hostages in Croatia. Serb forces also continued their aggressive opposition by firing a surface-to-air missile at NATO jets the day after the Udbina air strikes. NATO responded with what was termed "retrospective SEAD" (suppression of enemy air defenses), in which NATO aircrews would regroup after being fired upon and then conduct attacks against the offending missile system that fired at them. NATO conducted their "retrospective SEAD" strikes on 23 November, the day after the Serb air defenses fired at the NATO aircraft.

The Bosnian Serb Army's response to this was even more provocative. They took hundreds of UN peacekeepers hostage and reportedly forced three of the peacekeepers to lie on the runway at Banja Luka air field as human shields in case NATO decided to target the runway. At the same time, the Bosnian Serb Army continued its siege of Bihac.

Three days after the SEAD strikes, on 26 November 1994, American F-16s were again fired upon by Serb surface-to-air missiles while conducting routine no fly zone patrols. NATO air forces prepared a robust reconnaissance package, with SEAD and strike escorts, hoping to discover the location of the missile site. The mission was canceled after intense diplomatic discussions at NATO headquarters and the UN. With some 250 hostages already under Serb control, it was decided that any escalation would not be productive.

NATO pilots were directed to de-escalate their aggressive no fly zone patrols. They avoided Bosnian airspace and instead flew their combat air patrols over the Adriatic Sea. Once this change was made, several weeks of negotiations finally secured the release of all UNPROFOR hostages on 10 December 1994.

The events of the autumn of 1994 illustrate several key issues. First, although the attacks on the Udbina air base cannot be considered a meaningful success, they did succeed in preventing the Bosnian Serbs from continuing their flights out of Udbina. Second, the air strikes were not more effective in large part because the UN peacekeeping force was so small and so weak. Had the contributing states been willing to put a robust force in Bosnia that could defend itself and aggressively enforce the safe areas, air power would likely have been more effective. Third, NATO airmen found themselves struggling to respond quickly, decisively, and accurately after being fired on by Serb air defense missiles. At that time, no aircraft was capable of doing anything other than maneuvering to avoid a surface-to-air missile, and the aircraft systems were not advanced enough to pinpoint the location of the missile system. Consequently, NATO pilots found themselves in a cat-and-mouse game of evading the Serb air defenses when they were fired on, then seeking authorization for a "retrospective" strike through the generals and diplomats who approved the rules of engagement. The dilemma of aircraft self-protection, locating threats, and quickly responding is one that pilots and engineers continue to work on today. While one can appreciate the frustrations of the NATO pilots, and the risks they endured, it must be emphasized that throughout this protracted battle between NATO aircraft and the Serb air defense, no NATO aircraft were shot down. This speaks to the advances in American technology, tactics and proficiency in the years after Vietnam.

1995 witnessed a change in personalities, which also included a change in tactics and the use of air power. In January, Lieutenant General Rose completed his one-year tour of duty and was replaced by Lieutenant General Sir Rupert Smith as commander of UNPROFOR in Bosnia-Herzegovina. Smith brought a different perspective about air power: that its role could be more than just supporting troops on the ground. He believed the coercive potential of air power was significant. Smith had commanded an armored division during Operation Desert Storm in Iraq and had lost nine of his soldiers in a friendly fire incident. Politically savvy, Smith had spent the previous two years as the assistant chief of the defense staff of the British military.

In March, General de Lapresle finished his tour in Zagreb as the overall UNPROFOR commander and was replaced by a fellow Frenchman, Lieutenant General Bernard Janvier. Janvier was an infantryman who served in Algeria as a young lieutenant in 1960–1961 during the last years of the Algerian War. He also saw action in Chad during its civil war in 1979–1980 and again in Beirut as part of the multinational force. He commanded a French division during the 1990–1991 Gulf War and thus was one of the most operationally experienced officers in the French military.

The tactical situation in Bosnia did not improve during the winter and spring of 1995. Fighting continued around Bihac, and in March Bosnian forces launched an offensive. Fighting escalated, and Bosnian Serb forces shelled the safe areas of Gorazde, Sarajevo, and Tuzla. The peacekeeping forces remained deployed, undermanned and in vulnerable positions in the so-called safe areas. In April two French soldiers in Sarajevo were killed by sniper fire. The fighting did not abate throughout the spring, and finally in mid-May, General Rupert Smith requested NATO air strikes after continued Bosnian Serb shelling of Sarajevo. His request was disapproved by UN Secretary-General Boutros Boutros-Ghali.[15]

In the wake of this rebuff, Generals Smith and Janvier communicated to Boutros Boutros-Ghali their desire to redeploy their most vulnerable forces to safer places, especially in the eastern safe areas.[16] Then in the latter part of May, Bosnian Serb forces removed some heavy weapons from a UN weapons control site. General Smith warned the Bosnian Serbs that they would be subject to air strikes if they did not return the heavy weapons. He requested and received approval for NATO air strikes, and on 25 and 26 May, NATO aircraft bombed an ammunition facility near Pale.

The Bosnian Serbs responded to the air strikes by shelling the safe areas. The worst of these was an attack on Tuzla, which killed more than 70 civilians and wounded hundreds more. They also took as hostages more than 300

UN peacekeepers throughout Bosnia, placing several as human shields to guard against further air strikes.

Then on 27 May 1995, Bosnian Serb forces ambushed a French armored personnel carrier, taking the French soldiers hostage and donning the French uniforms. Dressed as French soldiers and driving the French armored personnel carrier, the Bosnian Serbs attacked the French checkpoints at the Vrbanja Bridge that crossed the Miljacka River in Sarajevo. The French responded with a force of 100 Marines, attacking the Bosnian Serb forces who held the bridge. After a short and violent battle, the French retook the bridge. Two French and four Bosnian Serb soldiers were killed.

This episode began to move international opinion and the Bosnian Serbs came to be seen at the United Nations as the aggressors. The desire to maintain the impartiality of UN forces was beginning to change. At the same time, General Smith began moving his soldiers away from UN weapons control points to less vulnerable positions, even as he had over 300 held hostage.

The Captain Scott O'Grady shoot-down

Days later, on 2 June 1995, American Air Force Captain Scott O'Grady was shot down by a Serbian SA-6 surface-to-air missile. It was a trap set by the Bosnian Serbs. The Bosnian Serbs had once again begun flying aircraft out of Udbina air field in Croatia, racing toward the border with Bosnia and then turning away. They had repositioned a mobile SA-6 missile just south of Banja Luka, which placed it directly beneath where NATO jets would fly to try to gain a missile shot against the jets approaching the border from Croatia. On this day O'Grady and his flight lead had previously been illuminated by SA-6 radar, but they continued their mission, only to have O'Grady targeted a second time and shot down.

Tense days followed the shoot-down. The Bosnian Serbs sought to gain advantage from O'Grady's shoot-down by offering to negotiate for his release in exchange for guarantees that no future air strikes would occur. O'Grady, however, managed to evade capture and was rescued by Marines from the 24th Marine Expeditionary Unit on 8 June 1995.

Negotiations with the Serbs over the UNPROFOR hostages continued after O'Grady's rescue, and eventually all UN hostages were released on 18 June 1995. These events fundamentally changed the UN mission and the no fly zone enforcement. NATO air commanders decided to reduce the risks they were willing to take and refused to allow pilots to fly no fly zone missions without robust SEAD (suppression of enemy air defenses) escorts, which meant tactical jamming aircraft such as the EA-6B Prowler and F-16CJ aircraft specifically designed for the SEAD mission, carrying radar sensing equipment and HARM (high-speed anti-radiation missiles). The vast majority of the no fly zone missions were required to remain over the Adriatic Sea rather than over Bosnian airspace.

The Bosnian Serbs responded to these new NATO tactics by beginning once again to fly aircraft out of the Bosnian air field of Banja Luka, seeking to demonstrate the ineffectiveness of the no fly zone, although those Bosnian Serb aircraft did not attack ground targets in Bosnia. The feasibility of enforcing the no fly zone was being called into question.

After the O'Grady shoot-down, General Janvier and Admiral Leighton Smith resolved to reduce risk in enforcing the no fly zone. Admiral Smith, the overall air commander in his role as Commander in Chief of Allied Forces Southern Europe, had flown in Vietnam. His perspective was fundamentally framed by that experience. He recalled many occasions in Vietnam when pilots were tasked with flying over enemy surface-to-air systems, baiting the North Vietnamese to target them in hopes of locating the missile systems. Once the North Vietnamese air defense operators radiated their systems or fired their missiles, they would reveal themselves, and this would allow the Americans to bomb the surface-to-air systems. It was an exercise that cost many lives. Admiral Smith was adamant in his unwillingness to expose NATO pilots to these risks.[17]

General Janvier was equally unwilling to accept risk. He seemed to accept Admiral Smith's logic: NATO and the UN did not have the political will to truly have an effect on the Bosnian Serb air defenses, and unless the pilots were allowed to significantly degrade the air defenses, which was a basic principle of self-defense, then he was unwilling to send them in harm's way. Moreover, because relatively few airplanes were violating the no fly zone, positioning aircraft over Bosnian airspace rather than over the Adriatic made little difference. He judged that the UN and NATO were unwilling to allow the degrading of what they believed was an increasingly capable and aggressive Serbian air defense system. He concluded that neither NATO nor the UN wanted to risk escalation, which he believed was highly probable based on the previous behavior of the Bosnian Serbs.[18]

Lieutenant General Sir Rupert Smith, the Bosnian UNPROFOR Commander, understood the situation in the same terms, especially the terrible vulnerability of his forces and that NATO could not take any aggressive or effective action with the UNPROFOR troops in such vulnerable positions and so few in number. General Smith also expected that more crises such as the hostage-taking after the Pale bombing would cause NATO and the UN to take action.

Operation Deliberate Force and the siege of Srebrenica

Lieutenant General Michael Ryan, the US Air Force officer serving as the Commander of Allied Air Forces in Southern Europe, also was involved in the rethinking that occurred in 1995. While the peacekeeping and no fly zone missions floundered in the spring of that year, he pushed his staff vigorously to devise plans for an air campaign against Bosnian Serb air defenses and ground forces, an exercise many felt to be futile. This planning, initially titled

Dead Eye, was renamed Deliberate Force, and having this plan in place would be crucial a few months later as events would come to a head toward the end of the summer of 1995.

The Bosnian Serbs apparently did not anticipate that the shoot-down of O'Grady would increase American and NATO support for taking action in Bosnia. Throughout the previous three years, as diplomats traversed the region trying to negotiate cease fires, declare safe areas, and compel the warring factions to cease their fighting, Washington and the European capitals had displayed passivity and inertia. They feared a spill over of the war into the rest of Europe, but they were unwilling to act beyond half-hearted contributions of peacekeepers that they insisted maintain impartiality and avoid risk. Or they were willing to contribute aircraft for the no fly zone which they believed was a nearly risk-free proposition. With the hostage taking after the Pale bombing and the shoot-down of O'Grady, they began to see failure as a real possibility, and serious thought about taking more decisive action began to take shape.

July 1995 would be the decisive month of the Bosnian conflict. The Bosnian Serb Army launched Operation Krivaja on 6 July 1995, an attack on the safe area of Srebrenica, a village of some 36,000 people. The Bosnian Serb forces moved rapidly and violently, eventually taking control of Srebrenica on 11 July 1995. The siege on Srebrenica revealed the UN peacekeeping force charged with protecting it to be completely inadequate and ineffective. And in one of the most tragic episodes of the war and the 1990s, the Serbs followed their seizure of Srebrenica by massacring 8,000 helpless Bosnians.

The UN force in Srebrenica was comprised of a 450-man Dutch battalion commanded by Lieutenant Colonel Karremans. Their headquarters was at a compound in Potocari, approximately five kilometers from Srebrenica. They manned some 30 observation posts around the city. As the assault began, Bosnian Serb forces shelled several of the Dutch observation posts, forcing them to flee. In the final assault Serbian forces took Dutch peacekeepers as hostages.

Lieutenant Colonel Karremans initially did not request air support, believing that the Serbs were not determined to seize the enclave, and he did not reverse his opinion until 10 July, four days into the attack and only one day before Srebrenica was overrun. On 11 July, the Dutch battalion compound was flooded with refugees seeking protection. Karremans requested air strikes to his chain of command, asking that over 40 targets be struck. He was expecting massive air strikes. The first air strikes were conducted on the afternoon of 11 July by Dutch F-16s, which destroyed two Serb tanks. General Mladic, the Bosnian Serb Commander, threatened to execute all the Dutch peacekeepers being held as hostages, and in response, Dutch Defense Minister Voorhoeve phoned the NATO air operations center and ordered an immediate cessation to the air strikes.[19]

Even had further strikes been authorized, it is unlikely that they would have had the effect many hoped for. The Serbs were conducting their siege in an urban environment, and locating and differentiating Serb forces from any other people on the ground would have been problematic. In reality, the outcome was largely predetermined once the Serbs did as they had done before, taking peacekeepers hostage and using them to deter NATO air strikes.

Most tragically, in the aftermath of the Bosnian Serbs' seizure of Srebrenica, the Dutch battalion handed over the civilian refugees they were protecting in their compound at Potocari. Those refugees were slaughtered by Bosnian Serb forces in the largest massacre in Europe since World War II.

Events shifted significantly after Srebrenica. Bosnian Serb forces moved quickly to seize the safe area of Zepa, only 30 miles from Srebrenica, leaving only four of the initial six safe areas under UN control. It appeared that General Mladic and the Bosnian Serb Army had their sights set next on Gorazde, the last safe area in the east and protected by a battalion of British soldiers. As the Bosnian Serb Army was seizing Zepa and the UNPROFOR soldiers were redeploying away from Zepa, General Rupert Smith was negotiating with General Mladic for the evacuation of Zepa's 17,000 Muslims, trying to avoid a repeat of Srebrenica.

At the same time, Croatian Serbs and rebel Bosnian Muslim forces joined together in an attack against Bosnian Serb forces in the safe area of Bihac in western Bosnia. This led NATO ministers and military leaders to consider expanding the threat of air strikes beyond even Gorazde. This would prove unnecessary, as Croatian government forces began their offensive, Operation Storm, in what would be the final decisive battle of the Croatian War of Independence, but which also reduced the Bosnian Serb Army threat to Bihac. From 4–14 August, the Croatian Army fought alongside the Army of the Republic of Bosnia and Herzegovina in what was the largest land battle in Europe since World War II. They regained control of much of eastern Croatia, and they also changed the military balance around the UN declared safe area of Bihac. This would be decisive a month in what was known as Operation Mistral, a Croatian/Bosnian ground offensive fought against the Bosnian Serbs concurrent with the NATO air campaign Operation Deliberate Force.

NATO ministers and military leaders held an intense series of meetings after the Srebrenica massacre. The first session was held in London on 21 July to discuss strategies after Srebrenica. At the London Conference the US and Britain agreed to use air power to protect Gorazde, though France and several other NATO countries dissented. A few days later at the North Atlantic Council meeting on 25 July, NATO ministers agreed to threaten forceful air strikes should Bosnian Serb forces attack Gorazde. NATO ministers also agreed on 1 August to expand the threat of air strikes to the three other safe areas of Bihac, Sarajevo and Tuzla. Then on 10 August Admiral Snuffy Smith and General Janvier signed a memorandum of understanding that expanded the authorization of air strikes and a new dual key arrangement which delegated both the UN keys and NATO keys to a lower level of approval.

The mood had changed. There was growing support for using NATO air power to degrade Bosnian Serb military capability. Srebrenica fortified world opinion that the Serbs were not only the aggressors in the conflict but criminals guilty of genocide. The Clinton administration became energized, in part by the exertions of Richard Holbrooke, the newly appointed envoy. The UN began redeploying its peacekeepers to more defensible positions. NATO began to act independently rather than purely in support of UNPROFOR.

These agreements to threaten air strikes to protect the safe areas would have been empty threats if not for the redeployment of UN peacekeepers to more defensible positions and the availability of a plan to degrade the Bosnian Serb Army's military capacity. This planning effort by Lieutenant General Ryan's staff had been ongoing since December of 1994.

The event that triggered what became known as Operation Deliberate Force was the Serbs' shelling of Sarajevo on 28 August. Once again, the Markale market was the target. Thirty-seven civilians were killed and 80 wounded during the shelling. General Rupert Smith was prepared for this possibility and was already pulling his peacekeeping forces out of their positions. The peacekeeper evacuation was complete by the end of the day on 28 August. Smith had redeployed his forces in Gorazde to Serbia and his forces in Sarajevo to defensible positions. Thus, without any threat of peacekeepers being taken hostage, the window was now open. UN and NATO officials received confirmation that the Serbs were responsible for the shelling of Sarajevo, and they approved air strikes for 29 August. General Rupert Smith asked for a 24-hour delay to commence air strikes in order to evacuate all UN peacekeeping forces to defensible positions.

Operation Deliberate Force began just after 4:00 am local time in Bosnia on 30 Aug. The military goal of the air campaign was twofold: first to roll back the Bosnian Serbs' integrated air defenses which were posing a consistent threat to NATO pilots, and second to degrade the Bosnian Serbs' military capability. The overall strategic goal of the campaign was to coerce the Bosnian Serb Army to remove all heavy weapons from inside Sarajevo's 20-kilometer exclusion zone, to cease attacks against the other remaining safe areas and to accept a cease-fire throughout all of Bosnia. These objectives were laid out in a letter sent by Lieutenant General Janvier to Bosnian Serb Army Commander General Ratko Mladic on the day that Deliberate Force began.[20]

Two days into the campaign, a bombing pause was initiated. Serbian President Slobodan Milosevic reached out through his contacts in Paris and the United Nations and proposed a meeting between General Janvier and General Mladic. US envoy Richard Holbrooke supported this initiative and convinced the NATO ministers and military leaders to cease bombing on 1 September. Generals Janvier and Mladic met in the Serbian border town of Zvornik on 1 September, but the meeting did not produce results. In response to the UN demands, Mladic brought with him a list of his own demands. Two days after the meeting Janvier sent Mladic a letter stating that his demands were unacceptable and that bombing would begin again on 5 September, if the Bosnian Serb Army did not comply with UN demands, specifically the removal of heavy weapons from the 20-kilometer exclusion zone around Sarajevo, the cessation of attacks against the safe areas, freedom of movement for UN forces and NGOs and unrestricted use of the Sarajevo airport.[21]

Bombing began again on 5 September and continued through 14 September. On the final day of bombing, Slobodan Milosevic met with Richard Holbrooke, imploring him to stop the bombing. Holbrooke stated that the Bosnian Serbs knew what they must do to stop the bombing. Milosevic in turn requested that Holbrooke speak with Bosnian Serb President Radovan Karadizic and General Mladic, which Holbrooke agreed to do. The two Bosnian Serb leaders agreed to accede to the UN demands, and NATO suspended air operations.[22] The suspension was initially planned for only 72 hours, but the Bosnian Serbs were granted another 72 hours to complete the withdrawal of heavy weapons around Sarajevo. The campaign officially came to a conclusion on 20 September when General Janvier and Admiral Smith announced that the Bosnian Serbs had complied with the demands of removing heavy weapons around Sarajevo and therefore continued bombing was unnecessary.

In total during the Deliberate Force campaign, NATO flew 3,535 sorties and dropped over 1,000 bombs, over 70 percent of which were precision guided.[23] NATO lost only one aircraft, a French Mirage 2000, which was shot down by a shoulder-fired surface-to-air missile near Pale on the first day of the bombing. The two-man crew was held by the Bosnian Serbs until 12 December.

The success of Operation Deliberate Force must be seen in terms of other actions taking place. Ivo Daalder makes this point, contending that three events changed the strategic landscape making possible the Dayton Peace Accords. First was the military ground offensive, Operation Mistral 2, an operation of the Croatian Army, the Croatian Defence Council and the Army of the Republic of Bosnia and Herzegovina that sought to create a security buffer between Croatia and Bosnian Serb held positions in western Bosnia. The offensive took place between 8 and 15 September. The second event was the agreement between Bosnian Serb leaders and Serb President Slobodan Milosevic that Milosevic would represent the Bosnian Serb side in peace negotiations. The third was the air campaign.[24]

After Admiral Smith and General Janvier officially declared the end of the air campaign on 20 September, the Bosnian, Croatian and Yugoslav ministers met in New York and agreed on 26 September to "Further Agreed Principles" for Bosnian peace. A cease-fire was announced on 5 October and went into effect on 10 October. The next day NATO approved its Implementation Force (IFOR) plan. These events paved the way for the Dayton proximity talks, which took place from 1–21 November, culminating in the Dayton Peace Accords, initialled on 21 November and signed on 14 December.

The Dayton Accords

The Dayton Accords established the State of Bosnia Herzegovina comprised of the Federation of Bosnia-Herzegovina and the Republika Srpska. Bosnia-Herzegovina encompassed 51 percent of the territory and the Republika Srpska encompassed 49 percent. The State of Bosnia and Herzegovina was highly decentralized, though it retained a central government with a rotating presidency, a central bank and a constitutional court.

The implementation of the agreement included the deployment of the NATO-led Implementation Force (IFOR), responsible for fulfilling the military aspects of the agreement and taking over for UNPROFOR. Initially, UNPROFOR soldiers remained in place and replaced their UN insignia with NATO IFOR insignia. Then on 29 December, some 60,000 NATO forces, joined by Russian, Moroccan, Egyptian, Ukrainian and Jordanian troops, began deploying to Bosnia. IFOR's mandate lasted for a year and was followed by the Stabilization Force (SFOR) that continued the military implementation for the next eight years.

Air operations in support of these events continued. Operation Deny Flight officially ended on 20 December and was followed by Operation Decisive Edge (December 1995–December 1996), Operation Deliberate Guard (December 1996–June 1998), and Operation Deliberate Forge (June 1998–September 2004). All of these operations were tasked with enforcing a no fly zone over Bosnia as well as providing air support to the IFOR and SFOR forces on the ground.

Operation Deny Flight lasted 983 days, from 12 April 1993 to 20 December 1995. In total, 100,420 sorties were flown. Operation Deliberate Force lasted for three weeks and totaled 3,535 sorties. The air operations after the Dayton Peace Accords lasted for nine years. Data is not available on the number of sorties flown, but it is noteworthy that no fly zone violations were not a factor, nor were any air strikes conducted during the duration of the air operations in Bosnia after the Dayton Peace Accords.

Operation Deliberate Force marked a turning point in the Bosnian war. It also marked a turning point in how people viewed the use of air power. The air strikes of Deliberate Force combined with the Croatian-Bosnian ground offensive created an environment that led to the Dayton Peace Accords. The confluence of events was twofold: first, the United States made a decision in August 1995 to change course from a policy of containment and disengagement to one of actively pursuing a solution in Bosnia; secondly, the UN and NATO ceased being impartial and used military force to try to coerce the Serbs to negotiate.

Ivo Daalder summarizes the change:

> Led by a US military still very much under the influence of the former JCS Chairman, General Colin Powell, the anti-interventionist camp had argued that nothing less than a full-scale involvement of tens, if not

hundreds, of thousands of troops designed to achieve a military victory could guarantee to bring the Serbs to heel while avoiding the risk of getting stuck in a Vietnam-like quagmire. Others . . . believed that the use of air power was desirable not only to punish the Bosnian Serbs for their barbarous ehaviour but also to force the Serbs to come to the negotiating table—to use air power in the service of diplomacy.[25]

Lieutenant General Briquemont, the Belgian commander of Bosnian UNPROFOR from June 1993 to January 1994, published his memoir in 1998. He aptly titled it *Do Something, General!*. Although he was a ground force commander, his book title sums up the oft-cited sentiment when people consider no fly zones. They most often amount to an effort by the international community to take action without taking on risks and costs.

Because the UNPROFOR forces were so undermanned, because political will to escalate was so lacking and because a lasting, agreed to, and enforceable cease fire could not be found, the utility of air power was minimal. To the critics of no fly zones and air power, Bosnia is viewed as a case study that exemplifies its limits. Time and again when air power was used, UNPROFOR found its forces taken hostage and was forced to negotiate with the Bosnian Serbs, unable to effectively use the threat or use of air strikes.

The Bosnia experience was in the end successful. When the UNPROFOR forces were removed from their vulnerable positions, and when the UN and NATO ceased trying to maintain the impartiality of the peacekeeping forces and instead took sides by bombing the Serbs during Operation Deliberate Force, coercive air power was effective. It drove the Bosnian Serbs to the negotiating table and resulted in the Dayton Peace Accords.

Deny Flight and Deliberate Force did not prove out the theory that a no fly zone is a slippery slope of inevitable escalation of involvement. The Bosnian no fly zone instead provided further options for using military force to bring about a lasting solution. NATO air power was used not just to stop the warring parties from flying, but also to lead the way to a settlement of the conflict.

The larger lesson from the use of air power in Bosnia is that a no fly zone is a low risk, low cost option, which is often low impact, though it must be said not without impact. A no fly zone is in many respects an expression of the limits of what a country or coalition is willing to do. NATO would experience this three and a half years later in Kosovo, when it again turned to air power alone, though not in the context or classification of a no fly zone, but rather as an air campaign.

Operation Allied Force – Kosovo

The Kosovo air campaign, known as Operation Allied Force, was never referred to as a no fly zone. It is nonetheless relevant to this work because it illustrates the difficulties involved in the exclusive use of air power in a narrowly limited intervention. NATO chose to intervene in Kosovo, seeking to stop the violence as Slobodan Milosevic turned his military and paramilitary forces on the Kosovar Albanians to expel them from their homes in Kosovo. Confident in the success of Operation Deliberate Force three and a half years earlier and the resultant Dayton Peace Accords, NATO's leaders believed a few days of air strikes would compel Milosevic to comply. Unable to coordinate a successful vote at the United Nations, they still had enough good will and acquiescence from the Russians that they proceeded without a Security Council resolution.

When a few days of air strikes did not coerce Milosevic, NATO found itself in a serious dilemma. Unwilling to escalate beyond air strikes, unable to influence events on the ground, much as in Bosnia, they muddled their way through, sustaining an air campaign for 77 days, threatening a ground invasion and working closely with a cooperative Russia to find a resolution that was successfully implemented through a robust international peacekeeping force.

As the violence in Bosnia de-escalated after the Dayton Peace Accords, the conflict in Kosovo grew. Kosovo, a landlocked province of Serbia and Montenegro, had long been an ethnically divided region filled with tensions between its Albanian and Serb populations. The Kosovo Albanians began challenging Serb rule in 1995 when the armed rebel group known as the Kosovo Liberation Army (KLA) began launching attacks against Serbian law enforcement in Kosovo. These attacks increased in March 1998, and Serb paramilitaries and regular forces began a campaign of retribution, an offensive that killed between 1,500 and 2,000 civilians and KLA rebels and also displaced many hundreds of thousands from their homes.

The US and the Europeans initially focused on imposing economic sanctions and seeking a settlement of Kosovo's political future, but this never extended to considering an intervention to separate the Serbs and Kosovars. The diplomacy was led by six contact group nations –France, Germany, Great Britain, Italy, Russia and the United States – who worked together, agreeing that any successful intervention required unity of effort as well as American involvement, but also believing that concerted pressure on Milosevic would be effective in convincing him to cease the violence and to begin a dialogue with the Albanian community in Kosovo. Their unanimity would not be sustained.

In response to the violence of March 1998, the US-led efforts resulted in United Nations Security Council Resolution 1160, adopted on 31 March 1998. It imposed an arms embargo and economic sanctions on the Federal Republic of Yugoslavia in hopes of dissuading Milosevic from continuing the violent offensive against the Kosovars. Nearly six months later, UNSCR 1199 was passed, which demanded that the Albanian and Yugoslav parties in Kosovo end hostilities, although there was no enforcement mechanism. This resolution specified what needed to be done, but it gave no indication on how it was to be accomplished. There was no consensus among any of the governments about what they were willing to do.

As the violence grew, US envoy Richard Holbrooke traveled to Belgrade in October of 1998 to try to convince Serbian President Slobodan Milosevic to end the offensive against the Kosovar population and the KLA. Holbrooke was able to secure from Milosevic an agreement to cease attacks on civilians, to grant access to humanitarian relief agencies, to allow refugees to return to their homes and to allow an international presence in Kosovo to verify compliance, a group known as the Kosovo Verification Mission (KVM). But enforcing compliance was not part of the agreement, and the international monitors were to be unarmed. This KVM mission was further codified through UNSCR 1203, adopted on 24 October 1998.

Conspicuously absent from all of these UN Resolutions was the threat or discussion of military force. The was primarily because Russia had made clear that it would veto any UN resolution authorizing the use of force against Serbia in Kosovo. This would prove to be one of the obstacles to intervention, though it was eventually overcome as the NATO alliance chose to act without UN authorization.

NATO had been planning steadily since the early months of 1998, from the use of ground and air power to a range of air-only options. Those air-only options included a limited air response of symbolic strikes on a few key targets and a full phased air campaign. As Ambassador Holbrooke was conducting his negotiations in October, NATO countries were polling each other about what forces they would be willing to contribute to an air-only option.

Ground power was effectively ruled out. The Clinton administration was unwilling to consider putting American troops on the ground, and the NATO allies, with the Bosnia experience still in the front of their minds, were not going to be in a position of Americans seeking to bomb while European peacekeepers were vulnerable on the ground.

It appeared that all parties had backed away from the brink after the Holbrooke-Milosevic agreement. The Kosovo Verification Mission of 2,000 unarmed monitors along with unarmed NATO aerial verification flights deployed to Kosovo.

In November 1998, however, Milosevic ordered the commencement of Operation Horseshoe, a campaign to eradicate the KLA and to engineer a fundamental shift in Kosovo's ethnic balance. The Serbs planned to empty the villages of their Albanian population and thus isolate the KLA fighters.

The offensive came to a head on 15 January 1999, when Serb paramilitary forces razed the village of Racak in southern Kosovo. They pounded the village with artillery, killing nearly 50 people. KVM monitors went to the village a day after the massacre and reported on the devastation and deaths.

Racak steeled the US and NATO to act but the discussions in Washington were far from unanimous. Some feared that air strikes would fail. Many worried that decisive action would lead to a long-term commitment that they were unwilling to make, especially in light of the continued presence of ground troops in Bosnia that were part of the implementation of the Dayton

Peace Accords. Here again it becomes evident that discussions of an aerial intervention in many cases are not an expression of determined intent, but rather an articulation of the limits of one's commitment to intervene.

The Clinton administration and NATO allies still believed that Milosevic could be coerced and that a credible threat of force would bring Milosevic around to make a political deal granting the Kosovar Albanians political autonomy. They launched one last diplomatic effort at the French town of Rambouillet near Paris, with a unanimous threatened use of force from NATO. The contact group's negotiation strategy put aside Kosovo's future political status and sought to limit the Serb military presence, to disarm the KLA, and to deploy a NATO force to implement this separation of hostile forces. The talks failed.

NATO was faced with a choice. They could allow the conflict to run its course, which would likely have been a humanitarian disaster. They could intervene on the side of the Kosovar Albanians, which if successful would likely have encouraged further Albanian nationalism and calls for independence in Macedonia and beyond the borders of Kosovo. Or they could limit their goals to stop the refugee crisis and depopulation of Kosovo and to secure by force the creation of an international protectorate in Kosovo. They chose the last option, though with a single tool – air power without any ground forces – a tool that was poorly matched for the task.

Significantly, Secretary of State Madeline Albright achieved the acquiescence of the Russians during a trip to Moscow in January, though without their willingness to support a UN Security Council Resolution. Thus, NATO made the decision to use force without the backing of a UN Security Resolution, knowing that they could not get one. They did, however, act with international backing – UN Secretary-General Kofi Annan in a speech to NATO in Brussels in January stated, "The bloody wars of the last decade have left us with no illusions about the difficulty of halting internal conflicts – by reason or by force – particularly against the wishes of the government of a sovereign State. But nor have they left us with any illusions about the need to use force, when all other means have failed. We may be reaching that limit, once again, in the former Yugoslavia."[26]

With the breakdown of talks at Rambouillet on 18 March, NATO began air strikes six days later on 24 March 1999. On the eve of the strikes, President Clinton stated at a press conference, "Our objective in Kosovo remains clear: to stop the killing and achieve a durable peace that restores Kosovars to self-government."[27] Two days later as the air campaign began, President Clinton in a nationally televised speech, continued to seek to articulate the objectives of the air campaign using three verbs – demonstrate, deter and damage – "Our mission is clear: to demonstrate the seriousness of NATO's purpose so that the Serbian leaders understand the imperative of reversing course; to deter an even bloodier offensive against innocent civilians in Kosovo and, if necessary, to seriously damage the Serbian military's capacity to harm the people of Kosovo."[28]

In the same speech he placed limits on the military force that would be used: "Hopefully, Mr. Milosevic will realize his present course is self-destructive and unsustainable . . . . But I do not intend to put our troops in Kosovo to fight a war."[29] Stating up front that ground troops would not be involved reflected President Clinton's judgment that it was crucial to keeping the alliance together and also that Congress and the US public were not prepared for such an escalation.

Similar to Bosnia a few years before, the commitment of air power did not carry with it the risk of escalation or the slippery slope of mission creep, but rather it was an articulation of the limits of what military action the administration was willing to take. Also, the logic of taking military action in the form of air strikes was that either Milosevic would be coerced by a few days of bombing and agree to the principles of the negotiations at Rambouillet (what most expected), or that the bombings would degrade Serb forces to such an extent that they would have to pull out of Kosovo.

On the night the bombing started, Secretary of State Madeleine Albright was interviewed and asserted, "I don't see this as a long-term operation. I think that this is something – the deter and damage is something that is achievable within a relatively short period of time."[30] NATO severely underestimated the pain threshold of Milosevic and the Serbs. They miscalculated and misunderstood what is the essence of coercion. Political scientist and economist Thomas Schelling wrote most convincingly (he used the term "compellence," and here it is used interchangeably with the term coercion), "compellence has to be definite: we move, and you must get out of the way."[31] What if the target has a much greater stake in the outcome and does not get out of the way? The only options are escalation or admission of failure.

NATO had some 344 aircraft deployed on the opening night of the campaign, 214 of them American, and there was not an aircraft carrier within range of Serbia at the beginning of the air campaign. The *USS Theodore Roosevelt* would not arrive on station until 5 April. By the end of the conflict, NATO would have over 1,000 aircraft deployed, 731 of them American.[32]

NATO initially failed in its air campaign. Milosevic and the Serbs did not capitulate, but rather hunkered down inside Serbia and accelerated Operation Horseshoe as they sought to eradicate the ethnic Albanians from Kosovo.

On the third night of the war, an F-117 Stealth Fighter was shot down about ten miles west of Belgrade. The aura of American air invincibility was broken. Moreover, the air campaign was not succeeding in coercing Milosevic to change his behavior. NATO was having no impact on the refugee crisis that was growing exponentially. By the first week of April, over 500,000 Kosovar Albanians had fled to Albania, Macedonia, Bosnia and Montenegro. The number of refugees who fled Kosovo would peak at over 800,000, and it is estimated that another 500,000 were internally displaced inside Kosovo.[33] Fortunately for NATO, the Serbian Army chose to expel the Kosovar Albanians and not to kill them, as occurred in Srebrenica less than four years earlier.

NATO's belief that the strikes would change Milosevic's calculus and drive him to the negotiating table was incorrect. NATO was caught off guard. It only had targets planned for three days of strikes, although the air campaign was generally planned in three phases. In Phase I, NATO would target anti-aircraft defenses and command bunkers, the standard doctrine of rolling back air defenses. Phase II would extend the strikes to Yugoslavia's infrastructure below the 44th parallel, well south of Belgrade. Then in Phase III NATO would strike targets in the capital.

The Serbian air defenses proved to be difficult targets. Using exceptional discipline, the Serbian air defense operators refused to radiate their radars for more than a few seconds at a time, and they moved their missile systems constantly. NATO moved slowly, struggling to gain a consensus within the alliance to expand the target list, with several countries vetoing targets outright. The alliance tended to operate through consensus, even in choosing targets to be struck, believing that maintaining alliance cohesion mattered more than anything. This would not be the case in Libya 12 years later when NATO would maintain its cohesion while only requiring approval of the individual country which was to strike a target.

The disagreements over how to wage the air campaign are well illustrated in an exchange between US Army General Wesley Clark, the Supreme Allied Commander and overall commander of the campaign, and US Air Force Lieutenant General Michael Short the air component commander. General Clark believed that the focus of effort should be targeting the fielded forces in Kosovo, going after artillery and tanks. General Short wanted to strike strategic targets such as power plants and the political ministries of Yugoslavia. During one of the daily secure video teleconferences, Short expressed his optimism that, at last, they were going to strike the Serbian special police headquarters in downtown Belgrade.

> "This is the jewel in the crown," Short said.
> "To me, the jewel in the crown is when those B-52s rumble across Kosovo," replied Clark.
> "You and I have known for weeks that we have different jewelers," said Short.
> "My jeweler outranks yours," said Clark.[34]

The air campaign seemed to be stuck, unable to find the limit of Milosevic's pain threshold. By 10 April, almost three weeks into the campaign, NATO had hit more than 150 targets, and on 12 April, the Pentagon estimated that Serbia's ability to produce petroleum products was 100 percent destroyed.[35]

NATO braced itself during its fiftieth anniversary summit from 23–25 April. In the statement issued by the alliance, they insisted that Milosevic cease all military action, violence, and repression in Kosovo, withdraw from Kosovo, and agree to the stationing of an international military presence in

Kosovo, declaring that they would continue the air campaign until their demands were met.[36] In many respects other NATO leaders seemed more committed than the Americans to expelling the Serbs from Kosovo, and they spoke forcefully of using ground forces. British Prime Minister Tony Blair in particular pushed President Clinton to take whatever action was necessary to win the war. Planning efforts were redoubled for a ground invasion, although President Clinton continued to publicly state that a ground invasion option was not under consideration.

Perhaps the most significant development to come out of the NATO summit was the change in the US-Russian relationship. Russian President Boris Yeltsin called President Clinton on 25 April to urge a dialogue on how to bring peace to the Balkans. He dispatched his former prime minister, Viktor Chernomyrdin, as his special envoy for discussions on finding a solution to the conflict.

In time the air campaign began to have an effect on Milosevic. By early June, the electricity grid in Belgrade and other cities was nearly destroyed. Many of the targets of greatest value to Milosevic and his cronies were being struck. Whereas during the first week of the war NATO was only able to muster around 50 strike sorties per day, by late May and early June, they were flying sometimes more than 300 strike sorties per day.

In May the task of defining the terms of the final agreement to cease the air campaign had fallen to Strobe Talbott, the US Deputy Secretary of State, representing NATO, Viktor Chernomyrdin representing Russia, and Martti Ahtisaari, the Finnish president representing the European Union. Over the course of a month they were able to gain agreement on the following: Yugoslavia's territorial integrity would be maintained, the UN would establish an interim administration for Kosovo, refugees would be allowed to return, international humanitarian relief agencies would be allowed into the area, and finally this would all have to be approved by the UN. They could not come to an agreement about NATO's demands that all Serb forces withdraw from Kosovo and that the international peacekeeping force would be under a unified command under NATO.

The three eventually agreed to NATO's demand that all Serb forces leave Kosovo with a stipulation that an agreed number of Yugoslav and Serbian personnel could return to Kosovo to perform such functions as conducting liaisons, marking and clearing minefields and maintaining a presence at Serb historical and cultural sites and key border crossings. They agreed to leave the NATO unified command unaddressed save a statement that the security presence would be under a unified command.[37]

Ahtisaari and Chernomyrdin presented the agreement to Milosevic on 2 June. Milosevic accepted, recommended that the Serb parliament approve it, and they did so on 3 June by a vote of 136 to 74. The Serb withdrawal and the deployment of the international peacekeeping forces (Kosovo Force, or KFOR) were spelled out in a military-technical agreement signed on 9 June. The next day, NATO ceased its air campaign, the same day the UN passed

96 *Bosnia*

Security Council Resolution 1244 that authorized the international presence in Kosovo and established the UN Interim Administration Mission in Kosovo (UNMIK).[38]

KFOR entered Kosovo on 12 June, tasked with establishing a secure environment, deterring new hostilities, demilitarizing the Kosovo Liberation Army and supporting the international humanitarian effort. KFOR's deployment into Kosovo and the Serbian Army's departure were conducted almost uneventfully with 36,000 troops, including 2,000 Russian troops, spreading out through Kosovo. No shots were fired, and KFOR was able to prevent any acts of retribution by the KLA. KFOR at its peak possessed over 50,000 troops from 39 countries. The implementation of the agreement has held.

In reflecting on the operation, John Keegan, the esteemed British military historian, summarized the conclusions of many: "The capitulation of President Milosevic proved that a war can be won by air power alone . . . . All this can be said without reservation, and should be conceded by the doubters, of whom I was one, with generosity."[39] Keegan's observations are correct, but only as far as they go. Milosevic did capitulate, though in part because he lost the support of the Russians. And what Keegan misses is the crucial role KFOR and the international constabulary played in the aftermath. What difference did an international ground presence make? Twelve years later air power would again win a war in Libya, and absent any will to complete the task and to assist in the aftermath of the fall of Qaddafi, NATO and her partners would lose the peace and find a Libya far less stable and more violent than before the air campaign.

Lessons learned from the Bosnia no fly zone

The no fly zone in Bosnia

- was the second test of the no fly zone option
- was not preceded by a war, so the integrated air defense systems were intact. Enforcing aircraft did not at the outset suppress the air defense systems but rather attempted to fly between the envelopes of the surface-to-air missiles and ground fire
- was an option that permitted the US to participate in the intervention but put troops at much lower risk than was the case for the troops of other nations such as Holland which intervened on the ground
- was a part of a complicated and sometimes contradictory set of efforts intended to support peacekeepers and to coerce the Serbs to comply with NATO and the UN's demands for a cessation of violence
- reflected an overselling of air power. Deny Flight was a central element of a program that the US and NATO believed, or pretended to believe, could accomplish all that was necessary to keep safe defenseless people in six designated "safe areas"

- demonstrated that the severely limited ground forces provided by the European Union actually weakened the effectiveness of the NATO air intervention forces
- was an attempt to engage without risk of casualties or of deeper involvement
- explored the use of dual-key authorization and found it a source of friction and delay.
- proved ineffective at keeping helicopters out of the air. This was a less grave failing since helicopters were not being used as attack aircraft
- pioneered the no fly zone as a close air support mission
- reflected partly wishful thinking, but mostly reluctance to act
- proved low risk in that only three aircraft were lost to enemy fire during the entire no fly zone enforcement. No lives were lost.

Notes

1 UN Security Council, 47th year. "Resolution 781," 9 October 1992. www.ohr.int/other-doc/un-res-bih/pdf/s92r781e.pdf. Accessed 27 May 2014.
2 UNSC Resolution 836, 4 Jun 1993, UN DocS/RES/836.
3 Ibid.
4 Beale, Major Michael O., USAF, *Bombs over Bosnia: The Role of Airpower in Bosnia-Herzegovina*, Maxwell AFB, AL: Air University Press, 1997, p. 2.
5 "NATO Operation Deny Flight – 15 Sep 95." www.hri.org/news/misc/misc-news/1995/95-09-15.misc.html. Accessed 31 March 2015.
6 Statement of the North Atlantic Council, 2 August 1993, www.nato.int/docu/comm/49-95/c930802a.htm. Accessed 22 August 2014.
7 Bucknam, Mark A., *Responsibility of Command: How UN and NATO Commanders Influenced Airpower over Bosnia*, Maxwell Air Force Base, Alabama: Air University Press, 2003, pp. 87–91.
8 Briquemont, Lt Gen Francis. *Do Something, General!: Chronique de Bosnie-Herzegovine 12 juillet 1993–24 janvier 1994*. Bruxelles: Editions Labor, 1997, pp. 111–112.
9 Bethlehem, D. L. and Weller, M., *The 'Yugoslav' Crisis in International Law: General Issues*. Cambridge: Cambridge University Press, 1997, pp. liii.
10 Bucknam, Mark A. pp. 133–138.
11 Bucknam, p. 137.
12 Interview with Lieutenant General Sir Michael Rose, personal interview, 18 March 2015.
13 Bucknam, pp. 161–162.
14 Rose, Lt Gen Sir Michael, *Fighting For Peace: Bosnia 1994*, London: The Harvill Press, 1998, p. 177.
15 Honig, Jan Willem and Both, Norbert, *Srebrenica: Record of a War Crime*, London: Penguin Books, 1996, p. 150.
16 Honig and Both, pp. 150–151.
17 Interview with Admiral Leighton Smith, personal interview, 22 January 2015.
18 Interview with Admiral Leighton Smith, personal interview, 22 January 2015.
19 Bucknam, p. 249.
20 Atkinson, Rick, "The Anatomy of NATO's Decision to Bomb Bosnia," *International Herald Tribune*, 17 Nov 1995, p. 2.
21 Daalder, Ivo, *Getting to Dayton: The Making of America's Bosnia Policy*, Washington, DC: Brookings Institution Press, 2000, p. 132.

22 Owen, Col Robert C., USAF, *Deliberate Force: A Case Study in Effective Air Campaigning*, Maxwell AFB, AL: Air University Press, January 2000, p. 193.
23 Owen, p. 168.
24 Daalder, p. 119.
25 Daalder, p. 136.
26 "Secretary-General Calls for Unconditional Respect for Human Rights of Kosovo Citizens, in Statement to North Atlantic Treaty Organization," UN Press Release SG/SM/6878, 28 January 1999.
27 "Remarks by the President on the Situation in Kosovo," White House, Office of the Press Secretary, 22 March 1999.
28 "Statement by the President to the Nation," White House, Office of the Press Secretary, 24 March 1999.
29 "Statement by the President to the Nation," White House, Office of the Press Secretary, 24 March 1999.
30 Albright, Madeleine K. interview with Jim Lehrer, *Newshour with Jim Lehrer*, PBS, 24 March 1999. http://1997-2001.state.gov/www/statements/1999/990324.html. Accessed 10 October 2015.
31 Schelling, Thomas C. *Arms and Influence*, New Haven, CT: Yale University Press, 1966, p. 72.
32 *Report to Congress: Kosovo? Operation Allied Force After-Action Report*, www.dod.mil/pubs/kaar02072000.pdf. Accessed 24 October 2015.
33 Daalder, Ivo H. and O'Hanlon, Michael E., *Winning Ugly: NATO's War to Save Kosovo.* Washington, DC: Brookings Institution, 2000, p. 109.
34 Priest, Dana, "The Battle Inside Headquarters: Tension Grew With Divide Over Strategy Series: The Commanders' War: 3/3," *The Washington Post*, p.. A1, 21 September 1999.
35 "DoD News Briefing," US Department of Defense, 12 April 1999. http://archive.defense.gov/Transcripts/Transcript.aspx?TranscriptID=584. Accessed 24 October 2015.
36 "NATO Press Release S-1(99) 62–23 April 1999," www.nato.int/docu/pr/1999/p99-062e.htm. Accessed 24 October 2015.
37 Daalder and O'Hanlon, p. 172.
38 Daalder and O'Hanlon, p. 174.
39 Keegan, John, "Please Mr. Blair, Never Take Such A Risk Again," *Daily Telegraph* (London), 6 June 1999.

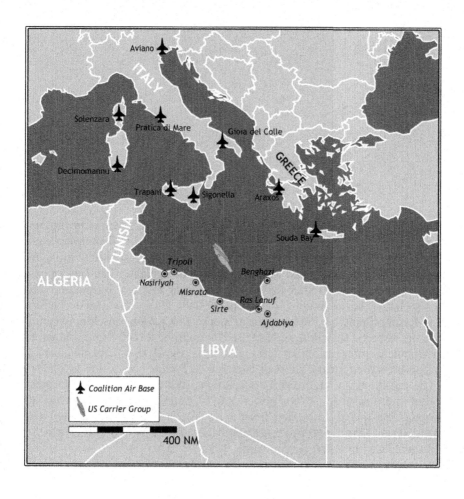

4   Libya

The no fly zone imposed over Libya in 2011, like its predecessors in Iraq and Bosnia, was aimed against a dictator who had created a humanitarian crisis. As in those cases, the no fly zone was part of a delayed response to gross and repeated atrocities committed against the dictator's peoples. The Libyan case, however, came 20 years after the no fly zones over Iraq and Bosnia and after a great deal of norm-building, including the 2005 United Nations declaration of a Responsibility to Protect. The response to Qaddafi was less uncertain than the response to Milosevic, and the UN imposed a no fly zone and gave a carte blanche authorization of "all measures necessary to protect civilians and civilian-populated areas," short of inserting "a foreign occupation force."

The coalition that enforced the resolution readily accepted the interpretation of "all measures" as "air power only." Content to operate from the air, the coalition quickly escalated from a no fly zone to an air campaign. It might be said that the no fly zone actually lasted only 24 hours, after which it was superseded by a full air campaign.

Uprising in Libya

When opponents of Qaddafi's regime rose against him, the uprising was taken to be another in the series of the sudden, unexpected waves of demonstrations and protests across the Middle East and North Africa demanding movement in the direction of modernization and democracy collectively labeled "the Arab Spring." The government of Tunisia was overthrown on 14 January 2011, when President Zine el-Abidine Ben Ali stepped down. In Jordan, demonstrations began on 14 January, and on 1 February, King Abdullah dismissed the Prime Minister and the cabinet. In Egypt, demonstrations began on 25 January, escalating and continuing for 18 days, most dramatically in Cairo's Tahrir Square. Police and supporters of the National Democratic Party (NDP) violently repressed the demonstrators, but the unrest continued. President Hosni Mubarak eventually ceded all presidential power to Vice President Omar Suleiman on 10 February, and on 11 February the Supreme Council of Armed Forces (SCAF) took control of Egypt, later dissolving the legislature and suspending the constitution. At the time of the demonstrations in Libya, it was uncertain whether the Egyptian government would be able to maintain the interval of calm, or whether they would use lethal force against the demonstrators.

Inspired by protests throughout the region, the people of Benghazi demonstrated on 15 February 2011, commemorating two events: the sixtieth anniversary of a massacre of Libyans by Italian colonial forces (an event normally marked with great solemnity) and the 1996 massacre of 1,200 inmates at the Abu Salim prison when Libyan security forces opened fire on the prisoners. The demonstrations were peaceful until security forces arrested Fathi Terbil, a well-known human rights lawyer and activist.

Demonstrations continued for four days, led by the National Conference for the Libyan Opposition, which declared a "Day of Rage" on 17 February. During that demonstration, Libyan military and police forces confronted the demonstrators and fired live ammunition at them, killing an estimated 232 protesters.[1] On 18 February, security forces withdrew from Benghazi after being overwhelmed by the protesters. By 21 February, the rebel forces controlled Benghazi, established a provisional government base there called the National Transitional Council and stated their intent to overthrow the Qaddafi government.

Libyan leader Muammar Qaddafi vowed he would fight to the death rather than leave Libya. Violence escalated as he turned his security forces against the protesters and rebels. While the extent of the regime's violence against its citizens is disputed, international opinion quickly settled around a belief that the Qaddafi government had in fact resorted to widespread violence and furthermore that the international community could not stand aside. The International Federation for Human Rights concluded on 24 February that "It is reasonable to fear that [Qaddafi] has, in fact, decided to largely eliminate, wherever he still can, Libyan citizens who stood up against his regime and furthermore, to systematically and indiscriminately repress civilians. These acts can be characterized as crimes against humanity, as defined in Article 7 of the Rome Statute of the International Criminal Court."[2]

The United Nations' response

UN Security Council Resolution 1973 was passed on 17 March 2011, only a month after the demonstrations in Benghazi were met with violence on 17 February. Why did the United Nations respond more rapidly to the acts of Qaddafi in 2011 than to the acts of Milosevic in 1992–1995, the period of Operation Sky Monitor and Operation Deny Flight? First, the air intervention in the former Yugoslavia, while initially modest and only marginally effective, grew in effectiveness with the increase of forceful ground actions. Second, the United Nations had pursued years of debate and exhortation leading to the 2005 world summit that produced the Responsibility to Protect doctrine.[3] Third, in the United States' the deep aversion to intervention that followed the loss of 18 American lives in the October 1993 Battle of

Mogadishu had diminished somewhat over almost 20 years. Reflection back on the refusal to intervene in Rwanda in 1994 and the casualty-free intervention in Haiti in 1994 also softened the aversion to use of force, while the experience of Northern Watch, Southern Watch and Deny Flight, all casualty-free, deepened the impression that intervention from the air could be managed in terms of risk, cost and escalation. Although the intervention was not an easy sell among the realists in the Obama administration, including the president himself, Secretary of Defense Gates, National Security Advisor Donilon and counter-terrorism chief Brennan, liberal internationalists like National Security Council member Samantha Power, UN Ambassador Susan Rice and Secretary of State Clinton argued strongly in favor of action. The Obama administration was attempting to disengage and disentangle itself from the events in Afghanistan and Iraq, but there was a sense that a limited air intervention in collaboration with Arab League partners might make that extrication easier. The outcome of the debate was the initiation of an 8-month aerial intervention classified as a no fly zone that would accelerate Libya's transition to a post-Qaddafi state but would not produce a country that was more stable or free of violence.

To call the 2011 air operations in Libya a no fly zone is misleading. It was a no fly zone, but it was also all of the following: an air campaign conducted, de facto, against the pro-Qaddafi forces, which led to the overthrow of the Qaddafi regime; an intervention that saved lives during the immediate crisis of Benghazi and that continued on because of the authority granted by a broad and general UN Security Council Resolution; an intervention without a specific end state or efforts to utilize other tools of national and international power beyond air power; an intervention of states that lacked the will to act beyond the low risk air campaign and minor ground operations that left chaos in its wake and a short term humanitarian effort that created instability and disorder in the longer term.

Qaddafi's actions and rhetoric of the third week of February were widely condemned. Qaddafi's violence against his citizens was denounced by the Arab League, the African Union and the Secretary General of the Organization of the Islamic Conference. Qaddafi's son and heir apparent, Saif al-Islam, appeared on Libyan television on 20 February and threatened that "thousands" would die and "rivers of blood" would flow if the rebellion did not cease.[4] This was three days after over 200 were killed at the demonstration in Benghazi. Two days later in a televised speech, Qaddafi, ever defiant, spoke in terms familiar from the Hutu Power propaganda in Rwanda in 1994, calling the protesters "rats," "cockroaches" and "cowards and traitors."[5] He ordered loyal Libyans to "come out of your homes, attack them in their dens." The speech heightened the already enormous fears at the UN of a possible genocide.

The states of Europe, especially the French, pushed hard for action. French President Nicholas Sarkozy, eager to show himself a leader in Europe, pushed others toward intervention. On 10 March Sarkozy summoned Mahmud Jibril and Ali al-Essawi of Libya's rebel national council to meet with him at the

Elysée Palace where he called them the only legitimate representatives of the Libyan people.[6] Other Europeans hesitated, arguing that Germany's rush to recognize the independence of Croatia and Slovenia in 1991 led to increased bloodshed in the Balkans.

Qaddafi, who had a history of behavior that made him seem capable of any atrocity, continued his provocative pronouncements. Qaddafi had been a major financier of the "Black September Movement" which perpetrated the massacre of Israeli athletes at the 1972 Olympics in Munich. Libyan state television had announced in 1986 that Libya was training suicide squads to attack American and European interests, and in April of that year, Libyan agents bombed the "La Belle" nightclub in West Berlin, an establishment frequented by American soldiers. Libyan agents also were responsible for the December 1998 bombing of Pan Am flight 103 over Lockerbie, Scotland. Perhaps most substantial to those fearing genocide, Qaddafi had previously ordered several thousand of his countrymen killed in prison, either through torture or deliberate mass killings, most famously the June 1996 massacre at Abu Salim prison when an estimated 1200 were killed.

On 21 February, Libya's Deputy Permanent Representative to the UN, Ibrahim O. Dabbashi, and much of the Libyan delegation, denounced Qaddafi and called on him to resign. Four days later, on 25 February, Libya's ambassador to the UN, Abdurrahman Shalgam, publicly denounced Qaddafi in a speech to the UN Security Council and called on the Security Council, saying "we need a courageous resolution from you."[7] Additionally, Libya's ambassadors to India, the United Kingdom, Poland, the Arab League, the United States, and several other countries resigned. Mustafa Abdel Jalil, the justice minister in the Qaddafi regime, defected to the side of the rebels. The fact that the Libyan delegation to the UN actually were working for a Security Council resolution against their own country had a considerable impact. It has been alleged that the Chinese ambassador to the UN had a close personal relationship with the Abdurrahman Shalgam, and that this affected the Chinese decision not to oppose the resolution calling for a no fly zone.

The resolution proposed a military operation that was feasible, did not pose unacceptable risks and could have an effect. Qaddafi's forces were advancing on Benghazi. Striking them from the air was a relatively simple tactical problem, especially if the critical task went no further than stopping them from reaching Benghazi and so preventing a massacre there. There are only two primary roads leading to Benghazi from the south, both traversing the open desert, making observation from the air straightforward. Moreover, the air defenses of the Libyan Air Force did not pose a considerable threat. If ever there was a case when air power could deny terrain, much like northern Iraq, this was it. Had Qaddafi's forces made their way into the city, the effectiveness of air power would have been far more limited, indeed almost negligible, and leaders knew they had to act before a battle for Benghazi ensued.

On 22 February, the United Nations Security Council held an emergency meeting and expressed "grave concern" about the situation in Libya.[8] The next day, President Obama stated that Qaddafi had a responsibility to refrain from violence, but his remarks were not strongly worded, nor did they imply much less specifically threaten military action. The very next day, Secretary of Defense Robert Gates gave a speech at West Point where he made the statement that "any future defense secretary who advises the president to again send a big American land army into Asia or into the Middle East or Africa should 'have his head examined,' as General MacArthur so delicately put it."[9] Those remarks were widely reported, but in fact no proposal to send a big American land army anywhere was on the table.

Major General Margaret "Maggie" Woodward, the commander of the US 17th Air Force and the first air component commander of the operation, noted that she and her superiors continued to believe that any military intervention was highly unlikely. On 25 February she was directed to develop plans for various courses of action, all under the label of a "no fly zone." She and her staff went to work, though still believing that it was only an exercise in preparedness and one that had an extremely low likelihood of being executed.[10]

On 26 February the United Nations Security Council unanimously passed resolution 1970 which made explicit reference to the responsibility to protect. It deplored what it called "the gross and systematic violation of human rights," demanded an end to the violence, referred the situation back to the International Criminal Court, imposed an arms embargo on Libya, imposed a travel ban, and froze the assets of Qaddafi's family and of certain government officials. These were significant coercive measures short of the use of military force, and they served to keep Libya in the headlines internationally, but events in Libya were competing for attention with the protests and rebellions in Tunisia, Yemen, Bahrain, Jordan and Egypt.

Violence escalated throughout Libya. Libyan citizens, empowered by the demonstrations of Benghazi, took up arms. Soldiers defected from the military, but the rebellion was disorganized and vulnerable to the greater military power of Qaddafi's forces. The most brutal and tragic example was the city of Zawiya, a city of 200,000 some 30 miles west of Tripoli. Qaddafi concentrated his efforts on Zawiya, and the rebellion was brutally put down over the course of a two-week battle that lasted from 24 February to 10 March.

As the battle for Zawiya was coming to a close, a rebel advance toward Tripoli was put down by pro-regime forces using tanks, artillery and some air strikes. The tide appeared to be turning against the rebellion and in favor of Qaddafi. On 9 March, the head of Libya's revolutionary council and former Qaddafi justice minister, Mustafa Abdel Jalil, claimed that if Qaddafi's forces were to reach Benghazi, the country's second-largest city, it would result in "the death of half a million" people.[11] On 11 March, French President Nicholas Sarkozy and British Prime Minister David Cameron sent a joint letter that called on NATO to draw up plans for a no fly zone.

In what would become one of the most significant events spurring the coalition to action, on 12 March, nine out of twenty-two members of the Arab League called for the establishment of a no fly zone.[12] This was unprecedented, and such a signal from the Arab League opened the door to United Nations action. It was also a political calculus by the members of the Arab League. In calling for a no fly zone, they could recommend military action without necessarily calling for the deaths of fellow Arabs. No fly zones are a uniquely limited and qualified use of force. They could also side with the people of Libya while deflecting attention from their own citizens who were calling for democracy.

NATO's response

As the battles raged during the second week of March, NATO found itself divided. France, Canada, and Britain favored action. Spain and others in the alliance insisted that a UN mandate accompany any action. The United States and Germany were the most reluctant. In the conversations within the US administration, the most articulate and forceful voice for restraint was Secretary of Defense Robert Gates. He made six arguments against intervention, and he:

1 warned against taking action without clear political objectives
2 stressed the lack of US and allied insight into the rebels
3 warned about the political fallout from another US-led attack on a Muslim country
4 stressed the potential "second- and third-order consequences" of action in Libya
5 argued that any intervention in Libya would draw US resources away from other higher priority operations, including Afghanistan
6 pointed out that the main strategy under discussion, a no fly one, would have little to no impact on the ground in Libya.[13]

Despite Gates' objections, the Obama administration changed course over the next week. President Obama called for Qaddafi to step down on 14 March, but he avoided any talk of intervention. As the week progressed, the situation developed quickly and reached a critical turning point. Qaddafi's forces began to overwhelm the rebels. As noted above, Zawiya fell to pro-Qaddafi forces on 11 March. In the west, the oil port of Ras Lanuf also fell to pro-Qaddafi forces on 11 March. Brega was overcome on 13 March as was Ajdabiya, the last city before Benghazi.

Secretary of State Hillary Clinton was in France at this time, and she met with government officials from Arab states who not only supported the operation but were willing to contribute militarily. She reported this information back to the President. Her reports framed discussions at a meeting of the National Security Council on 15 March.[14]

During this meeting, the president's advisors were reluctant. Secretary of Defense Robert Gates, National Security Advisor Tom Donilon and Chairman of the Joint Chiefs Admiral Mike Mullen were all skeptical of intervention. The term no fly zone was still being used, and there was a fear that absent troops on the ground, the situation could degenerate into a scene where aircraft would fly overhead and do no more than watch Qaddafi's forces massacre civilians below. That is of course what had happened in Srebrenica 16 years earlier. President Obama was dissatisfied with the options he was being given. The group adjourned in order for the president to attend a dinner while the president's advisors worked on more options. The group ultimately determined that the US and the coalition could save lives in Libya, and specifically Benghazi, but that they would need a UN resolution that permitted aggressive military measures involving attacks on Qaddafi's forces on the ground from the air.

Had this crisis occurred in 1991, the first options considered may well have been to insert ground forces – peacekeeping troops. An empowered and emboldened United Nations under the leadership of Boutros Boutros-Ghali, exuberant after the end of the Cold War and optimistic about the prospects for peacekeeping, turned to such actions in the Balkans. Had this been 1994, there may have been complete reluctance to act, as the memory of the casualties of the Somalia intervention weighed heavily on the minds of decision makers. Had this occurred in 2000, there may have been reluctance to look to air power as an option. At that moment, there was much concern that the Air Force was being stretched to the limit after Bosnia, Kosovo and the enduring Iraqi no fly zones.

In 2011, however, there was more confidence in the effectiveness of air options, matched with a strong determination not to commit ground troops. Intervention fatigue after nearly a decade of war in Afghanistan and 8 years in Iraq weighed against ground forces, but in the wake of the operations in Iraq and Afghanistan, with the advances in technology and the efficacy of air power, it was believed that air power alone could make a difference, if given the leeway to act and not overly restricted in how it operated; in other words: permissive rules of engagement.

After the President returned from his dinner, he was presented with options that included strikes to stop Qaddafi's forces from advancing on Benghazi. Ambassador Rice believed that a UN resolution that permitted this more aggressive action was within reach. She was instructed to negotiate a resolution that would allow military action that included attacking Libyan forces on the ground.[15]

On 17 March, the United Nations Security Council passed Resolution 1973, with ten members voting for the resolution and five members abstaining (China, Russia, Brazil, India and Germany). The resolution authorized "member states ... to take all necessary measures ... to protect civilians and civilian populated areas under threat of attack in the Libya Arab Jamahiriya, including Benghazi, while excluding a foreign occupation force of any form . . . . "[16] Russia and China's abstention from UNSCR 1973, in reality and acquiescence, rested on a political calculation that they could distance themselves from the military action once it began.

UNSCR 1973 was remarkable for its permissiveness. The three words, "all necessary measures" were used throughout the operation to justify aggressive rules of engagement or the escalation and expansion of target lists. They became a source of conflict within the United Nations, as China and Russia objected to some of the actions taken, believing that the coalition was overstepping the mandate given by UNSCR 1973.

Military planners were taken by surprise when UNSCR 1973 was passed. The speed of the crisis was hard to appreciate; the Arab world had gone from quiet to chaos in a matter of weeks. But also, military leaders had been closely watching and parsing the statements of administration officials. Leading the administration's public words were those of Defense Secretary Robert Gates. A week after his West Point speech where he cautioned against involving the country in a land war in Asia or the Middle East, Gates warned during congressional testimony that even a modest no fly zone would require an attack on the Libyan air defenses, "Let's just call a spade a spade. A no fly zone begins with an attack on Libya to destroy the air defenses . . . and then you can fly planes around the country and not worry about our guys being shot down."[17] He clarified those remarks 12 days later in speaking with reporters, and in response to criticism of inflating the dangers of imposing a no fly zone, he said, "A little bit too much has been read into some of my remarks last week. If we are directed to impose a no fly zone, we have the resources to do it. This is not a question of whether we or our allies can do this. We can do it. The question is whether it's a wise thing to do. And that's the discussion that's going on at a political level. But I just want to make clear that we have the capacity to do it."[18]

US military planners at the very highest levels were convinced that this would not come to action. During discussions with the Secretary of Defense and his military commanders, Gates agreed to reposition assets near Libya, but in scant numbers, and notably excluded from the list was the aircraft carrier *USS Enterprise.* He did reposition the amphibious assault ship, *USS Kearsarge,* which possessed six AV-8B Harrier jump jets as well as MV-22 Osprey tilt rotor aircraft, which could be used for combat search and rescue. But the Kearsarge with its complement of Harriers possessed only a fraction of the sortie rates and capability of an aircraft carrier. Secretary Gates did, however, reposition ships and submarines capable of shooting Tomahawk cruise missiles. These included the two guided missile destroyers *USS Barry* and *USS Stout,* the nuclear attack submarines *USS Providence* and *USS Scranton* and the cruise missile submarine *USS Florida.* These ships would launch the bulk of the initial attacks.

In reflecting on the first hours and days of the operation, Major General Woodward noted that she first became convinced that the operation would be executed as she watched the passage of UNSCR 1973 on CNN. General Woodward's staff had developed a comprehensive plan, but the Secretary of

Defense and the Chairman of the Joint Chiefs of Staff had not prepositioned forces – only five of the 98 assets that were deemed to be required by General Woodward were in place on 19 March, the night of the first strikes.[19]

After the passage of UNSCR 1973, President Obama sent Secretary of State Hillary Clinton back to Paris on 19 March where she joined leaders from the countries supporting the intervention. There was still hope that military action could be avoided, but French President Sarkozy walked out of the meeting and announced that French Rafale fighters had struck targets in Libya, to the surprise of almost everyone.[20]

Executing Odyssey Dawn

The US Commander of the operation during those first 13 days was General Carter Ham. The Joint Task Force Commander was Admiral Samuel Locklear who, in his role as the Commander of US Naval Forces Europe-US Naval Forces Africa, would also play a role during the subsequent NATO operation. The air component commander was Major General Margaret Woodward.

General Woodward was given the green light to begin execution on 19 March, though as noted, few of the assets were in place save the ships capable of shooting Tomahawk missiles. During the first night of strikes, the US was only able to muster a 4-ship (four aircraft) of F-15E Strike Eagles from Lakenheath Air Base, England, which recovered at Aviano Air Base, Italy, four AV-8B Harriers from the *USS Kearsarge* and three B-2 bombers from Whiteman Air Force Base in Missouri. General Woodward even had to order that the B-2 bombers launch for the 26-hour mission without an execute order from the Joint Staff, the order finally being released more than six hours after the B-2s had taken off from Missouri on their transit across the Atlantic. She summarized the circumstances thus: "It was a great plan without the assets to execute the plan."[21]

The operation began as an international coalition led by France, the United Kingdom, and the United States, due to an initial lack of consensus among NATO members. Joining the coalition were Belgium, Canada, Denmark, Italy, the Netherlands, Norway, Qatar, Spain and the United Arab Emirates. The operation was titled Joint Task Force Odyssey Dawn. Each country had its own name for the operation: the US called it Operation Odyssey Dawn, the British named it Operation Ellamy, the French named it Operation Harmattan, and the Canadians called it Operation Mobile. As NATO worked out its consensus, the organization took control of the no fly zone enforcement on 24 March under the title Operation Unified Protector, and then on 31 March NATO took control of the air strikes as well, ending the more hastily-coordinated Operation Odyssey Dawn.

Planners for the operation faced unique mission challenges. First, and most significant was the requirement to plan air operations over vast distances. The closest air base to Libya for fighter aircraft was Sigonella, Sicily, which is well

Table 4.1 Summary of the coalition forces

Country	Air base	Type of aircraft (mission)	# A/C
Belgium	Araxos, Greece	F-16 Falcon (strike)	6
Canada	Trapani, Sicily	CF-18 Hornet (strike)	7
	Trapani, Sicily	CC-150 Polaris (refueling)	2
	Valletta, Malta	CC-17 Globemaster (transport)	2
	Valletta, Malta	CC-130J Super Hercules (tactical transport)	2
	Sigonella, Sicily	CP-140 Aurora (maritime patrol)	2
Denmark	Sigonella, Sicily	F-16AM Falcon (strike)	6
	Sigonella, Sicily	C-130J-30 Super Hercules (tactical transport)	1
France	Solenzara, Corsica, France	Dassault Rafale (strike)	7
	Solenzara, Corsica, France	Mirage F-1 (strike)	3
	Sigonella, Sicily	Dassault Rafale (strike)	5
	Souda Bay, Crete	Mirage F-1 (strike)	16
	Souda Bay, Crete	Atlantique (maritime patrol)	1
	Various, France	Super Étendard (strike)	6
	Various, France	E-2 Hawkeye (airborne early warning)	2
	Various, France	C-2 Greyhound (tactical transport)	2
	Sigonella, Sicily	Harfang (unmanned system)	UNK
	Avord, France	E-3F AWACS (airborne early warning)	1
	Istres, France	C-135 (refueling)	6
	FS Charles de Gaulle	E-2C Hawekeye (airborne early warning)	2
	FS Charles de Gaulle	Rafale (strike)	6
	FS Charles de Gaulle	Super Étendard (strike)	6
	FS Tonnere	Tigre (attack helicopter)	UNK

Country	Air base	Type of aircraft (mission)	# A/C
Italy	Trapani, Sicily	Tornado ECR (SEAD)	4
	Trapani, Sicily	Tornado IDS (refueling)	6
	Trapani, Sicily	F-16 Falcon (strike)	4
	ITS Giuseppe Garibaldi	AV-8B Harrier (strike)	4
	ITS Giuseppe Garibaldi	SH-3D (CSAR helicopter)	UNK
	Trapani, Sicily	Typhoon Eurofighter (strike)	4
	Undisclosed	KC-130J Super Hercules (refueling)	UNK
	Undisclosed	KC-767A (refueling)	UNK
Jordan	Aviano, Italy	F-16 (strike)	6
NATO	Trapani, Italy	E-3A AWACS (airborne early warning)	3
Netherlands	Decimomannu, Sardinia	F-16AM Falcon (strike)	6
	Decimomannu, Sardinia	KDC-10 (refueling)	1
Norway	Souda Bay, Crete	F-16AM Falcon (strike)	6
Qatar	Souda Bay, Crete	Mirage 2000–5EDA (strike)	6
	Souda Bay, Crete	C-17 Globemaster (transport)	2
Spain	Decimomannu, Sardinia	F-18 Hornet (strike)	6
	Decimomannu, Sardinia	KC-707–331B (refueling)	2
Sweden	Sigonella, Sicily	JAS-39 Gripen (strike)	8
	Sigonella, Sicily	Saab 340 (airborne early warning)	1
	Sigonella, Sicily	C-130 Hercules (transport)	1
Turkey	Sigonella, Sicily	F-16 Falcon (strike / non-combat)	6
	Sigonella, Sicily	KC-135 (refueling / non-combat)	1
UAE	Decimomannu, Sardinia	F-16 Falcon (strike)	6
	Decimomannu, Sardinia	Mirage 2000 (strike)	6

Country	Air base	Type of aircraft (mission)	# A/C
United Kingdom	Gioia del Colle	Tornado (strike)	16
	Gioia del Colle	Typhoon Eurofighter (strike)	10
	Akrotiri, Cypress	Nimrod R1 (surveillance)	1
	Akrotiri, Cypress	Sentinel R1 (surveillance)	1
	Akrotiri, Cypress	E-3 AWACS (airborne early warning)	1
	Brize Norton, UK	VC10 (refueling)	UNK
	HMS Ocean	AH-64 Apache (attack helicopter)	UNK
United States	USS Kearsarge / USS Bataan	AV-8B Harrier (strike)	6
	Aviano, Italy	A-10 Warthog (strike)	UNK
	Aviano, Italy	EA-18G Growler (SEAD)	5
	Aviano, Italy	EA-6B Prowler (SEAD)	5
	Aviano, Italy	F-15E Strike Eagle (strike)	UNK
	Aviano, Italy	F-16 Falcon (strike)	18
	Whiteman, USA	B-2 Stealth bomber (strike)	UNK
	Akrotiri, Cypress	U-2 (reconnaissance)	UNK
	Mildenhall, UK	AC-130U Spectre (strike)	2
	Souda Bay, Crete	RC-135 Rivet Joint (reconnaissance)	2
	Rota, Spain	E-8C JSTARS (reconnaissance)	1
	Rota, Spatin	E-3B AWACS (airborne early warning)	2
	Sigonella, Sicily	MQ-1 Predator (UAVS strike & reconnaissance)	UNK
	Sigonella, Sicily	RQ-4 Global Hawk (UAS reconnaissance)	UNK
	Moron, Spain	KC-135 Stratotanker (refueling)	15
	Moron, Spain	KC-130 Extender (refueling)	4

over 200 miles from Tripoli. American fighters based out of Aviano, Italy, had a one-way transit of over 1,100 miles to get to Benghazi. Libya is a large country, the 17th largest in the world, and four times as large as Iraq. Unlike Iraq, however, nearly all of the Libyan population is concentrated in one area, along the Mediterranean coast. Operations were focused on two objective areas – one in the west that ran from Zawiya to Tripoli to Misrata, and one in the east that ran from Brega to Ajdabiya to Benghazi. It is roughly 400 miles between these areas, which is an hour-long transit for a fighter, or a 4-hour transit for a Predator drone.

The first actions of the operation necessarily entailed neutralizing, or rolling back, the Libyan air defenses to ensure that coalition aircraft could fly without undue risk. Simultaneously, or nearly simultaneously, the coalition had to prevent the pro-Qaddafi forces from killing civilians. Both Misrata and Benghazi were threatened by pro-Qaddafi forces. Stopping that advance was the critical task – a task for which many would contend air power is not the most appropriate tool.

It was a large coalition that eventually expanded to 19 states, with the newer states mostly enforcing the no fly zone and the naval blockade (but not conducting air strikes) or providing military logistical assistance. The initial sorties in the campaign were flown by American, French, British and Canadian air forces. A naval blockade was also immediately imposed. French aircraft conducted the first air strikes.

The tactical challenge facing the coalition was substantial, but it was not insurmountable. Qaddafi had drawn on his oil money to equip Libya with one of the most robust air defense networks on the African continent. He had 17 active early warning sites comprised of Spoon Rest, Tall King, Bar Lock, and Back Net radars, all vintage Soviet era radars that were vulnerable to the advanced jamming capabilities of the coalition. The Libyans possessed 31 active strategic surface-to-air missiles sites, a mixture of Soviet SA-2, SA-3, and SA-5 SAMs. They also possessed a handful of mobile SA-6 and SA-8 SAMs. None of these SAMs were the most modern of weapons; all were decades old and were ones which the coalition had seen throughout their experiences in Iraq and the Balkans. Whatever public statements were made about how strong and formidable the Libyan air defenses were, it was known from the beginning that this was not a force that could significantly challenge coalition air power. Moreover, if the Libyan air defenses chose to aggressively oppose the no fly zone, they would not survive for long.

Far more challenging than the Libyan air defenses were the distances involved. There were no air bases in close proximity to Libya, and the coalition aircraft were stationed at bases spread throughout the Mediterranean. Below is a summary of the coalition air forces[22]:

The coalition chose to aggressively target the Libyan air defenses, something which did not occur during the Iraqi and Bosnian no fly zone operations. All air strikes against Libyan airbases and air defense targets were classified as "no fly zone enforcement." In the first 24 hours, the coalition launched 124 Tomahawk missiles against the Libyan strategic missile sites. Three B-2 bombers from Whiteman Air Force Base conducted strikes against airbases.

By way of comparison, this was a smaller military effort than the Desert Fox campaign of December 1998. During that four-day campaign over Iraq, 415 cruise missiles were fired, and over 600 bombs were dropped. Over 300 combat aircraft flew in that campaign. As detailed above, the Libyan coalition had fewer than 300 aircraft that participated in the operation. In the first week, the total number of strike sorties was less than 500 among the entire coalition.

The Libyans did not oppose the coalition. Two days into the operation, Vice Admiral William Gortney, the Director of the Joint Staff, in his press briefing on 20 March, noted "there has been no new air activity by the regime and we have detected no radar emission from any of the air defense sites targeted, and there has been a significant decrease in the use of all Libyan air surveillance radars."[23] By 23 March the Libyan Air Force was largely destroyed, and Libya's air defenses were degraded to the point that the coalition was able to operate unimpeded.

The greatest threat to mission failure was not the Libyan air defenses, but rather the threatened siege of Benghazi. General Woodward noted that her greatest fear was that they might be too late to prevent the pro-Qaddafi forces from reaching Benghazi. Ajdabiya had fallen only six days before the campaign, on 13 March, and an armed convoy of pro-Qaddafi forces were pushing toward Benghazi, a distance of only 100 miles. In the event, however, the pro-Qaddafi forces were struck before they reached Benghazi so the promised slaughter in that city did not occur. The convoy ceased its advance, halting in the desert outside Benghazi, and because of the terrain, they became easy targets to spot and destroy from the air.

The initial days of the operation found NATO in heated negotiations about whether or not they would take control of the operation. The US and Britain pushed to bring the operation under NATO command. Belgium and Norway were in this pro-NATO camp, arguing that it was more palatable politically for the operation to be under NATO command. The French objected to this and strongly favored a coalition of the willing, arguing that the NATO operation in Kosovo had experienced unnecessary difficulties in trying to coordinate consensus. In the end, Secretary of State Hillary Clinton, with the help of US NATO Ambassador Ivo Daalder, was able to negotiate an agreement for NATO to take the lead, and the handover took place on 31 March.

While these negotiations were taking place, General Woodward was overseeing an aggressive air campaign. The three words "all necessary measures" from UNSCR 1973 allowed her the leeway and flexibility to strike any targets that could threaten civilians. The initial strikes were against tanks, technicals (pick-up trucks with guns mounted in their beds), multiple launch rocket systems and self-propelled artillery that could be verified as actively attacking targets. Woodward and her staff almost immediately expanded the authorized targets to include equipment sitting stationary and not actually engaged in any activity, but which they determined could threaten civilians at some moment in the future. It was with that same logic that coalition aircraft later, a few more days into the campaign, attacked weapons storage facilities and command and control facilities of the pro-Qaddafi forces, noting that they could pose a threat to civilians in the future.

General Woodward ordered that protecting civilians should be the sole rationale for attacking any target. She wanted to avoid the appearance that the coalition favored one side over the other, and if anti-Qaddafi forces were observed to be threatening or attacking civilians, then they too, would be targeted by the coalition.

Target approval was much simpler than during the Balkan air operations. Approval did not require a consensus among all the coalition members, as was the case in Bosnia and Kosovo in the 1990s. If a target was nominated or discovered during a mission, General Woodward would consider the reasons for nominating the target, and if sound, would validate the target as legitimate. She then would approach a coalition member with air assets on station and inquire if they were willing to strike the target. That coalition member would request through their national chain of command approval to attack the target. If approved, they would strike the target. If not, General Woodward would request a strike from another coalition member. Other countries in the coalition did not have veto authority over target selection but were limited to deciding if their assets would be used to attack targets. This led to a much smoother approval process than the experience in the Balkan air operations.[24]

One of General Woodward's gravest concerns was the coalition's ability to rescue any downed pilots. Complete combat search and rescue (CSAR) assets were not in place when the operation began, and even when they finally were in place, the enormous distances involved meant that the coalition was assuming great risk should an aircraft go down.

These fears were realized only three days into the operation when on 21 March a US F-15E Strike Eagle experienced a malfunction near Benghazi. Both crew members ejected, and they were separated from each other during their ejection. One crew member was picked up by pro-rebel forces and returned to safety. The other was picked up by Marines from the *USS Kearsarge* flying MV-22 Osprey aircraft less than four hours after the aircraft went down.[25] Again, fortune favored the coalition in this instance.

Executing Unified Protector

The operation transitioned to NATO command on 31 March and changed its name from Operation Odyssey Dawn to Operation Unified Protector. During those first 14 days of Operation Odyssey Dawn, the coalition had accomplished a great deal. The Libyan air force was decimated and its air defenses and command and control systems were significantly degraded. The possible siege of Benghazi was halted, and potentially thousands of lives were saved.

Just as important, civilian casualties and collateral damage were minimal as was damage to the civilian infrastructure of Libya.

When NATO assumed control of the operation, the situation had developed into a two-front war. The rebels controlled the east, including Benghazi, which would prove crucial to their ability to arm, train and equip themselves as the anti-Qaddafi forces. In the west, however, Zawiya and Mistrata were still threatened, and pro-Qaddafi forces controlled Tripoli. US Navy Admiral James Stavridis, the Supreme Allied Commander, assumed the role of the overall commander. The operational commander (the joint task force commander) was Lieutenant General Charles Bouchard of the Royal Canadian Air Force. The air component commander was US Air Force Lieutenant General Ralph Jodice.

General Jodice began with very little guidance. There was no mission statement or end state articulated and there was no specific North Atlantic Council guidance. In announcing that NATO would take over the mission, NATO Secretary General Anders Fogh Rasmussen stated, "Our goal is to protect civilians and civilian-populated areas under threat of attack from the Gaddafi regime. NATO will implement all aspects of the UN resolution. Nothing more, nothing less."[26] While this sounds definitive, in fact it is quite open-ended, reaffirming the UN "all necessary measures . . . to protect civilians and civilian populated areas" standard from UNSCR 1973. It certainly offered more than enough rationale for a no fly zone, although NATO's air operations had gone far beyond a no fly zone by then.

Policymakers characterized this as the most benign intervention possible, aimed at preventing either side from killing civilians but not taking a side in the conflict. Pilots and planners consistently questioned how they could use aircraft alone to carry out that mission. How, for instance, would a fighter aircraft prevent a massacre in Misrata if pro-Qaddafi forces started rounding up civilians and shooting them? What force could aircraft interpose? The UN and NATO, they argued, were offering fighter aircraft to do what only ground troops could accomplish. They were imposing an embargo and a naval blockade, and they were asking air power to protect civilians, but were unwilling to entertain the idea of ground forces, peacekeepers or constabulary forces to protect humanitarian efforts. They were hoping that such action might shape the tactical situation, though without much idea what a suitable end state might look like. It was reasonable to suppose that the objective behind the ostensibly humanitarian effort was a transition away from a Qaddafi regime.

Because of terrain, the vast open desert, the remarkable intelligence, surveillance, and reconnaissance capability of the coalition and a great deal of luck, air power did prove able to influence the situation on the ground. When General Jodice took over the leadership of the air campaign, he immediately focused on the four tasks outlined in UNSCR 1973: enforcing the arms embargo, providing humanitarian relief, enforcing the no fly zone and protecting civilians. During the day prior to the handover, General Jodice had a conversation with Admiral Locklear that framed his thinking throughout the operation. Admiral Locklear, who would step down as the joint task force commander but would play a key role as the US maritime component commander, emphasized to General Jodice that he should "be bold and aggressive but not reckless." Jodice in turn delivered his commander's guidance to his staff at the air headquarters by making it an oft-repeated warning, practically a mantra, "be bold, be aggressive, be relentless, but don't be reckless." He told them to relentlessly pursue any forces (either pro-Qaddafi or anti-Qaddafi) that appeared intent on harming civilians.[27]

The North Atlantic Council had little interest in involving themselves in the execution of the operation, save an initial mandate that there be no civilian casualties. Jodice's lawyers strongly objected to this mandate, noting that civilian casualties are to be avoided, but a commander cannot be told to eliminate all possibility of civilian casualties. The council's decree did, however, set the tone for operations and led to his decision to utilize only precision guided munitions from fixed wing aircraft, although there were occasions when non-precision munitions were utilized from the French and British helicopters later on in the operation.

General Jodice's first task was to establish what the focus of effort would be. He never had enough assets to fill the vast skies over Libya with NATO air, so difficult and extensive prioritization was necessary. He gathered his staff, and under the normal 72-hour planning cycle would decide where to focus resources for each day's ATO (air tasking order.) Almost without exception, they decided to accept risk in the east, acknowledging that the anti-Qaddafi forces controlled the east and were not going to threaten civilians. They would focus their efforts in the west.

Jodice's staff began by asking the question, "What does it mean to protect civilians?" It was with this mind that Jodice developed his mission statement and commander's intent. They began by seeking impartiality and focusing on the protection of civilians. To this end, they divided the engaged forces into two categories, pro-Qaddafi forces and anti-Qaddafi forces, avoiding any more specific categorization of factions. If the hostile forces chose to engage each other in battle, as long as civilians were not threatened, General Jodice chose to avoid intervening. He was adamant that they would not intervene in the "battle of pick-up-trucks-with-guns fighting pick-up-trucks-with guns."[28]

Lacking any more specific guidance from NATO or the North Atlantic Council, Jodice constructed a mission statement that declared that NATO would "protect civilians through the employment of kinetic and non-kinetic means against belligerent actors while enforcing the arms embargo and no fly zone while permitting approved non-NATO flight activity and enabling the delivery of humanitarian assistance." From there, he gave his commander's intent (again, lacking any such guidance), that stated "by conducting a coercive air campaign to compel armed factions attacking or threatening to attack civilians to agree to an enduring cease fire in accordance with the terms of UNSCR's 1970 and 1973 and the Berlin declaration by isolating them."[29]

General Jodice's headquarters was in Izmir, Turkey, but only two days into the operation he moved the headquarters to Poggio Renatico, Italy, a more capable facility. Among his greatest challenges was the lack of intelligence, surveillance and reconnaissance assets. He had only two Predator drones available, flying out of Sigonella, Sicily. He had a single RC-135 Rivet Joint Signals Intelligence aircraft and a single E-8 JSTARS ground surveillance and command and control aircraft. He was given only two to six U-2 reconnaissance flights per month. Coupled with that, the US withdrew all strike assets on 4 April, which meant he no longer had the use of F-15E Strike Eagles, A-10 Thunderbolts, B-2 bombers, or F-16CG aircraft. He did, however, still have the use of "unique enablers" which included F-16CJs (suppression of enemy air defense, or SEAD assets), the EA-18G Growlers (also a SEAD asset), air refueling aircraft and the ISR (intelligence, surveillance and reconnaissance) platforms the US possessed.

As the NATO operation began, fourteen NATO nations were participating along with four non-NATO partners. General Jodice created a group that came to be known as the "striker group" consisting of those countries conducting air-to-ground strikes (Belgium, Britain, Canada, Denmark, France and Norway). The group would add Italy and the US when they joined strike operations (though the US participation was only Predator strikes with Hellfire missiles and F-16CJ assets in a SEAD role). The target approval deliberations were fast-tracked through an innovative process learned from the Kosovo air campaign (when NATO countries frequently disapproved target nominations), by keeping decisions at the operational level, much like the process used by General Woodward, and whereby a target did not require the approval of all partners but only by the country who would attack the target.[30]

The NATO operation did not begin auspiciously. Pro-Qaddafi forces repulsed an anti-Qaddafi forces breakout that had nearly reached Qaddafi's home town of Sirte. The anti-Qaddafi forces in the east were pushed back to Ajdabiya, a mere 100 miles from Benghazi. Sandstorms prevented NATO aircraft from operating, and suddenly the pro-Qaddafi forces were again threatening Benghazi. The rebel military chief, Abdel Fattah Younes publicly proclaimed his disappointment in the support he was received from NATO.[31]

In the west, pro-Qaddafi forces threatened Misrata and were indiscriminately shelling the city of 300,000. General Jodice was unable to focus his efforts, splitting assets between the battle in the east and the siege of Misrata in the west. This development represented General Jodice's greatest fear. He consistently maintained that the greatest threat to the success of the operation was if the pro-Qaddafi forces were able to "round the corner" to Benghazi.

General Jodice also had to overcome a critical shortfall of ISR and of staff capable of performing the work of targeteers – individuals who can assess, analyze and prosecute potential targets. Most of the coalition partners did not have expertise or experience in offensive air operations. The US sent augments to Jodice's staff, and the slow start of operations picked up after a few weeks.

118 *Libya*

In reflecting back on these events, General Jodice emphasized the enormous backbone of intelligence, surveillance, and reconnaissance capabilities that must underpin any air operation, ranging from the geo-spatial intelligence of satellite imagery to full-motion video from drones such as the Predator and Reaper, from human intelligence (which was severely lacking in Libya) to signals intelligence. These capabilities, he argued, are where the US has truly lapped everyone in the world, but is also unappreciated by most.[32]

NATO found its stride after a few weeks, but the larger question of the strategic end remained unanswered. With the imminent attack on Benghazi halted, what was NATO supposed to achieve, and how far were they authorized to go to achieve it? NATO held a foreign ministerial meeting in Berlin, and from that meeting they published a statement. They agreed that Qaddafi had "lost all legitimacy" and had to step down and stated that NATO would continue its operation until the following three conditions were met:

1   All attacks and threats of attack against civilians and civilian populated areas have ended
2   The regime has verifiably withdrawn to bases all military forces, including sniper, mercenaries and other para-military forces, including from all populated areas they have forcibly entered, occupied or besieged throughout all of Libya, including Ajdabiyah, Brega, Jadi, al Jebal al Gharbiyah, Kikla, Misrata, Nalut, Rslanuf, Yefrin, Zawiyah, Zintan, and Zuara
3   The regime has committed to permit immediate, full, safe and unhindered humanitarian access to all the people in Libya in need of assistance.[33]

The last point is the most revealing as it indicates the irony and the limits of NATO's commitment. NATO demanded "unhindered humanitarian access" without saying what the humanitarian organizations were to do once this access was granted or how the organizations would be kept safe. These issues were both raised and resolved by those humanitarian organizations themselves, largely without the input or assistance of NATO.

The statement did not call for regime change, but it did permit General Jodice to continue to attack targets that would threaten civilians. Like General Woodward, he determined that legitimate targets included weapons that could threaten civilians, such as tanks, artillery and multiple launch rocket systems, even if those weapons systems were not being used. He also chose to target any surface-to-air missile systems, as these could threaten NATO aircraft. Legitimate targets also included weapons storage facilities, as these weapons, if pulled out of storage, could be used to target civilians. Command and control facilities were also deemed legitimate, as these facilities could be used to control forces that could attack civilians. They avoided targeting Qaddafi himself, although Qaddafi's military headquarters at Bab al-Azizia (the Splendid Gate) in the southern suburbs of Tripoli was targeted due to its use as a command and control facility. In short, the target list was easily expandable. This proved to be a practical and simple way to provide air planners with the most flexibility.

Every target required a collateral damage estimate (CDE), based on a 5-level numerical system which looked at the potential for collateral damage of the buildings and people surrounding the target. Any target with a CDE of 1 or 2 could be approved in the cockpit of the aircraft that was to strike the target. Any target with a CDE of 3 or 4 had to be approved by General Jodice. Any target with a CDE of 5 had to be approved by Admiral Locklear.

A few examples illustrate the care with which NATO executed its targeting. In June targeteers nominated a POL (petroleum, oil, lubricant) facility near Brega. Striking POL facilities was not permitted. Such facilities could reasonably be assumed to be of use to either side and to civilians, so striking the facility could be interpreted as harming the people of Libya. NATO targeteers continued to monitor the facility, and it was eventually determined that it was only being used by pro-Qaddafi forces for their armored vehicles and technicals. At that point it was put on the target list.

In another instance, a Predator discovered an SA-8 mobile surface-to-air missile in a compound that was located near a soccer pitch. The SA-8 is a missile system in which the engagement radar and missiles are all self-contained on a single self-propelled three-axle vehicle. The video showed that there were teenagers playing on the field. Although the SA-8 system was sufficiently far away from the pitch and could be struck using a run-in heading that would ensure that the missile would not threaten the people, General Jodice decided to wait. Later on in the night, when the soccer pitch was empty, NATO struck the SA-8, ensuring not only that the civilians were not hurt, but that the commotion from such a strike was also avoided.[34]

As the operation continued into May, the faceoff in the west around Benghazi was at a standstill. Misrata was the focus, and pro-Qaddafi forces continued to shell the city with heavy weapons, self-propelled artillery, and mortar fire, killing indiscriminately. Eventually the anti-Qaddafi forces retook the airport at Misrata and some of the suburbs, but it looked like a resolution was not coming soon, and many in NATO believed that a negotiated settlement on favorable terms was impossible. The NATO authorization was only for 90 days, and that deadline was fast approaching. The most vulnerable aspect of the coalition was its cohesion, and that was becoming suspect. In order to maintain its cohesion, NATO had to remain within the UN civilian protection mandate and avoid going any further.

NATO reached a compromise, continuing meetings of what was known as the Libya Contact Group and pushing forward with negotiations for a settlement. The Libya Contact Group was a NATO-led group that also included all partner countries participating in the operation. It was directed to provide "leadership and overall political direction to the international effort in close coordination with the United Nations, African Union, Arab League,

Organization of Islamic Cooperation, and European Union to support Libya, provide a forum for coordinating the international response on Libya, and provide a focal point in the international community for contact with the Libyan parties."[35]

In June France and Great Britain added helicopters to the air campaign, the French flying Tigre attack helicopters from the FS Tonnere and the British flying Apache attack helicopters from the HMS Ocean. The French and British claimed that these assets would be useful in targeting pro-Qaddafi forces that were seeking cover and concealment. General Jodice was wary of this action. He was told by his French and British counterparts that it was highly likely that a helicopter would be lost, and he was unconvinced that assuming such risks was warranted. Their contribution was minimal, although the positive psychological effect on the anti-Qaddafi forces was significant.[36]

NATO defense ministers met in June and agreed to extend the mission for another 90 days, but the commitment of coalition members was fraying. Norway announced that they would curtail their role and pull out completely by August. The US was equally ambivalent. In a remarkable episode, Congress showed its strange unwillingness to take on the issue. On 24 June Speaker of the US House of Representatives John Boehner brought two bills to the floor. The first was a resolution that would fully authorize combat operations in Libya (HJ Resolution 68) and a second was an opposite measure that would eliminate funds for further US strikes and limit US participation to ISR, refueling, search and rescue and planning (HR Resolution 2278). Both bills failed.[37] Members of Congress could claim whatever they wanted, either that they supported the war, that they wanted the intervention limited or that they wholly opposed the war, depending on which bill they chose to cite as they offered explanations of their votes. What this congressional inaction indicated was that if NATO was going to escalate its actions, it had to do so without a firm commitment or leadership from United States.

By mid-July, the situation had changed very little. Anti-Qaddafi forces were still fighting south of Benghazi in Ajdabiyah. They were also fighting to break out from Misrata in the west toward Tripoli. At the same time, some NATO members were preparing for their normal summer vacations in August, much to the amazement of many in the coalition. Negotiations with the contact group continued, with little progress.

What turned the tide was not the efforts of the air campaign, but rather that the anti-Qaddafi ground forces improved their capabilities and developed a strategy. NATO had little influence on this, although some coalition members played a role. Special forces from France, Britain, Italy, Qatar and the United Arab Emirates were on the ground throughout the conflict, and they became more and more engaged as the conflict progressed. Qatar played a particularly important role, "sending some 20,000 tons of weapons in at least eighteen separate arms shipments to specific rebel leaders, along with tens of millions of dollars in aid, as well as at least twelve ammunition shipments, via Sudan."[38]

In this respect the experience of the no fly zone in Libya echoes that of the no fly zone in Bosnia: the air campaign achieved its end only when the forces on the ground became more effective.

The advance of the anti-Qaddafi forces was quick and unexpected. In late July, Commander Abdul Fattah Younes, the rebel commander and former Qaddafi interior minister, was killed. It is not known who killed Younes, but his death threatened to break apart the anti-Qaddafi forces and initiate a bloody internal struggle. The anti-Qaddafi forces in the west, however, began an advance on Tripoli just as they were fighting among themselves in the east.

The advance on Tripoli was accompanied by increased NATO air strikes on the capital. Tripoli fell on 23 August as anti-Qaddafi forces overran Qaddafi's compound, Bab al-Aziziya. Qaddafi fled to Sirte, although his whereabouts remained uncertain at the time.

NATO's role from the air after the rebels took Tripoli was extremely limited. Very few air strikes were conducted, and NATO aircraft primarily observed the battles from overhead. Most political leaders continued to believe that some kind of negotiated settlement would be found, and the contact group continued to meet.

The culminating event occurred on the night of 19 October. A Predator discovered a column of about 150 vehicles in Sirte, which they knew to be pro-Qaddafi forces. They were expecting these forces to make a run for Sabha in the south. It was believed that Qaddafi's son was in the convoy, but no one was aware that Qaddafi himself was in the convoy as well. General Jodice authorized the Predator to strike a vehicle in the middle of the convoy, which split it apart. One group of vehicles gathered near a power station. General Jodice then authorized two French Mirages to strike this group of vehicles, which scattered the pro-Qaddafi forces even further. As it turned out, Qaddafi was in that group of vehicles and fled into a drainpipe. He was pursued by anti-Qaddafi forces, who pulled him out, abused him and executed him.[39]

NATO's no fly zone officially ended on 31 October. In total, the coalition committed approximately 8,000 troops, over 260 air assets and 21 naval assets. They flew over 26,500 sorties, including over 9,700 strike sorties, destroying over 5,900 military targets including over 400 artillery or rocket launchers and over 600 tanks or armored vehicles.[40]

Assessing the Libya no fly zone

Judging strictly by its stated objectives, the operation was a success. The coalition maintained an arms embargo, facilitated humanitarian relief, created and sustained a no fly zone and protected thousands of Libyan civilians. Most significantly, the operation forestalled what would likely have been a huge slaughter in Benghazi in the opening hours of the campaign. The operation was accomplished with relatively little cost and risk. It must be acknowledged that NATO had the good fortune of fighting against forces loyal to Qaddafi that were almost universally despised and also tactically and strategically incompetent. The geography of the desert made the application of air power far easier than in most other environments.

Moreover, the cohesion of the alliance was one of the remarkable successes of the operation. The political leaders of NATO were able to agree on objectives, giving the military commanders the leeway they needed to execute the operation. The military leaders, in turn, were able to create a productive environment of collaboration and teamwork.

Strategically, however, the Libyan intervention was marred by its aftermath. The barely sufficient determination of the coalition and their commitment of air power was not matched by the diplomatic, political, economic and military constabulary forces that were required to secure the peace after the fall of Qaddafi. Operation Unified Protector ended and the situation in Libya deteriorated soon thereafter. The West and the Arab world remained largely disengaged. Rival militias turned against each other in the postwar power vacuum, drawing support from foreign sponsors. Libya remains in the throes of extended violence to determine its future, only without the benefit of engaged and committed outside powers to facilitate a political resolution to the conflict.

Lessons learned from the Libya no fly zone

The no fly zone over Libya

- had to overcome much reluctance from American policy makers, especially Secretary of Defense Robert Gates
- was authorized by United Nations Security Council Resolution 1973 which authorized "all necessary measures . . . to protect civilians and civilian-populated areas."
- used that authorization to morph quickly from a no fly zone operation into an outright, comprehensive and sustained offense counter air operation
- was begun by a coalition of states hastily assembled
- prevented ground forces loyal to Qaddafi from entering Benghazi
- began as a hasty coalition, became a NATO operation 13 days after it began and changed its title from Operation Odyssey Dawn to Operation Unified Protector.

Notes

1 Human Rights Watch, "Libya: Government Should Demand End to Unlawful Killings," www.hrw.org/en/news/2011/02/20/libya-governments-should-demand-end-unlawful-killings. Accessed 23 April 2014.
2 "Libya: Strategy of Scorched Earth, Desire for Widespread and Systematic Elimination" (Press release). International Federation for Human Rights, 24 February 2011. Accessed 23 April 2014.

3 United Nations General Assembly, *60/1. 2005 World Summit Outcome*, New York: United Nations, 24 October 2005, p. 30, www.un.org/womenwatch/ods/ A-RES-60-1-E.pdf. Accessed 2 December 2015.
4 Walt, Vivienne, "Gaddafi's Son: Last Gasp of Libya's Dying Regime," *Time*, 21 February 2011, www.time.com/time/world/ article/0.8599.2052842.00.html. Accessed 30 March 2015.
5 "Libya Protests: Defiant Gaddafi Refuses to Quit," BBC News, 22 February 2011, www.bbc.co.uk/news/world-middle-east-12544624. Accessed 30 March 2015.
6 Cowell, Alan and Erlanger, Steven, "France Becomes First Country to Recognize Libyan Rebels," *The New York Times*, 10 March 2011, www.nytimes.com/2011/03/11/world/europe/11france.html. Accessed 2 December 2015.
7 "Libya's UN Ambassador Denounces Gaddafi," *The Telegraph*, 25 February 2011, www.telegraph.co.uk/news/worldnews/africaandindianocean/libya/8349048/Libyas-UN-ambassador-denounces-Gaddafi.html. Accessed 30 March 2015.
8 United Nations, "Security Council Press Statement on Libya," 22 February 2011, http://www.un.org/press/en/2011/sc10180.doc.htm. Accessed 19 April 2015.
9 Gates, Robert, "Secretary of Defense Speech," West Point, NY: United States Military Academy, 25 February 2011.
10 "Interview with Major General Margaret Woodward, USAF (Ret.)," personal interview. 8 April 2015.
11 McGreal, Chris,"Gaddafi's Army Will Kill Half a Million, Warn Libya's Rebels," *The Guardian*. Accessed 16 May 2014.
12 "Arab States Seek Libya No Fly Zone," *Al Jazeera,* 12 March 2011.
13 Chivvis, Christopher S., *Toppling Qaddafi: Libya and the Limits of Liberal Intervention*, New York: Cambridge University Press, 2014, pp. 44–47.
14 Chivvis, p. 56.
15 Sanger, David E. and Shanker, Thom, *Confront and Conceal*, New York: Crown Publishers, 2012, pp. 343–345.
16 "Security Council Approves 'No Fly Zone' Over Libya, Authorizing 'All Necessary Measures' to Protect Civilians, by Vote of 10 in Favour with 5 Abstentions" (Press release), United Nations Department of Public Information, 17 March 2011.
17 "No Fly Zones for Libya Would Require Attack: Gates," *Reuters*, 2 March 2011, http://www.reuters.com/article/2011/03/02/us-libya-usa-pentagon-idUS TRE7214EX20110302. Accessed 12 April 2015.
18 Finn, Peter and Wilson, Scott, "Gates Says US Military Could Enforce a No Fly Zone in Libya if Obama Ordered One," *Washington Post*, 14 March 2011, www.washingtonpost.com/wp-dyn/content/article/2011/03/12/AR2011031204978.html. Accessed 13 April 2015.
19 Woodward interview.
20 "Libya: French Plane Fires on Military Vehicle – BBC News," *BBC News*,19 Mar 2011, www.bbc.com/news/world-africa-12795971. Accessed 4 December 2015.
21 Woodward interview.
22 Chivvis, p. 209–213.
23 Department of Defense, DOD News Briefing with Vice Admiral Gortney from the Pentagon on Libya Operation Odyssey Dawn, 20 March 2011, www.defense.gov/transcripts/transcript.aspx?transcriptid=4787. Accessed 7 March 2015.
24 Woodward interview.
25 Department of Defense, Public Affairs Office, "Transcript: DoD News Briefing with Admiral Locklear via Teleconference from *USS Mount Whitney*," 22 March 2011, www.navy.mil/submit/display.asp?story_id=59247. Accessed 5 December 2015.
26 North Atlantic Treaty Organization, "Statement by NATO Secretary General Anders Fogh Rasmussen on Libya," 27 March 2011, www.nato.int/cps/en/natohq/news_71808.htm?selectedLocale=en. Accessed 5 December 2015.

124 *Libya*

27 "Interview with Lieutenant General Ralph Jodice, USAF (Ret.)," personal interview, 27 April 2015.
28 Jodice interview.
29 Jodice interview.
30 Jodice interview.
31 Smith, Graeme, "Rebel Military Chief Rebukes NATO," *Globe and Mail*, 16 April 2011, p. A14.
32 Jodice interview.
33 NATO Press Office, "Statement on Libya Following the Working Lunch of NATO Ministers of Foreign Affairs with Non-NATO Contributors to Operation Unified Protector," 14 April 2011.
34 Jodice interview.
35 UK Foreign Secretary William Hague statement following the London Conference on Libya, 29 March 2011, www.fco.gov.uk/en/news/latest-news/?view=News&id=575592482. Accessed 18 October 2015.
36 Jodice interview.
37 Chivvis, p. 142.
38 Chivvis, p. 155.
39 Jodice interview.
40 "Operation Unified Protector Final Mission Stats," North Atlantic Treaty Organization, 2 Nov 2011, www.nato.int/nato_static/assets/pdf/pdf_2011_11/20111108_111107-factsheet_up_factsfigures_en.pdf. Accessed 30 March 2015.

5 The politics and prospects for no fly zones

Politics

The no fly zone option was quite highly regarded after the experience in Libya, but only briefly. When Qaddafi was killed by rebel forces in October 2011 and Operation Unified Protector was closed out just 11 days later, the intervention appeared to have been a great success. The dictator had been prevented from carrying out his threat to purge the city of Benghazi of what he called "rats" (meaning citizens of Libya who resisted his rule), and he had been blocked from fulfilling his promise to cleanse Libya house by house. Moreover, the American portion of the intervention had been carried out entirely from the air, and it had been done with the support of allies in the region. The US and NATO had been joined by Jordan, Qatar and the United Arab Emirates and had been called on and authorized to act by the Arab League as well as by the United Nations. All this had been carried out with impressive care and discrimination. Over 8,000 strike sorties had resulted in fewer than a dozen unintended casualties.[1]

Libya had offered from the outset near ideal conditions for a no fly zone. Qaddafi had been isolated in his region and was effectively without allies. The UN Security Council had called for the intervention, and the International Criminal Court had charged him with crimes against humanity. The great geographic expanse of Libya, the dry, clear air, the few roads and the limited air defenses (all of which were knocked out in the first 72 hours) had favored air operations. In short, Operation Unified Protector might have been taken as proof of the "no fly zone plus no-ground-forces intervention" concept in the sense that the humanitarian atrocities were ended, no alliance lives were lost, few innocent lives were taken, Qaddafi was neutralized and removed, and NATO's tactical capabilities were displayed and confirmed. It was not surprising when the US ambassador to NATO and the Supreme Allied Commander together wrote an article about the operation they conducted and titled it "NATO's Victory in Libya: The Right Way to Run an Intervention."[2]

But within three months after air operations ended there were clashes between rebel groups and eight months after that the US ambassador was killed along with three other Americans in an attack in Benghazi. Less than three years after NATO's victory in Libya the UN staff had been withdrawn, the embassies had been shuttered, foreigners had been evacuated, the airport in Tripoli had been destroyed and the Islamic State had established itself. The intervention, which had helped destroy an oppressive regime, had quickly opened the path to a failed state. Hundreds of thousands of refugees had fled the country, their decision to flee underlining their judgement that their families had been safer under Qaddafi's brutal rule than under the chaos that followed the intervention.

No fly zones in a new light

The outcome in Libya cast no fly zones in a new light. The no fly zone operations in Iraq and Bosnia had been criticized for being ineffective, but they had never been blamed for producing chaos and violence.

By contrast, the operations in Libya had proven catastrophic in their outcome, despite having begun with good intentions and pursued with careful limitations. Provide Comfort and Northern and Southern Watches had constrained Saddam for a dozen years, Deliberate Force had brought the Bosnian War to a conclusion, and both regions were left more stable than before. Operation Unified Protector, by contrast, opened the way to chaos and suffering for the people it had been designed to help. Moreover, it led to the foreign powers that carried out the intervention abandoning the region to an array of insurgent groups who exercised few limits on their use of force and presented no discernible progress toward good governance or even relief from violence.

Even such a model intervention, one carried out with such good intentions at such low cost, at such low risk and with such discrimination, was arguably worse than doing nothing at all. This outcome greatly colored the subsequent debate over intervention in Syria and altered the value set on no fly zone operations, especially ones that grew into air-only interventions.

Darfur

The Libya intervention and the debate surrounding it had been preceded and presaged by one over Darfur. Since 1983 the black population of southern Sudan had suffered violence inflicted by the Arab government in the north which incited brutal attacks south by armed and mounted bands that raped, pillaged and killed. Outside powers' failure to intervene brought comparisons to Rwanda, and the persons who championed a humanitarian intervention declared themselves unwilling again to be "bystanders to genocide," to quote the title of an article by one of them.[3]

The debate was made more urgent and harder to ignore by the fact that in previous years in response to Rwanda and other humanitarian atrocities, the United Nations had been feeling its way toward a formal declaration of the

"Responsibility to Protect" principle or "R2P." The Save Darfur movement was the concrete expression and case in point for the R2P principle that was promulgated and adopted by a unanimous vote at a UN special summit in 2005.

The Bush administration was extremely reluctant to intervene, especially with ground troops, but the pressure "not to do nothing" was significant. Darfur might have been an occasion when a no fly zone would have both relieved pressure to do something and avoided repeating the errors that had led to loss of life and rapid withdrawal in Somalia under the Clinton administration.

The situation presented many conditions that made a no fly zone a particularly attractive policy response. First, it was morally compelling. A predatory Arab militia backed, encouraged and paid for by an Arab government in Khartoum, was terrorizing undefended black people. Sudanese leader Omar al-Bashir was charged with crimes against humanity in 2008.

The situation also was both tactically promising and geographically favorable for a no fly zone. Only one side in the conflict, the Sudanese government, possessed significant air assets, and this fact constituted an important advantage over the people in the south. The distances involved were great, ground transportation was poorly developed and air operations were crucial. The non-governmental organizations offering aid to the villagers who were brought under attack also depended on air transport, but their small civilian planes could be marked, tracked and avoided as they came and went principally from Juba. Airfields for the planes used for no fly zone enforcement were available in Chad, and France had close relations with that country.

The geography was not perfectly favorable for a no fly zone intervention, however, in three ways. First, there was no way from the air to impose a physical separation between the Janjaweed and their victims, so a no fly zone would not stop the killing. Second, the Janjaweed did not present an air interdiction target comparable to the armored columns of Qaddafi five years later in Libya, so air operations in Darfur would not have the kind of dramatic impact they later had in Libya. Third, the distance between the site of the conflict and Europe meant that refugees from the Darfur conflict had to cover thousands of arid miles before their presence would pose an issue to be dealt with by European powers. This made the strategic necessity of acting much less urgent. The distance from Darfur to the Mediterranean at Alexandria, for example, is 3,000 miles as the crow flies and that route runs through Khartoum. That meant there would be limited refugee pressure that would make European countries feel the need to intervene to stop the flow of displaced persons.

Despite these predominantly favorable conditions, plus the simultaneous global commitment to the Responsibility to Protect principle, no multilateral air intervention to supplement a very limited African Union peacekeeping force was attempted. There was no response on the order of the intervention in Libya. Instead, Darfur resembled Rwanda both in being a place of very limited strategic importance to European powers and in being left to resolve itself without sufficient multilateral outside intervention to stop a humanitarian disaster.

As the Bush administration gave way to the Obama administration in January 2009, some of the people who were inclined to intervene assumed posts that made them able to exert pressure for a response. Assuming these posts of responsibility made them cautious activists. They included Anne Marie Slaughter, Director of Policy Planning at the Department of State (2009–2011), Susan Rice, US Ambassador to the UN (2009–2013) and National Security Adviser (2013–2017), Samantha Power, National Security Council Senior Director for Multilateral Affairs and Human Rights (2009–2013) and US Ambassador to the UN (2013–2017) and Hillary Clinton, US Secretary of State (2009–2013). In 2005 even Senator Barack Obama of Illinois had called for intervention in Darfur.[4]

Moral hazard and the Responsibility to Protect

Outside the administration, Madeleine Albright, Michael Ignatieff and Anthony Lake expressed their desire for action. Retired Air Force General Merrill McPeak also argued strongly for action in an essay titled "Creating a No Fly in Darfur is the Best Way to Stop the Atrocities."[5] Like most of the American proponents of a no fly zone for Darfur, or later, one for Syria, McPeak envisioned limited American participation in shared air operations, with the US contributing such services as inflight refueling, while other members of the UN or the African Union provided increased forces on the ground. In other words, as in previous cases the pattern was US participation limited to air operations, matched with operations on the ground outsourced to others. McPeak's argument came just three months into Obama's first term and had additional weight since he had been both a specialist in the application of air power for 30 years as an officer in the Air Force and, more recently, a deputy director of the Obama campaign.

In contrast to these voices, and in reply to General McPeak, there emerged a contrarian position in the Darfur debate which is worth exploring because it was made stronger, was more widely held and was strengthened as well by the deterioration of order in Iraq after the invasion in 2003. It also became a factor in the debate over Syria where uprisings began in March 2011. The contrarian argument was made in the first instance by Alan Kuperman of the University of Texas who argued against a no fly zone over Darfur even though, and in fact precisely *because*, he thought it would be effective:

> In Darfur's civil war, only the government has aircraft, so a no fly zone would tilt the military balance and thereby embolden the rebels to go on the offensive.[6]

The fact that a no fly zone would tip the balance in some degree against the regime was of course its greatest virtue in the eyes of those who welcomed the recently-proclaimed Responsibility to Protect principle. To Kuperman, that virtue was actually a fatal problem because it would tend to prolong the violence:

> The government would retaliate by unleashing Arab militias to attack civilian areas perceived to support the rebels and by interrupting vital humanitarian aid to these areas. The net effect of imposing a no fly zone, therefore, would be more dead civilians in Darfur.[7]

Moreover, intervention would delay a negotiated settlement while it incentivized provocative risk-taking:

> The rebels, much weaker than the government, would logically have sued for peace long ago. Because of the Save Darfur movement, however, the rebels believe that the longer they provoke genocidal retaliation, the more the West will pressure Sudan to hand them control of the region.[8]

Worse, he argued, it was foreseeable that struggles, if prolonged, tend to spiral down into greater chaos and killing. He predicted that factions among the rebels would form, strengthen, radicalize, become more violent and indiscriminate and create victims among the people whose cause they claimed to champion. Unless a government becomes far more brutal and closed to negotiations than the one in Khartoum, he held, intervention on humanitarian grounds is a poor option. It is, he concluded, counterproductive and actually *anti*-humanitarian.

Kuperman did not see particular virtue in the rebels' cause. He held that promoting their cause mattered less than ending the violence. Protecting the innocent, by his logic, required withholding military measures against the regime and exerting pressures on both the regime and the insurgents to seek a negotiated resolution. External military interventions that strengthened the rebel groups would make them less inclined to seek political solutions and more inclined to continue and to widen the fighting. In moral terms, his argument rested on an assessment of the consequences of an action only and not on a judgment of the intentions behind the action.

Kuperman's warning against more ambitious interventions resonated in 2009 because other interventions were going poorly in Afghanistan and Iraq. He appended to the Sudan debate the phrase "moral hazard," a term of art made current in 2008 by the great financial collapse of that year, and explained that if an outside power backed up the rebels the way the Federal Reserve backed up banks like Bear Stearns in 2008, it would encourage more risk-taking by the rebels. The proper goal of an outside power, he held, is to encourage restraint, to limit risk taking and to drive all sides toward a settlement in the shortest possible time and so bring the fighting to a close.

This argument looked heartless in Darfur in 2006 through 2009. It looked somewhat better in the context of the grim outcome in Libya six years later.

130 *Politics and prospects*

Kuperman seemed perverse when he called on the government of Sudan to bring the violence to an end, which predictably they would do by crushing the rebels. This of course was anathema to the "do something" advocates:

> Ultimately, if the rebels refuse, military force will be required to defeat them. But this is no job for United Nations peacekeepers. Iraq, Afghanistan and Somalia show that even the United States military cannot stamp out Islamic rebels on their home turf; second-rate international troops would stand even less chance.[9]

He made a small concession to the R2P principle in that he would not allow entirely free rein to a government as abusive as Khartoum. He argued:

> [W]e should let Sudan's army handle any recalcitrant rebels, on condition that it eschew war crimes.[10]

But directly contradicting the spirit of the Responsibility to Protect principle, he granted great priority to sovereignty:[11]

> This option will be distasteful to many, but Sudan has signed a peace treaty, so it deserves the right to defend its sovereignty against rebels who refuse to, so long as it observes the treaty and the laws of war.[12]

To generalize this policy of non-intervention, and in contradiction of the Responsibility to Protect principle, he argued in 2006:

> Indeed, to avoid further catastrophes like Darfur, the United States should announce a policy of never intervening to help provocative rebels, diplomatically or militarily, so long as opposing armies avoid excessive retaliation. This would encourage restraint on both sides. Instead we should redirect intervention resources to support "people power" movements that pursue change peacefully, as they have done successfully over the past two decades in the Philippines, Indonesia, Serbia and elsewhere.[13]

Kuperman offers a harsh assessment of the Responsibility to Protect principle:

> Thus, the emerging norm resembles an imperfect insurance policy against genocidal violence. It creates a moral hazard that encourages the excessively risky behavior of rebellion by members of groups that are vulnerable to genocidal retaliation, but it cannot fully protect these groups against the backlash. The emerging norm thereby causes some genocidal violence that otherwise would not occur.[14]

Kuperman isolated two rules out of the Darfur, Iraq, Libya and Syria experiences. First, do not let intervening forces become an asset to either side. In the Libya case, he argued, NATO effectively became the rebels' air force. It drove Qaddafi from the skies, destroyed his ground anti-air defenses, crippled his mechanized ground forces, interdicted his advance on Benghazi, provided surveillance and intelligence to the rebels, intercepted Qaddafi's convoy when he attempted to flee, guided the final hunt for Qaddafi and observed his death at the hands of the rebels.

Second, Kuperman argued, never aim for regime change because the vacuum left behind will itself be a stimulus to further violence. This second rule, reinforced by the dismal outcome in Libya and strengthened by the continuing and metastasizing disorder in and emanating from Iraq, gained increasing weight and power after the 2011 intervention in Libya and did much to shape the US response to events in Syria.

The sustained but unsuccessful efforts by outside powers to create a government and order in Iraq and Afghanistan made the prospect of doing the same in Libya so daunting that little was attempted. The Iraq and Afghanistan experiences suggest that post-conflict reconstruction and the creation of a new political order requires immense expense and decades-long presence by victorious occupying forces, and that such efforts still are likely to fall short. The minimal engagement represented by a no fly zone is a much less burdensome option than the open-ended and expansive commitment on the Iraq model. The animating spirit of the no fly zone is a spirit of caution and reluctance. It is a reluctance to get involved matched with the desire to keep US boots off the ground. As Libya confirms, an administration that chooses the no fly zone option will not likely follow up with a sustained, extended and costly effort at creating and protecting new institutions of order.

The core of the Responsibility to Protect proposition is simple and forceful: do not be "bystanders to genocide" yet again. The R2P proposition cannot be satisfied with a no fly zone only. It implies a readiness to do more – to provide sanctuaries, corridors, no-drive zones, no-kill zones, ground operations and then post-conflict stability operations and open-ended engagement. By contrast, the proposition laid out by Kuperman can be satisfied by diplomatic operations only. It offers a rationale for military inaction altogether.

The experience in Darfur and Libya, and in Iraq and Bosnia as well, underlines the fact that no fly zones are not preventers of chaos. They do not provide protection for the innocent unless they can impose separation between the perpetrators and their victims. They do not end violence between warring factions unless they can deter them by denial or by punishment, both very hard to accomplish solely from the air.

The first day of Odyssey Dawn did prevent Qaddafi's forces from closing on Benghazi, but even if that operation was labeled a no fly zone it morphed immediately into an offensive air campaign and it worked largely because of the peculiar circumstances of Benghazi: that an armored column was caught isolated traversing an open space in a lightly populated area. Such circumstances

132 *Politics and prospects*

will not occur frequently. Much more commonly there will be dispersed forces presenting targets compromised by proximity to innocents. It is much easier to destroy an exposed and concentrated column of soldiers than to control, separate, contain or even monitor a dispersed militia.

No fly zones offer the temptation of intervention without deep engagement. Indeed, the option's greatest attraction is that it offers a way to intervene without running the risks of deep engagement, or even ground engagement of any kind. Yet the example of Libya suggests that the outcome can nonetheless be catastrophic, especially if regime change is involved.

If one is skeptical of nation-building based on the experience in Beirut, Mogadishu, Iraq, Afghanistan and Libya, if one believes nation-building is bound to fail or is an inappropriate use of military resources, then one is likely to view no fly zones either as a welcome way to keep nation-building at arm's length and to keep American boots off the ground, or as a possible "gateway intervention" and a slippery slope.

If, by contrast, one believes that nation building is appropriate and necessary, and probably feasible if enough effort and time and resources are committed, then one may still be inclined to oppose the no fly zone option, but for the opposite reason: not because it is potentially entangling but because it is inadequate.

To either point of view, no fly zones were bound to seem unsatisfactory, to the first group because they may prove too open-ended and to the second because they are too faint-hearted. Three years after the end of the Libya intervention, no fly zones had few fans from either side.

Syria

Inaction in Darfur notwithstanding, intervention in Syria appeared likely in 2011. The uprising in Syria against Assad began in the same month that the no fly zone in Libya was established against Qaddafi. Calls for another no fly zone began almost at once, and the calls were given momentum by reliable reports that Assad's forces were refusing his orders and deserting and by the perception that Assad was on the way out. In August 2011, Obama, then in the third year of his presidency, released a statement saying "The time has come for President Assad to step aside." The so-called "Arab Spring" had already swept aside leaders in Tunisia and Egypt.

Options under discussion ranged from a passive air monitoring operation like Sky Monitor over Bosnia in 1992, an enforced no fly zone like Deny Flight over Bosnia in 1993–1995, an enforced no fly zone with one or more ground sanctuaries like Operation Provide Comfort and Northern Watch in Iraq in 1991–2003 or an air campaign to push back Assad's forces like Operation Unified Protector which was under way at that time over Libya.

Parallels were drawn to Operation Provide Comfort, a no fly zone supported by ground troops. In that operation, begun immediately after Operation Desert Storm in March 1991, 20,000 troops from 13 nations were deployed to the north of Iraq to clear a space for the Kurds to return from the Zagros Mountains. The troops were removed in under 60 days and air operations subsequently served to enforce a separation between Iraqi forces and Kurds.[15]

However, there were major differences. The forces of Saddam Hussein had just been crushed in the Gulf War of 1991. The defeat had left him militarily and psychologically depleted and without sympathizers or supporters. Also, unlike the opposition in Syria, Saddam's victims in northern Iraq, the Kurds, were a single, cohesive people ready to collaborate with outside powers for their own defense. In addition, British and American forces and materiel were already deployed to the region, having been sent there in Operation Desert Storm, and the target's air defenses had already been dismantled. In Syria the air defenses were intact and more modern and extensive.

There could be no assurance that the more sophisticated surface-to-air missile systems deployed in Syria would prove as ineffectual as those in Iraq had been. Even the fairly basic mobile surface-to-air missiles in Bosnia had brought down an American plane. The potential vulnerability of planes enforcing a no fly zone over Syria remained open to question.

From August 2011, when Obama called on Assad to step aside, through all of 2012, no fly zone options were continually discussed but no action was taken. Although the debate intensified each time Assad used barrel bombs on his population, as he did on at least three occasions in 2012, resistance to engaging in another war in the Middle East made even a no fly zone seem a step too far.

In early 2012 Chairman of the Joint Chiefs General Martin Dempsey presented a power point in the Situation Room at the White House.[16] He warned that it would require 70,000 troops to dismantle Assad's air defenses and establish a 24-hours-per-day, 7-days-per-week enforced no fly zone. He was not challenged about these very high numbers, which were far out of line with numbers from Northern Watch or Deny Flight, nor was it pointed out that effective no fly zones have functioned in the past without the dismantling of the target country's air defenses and with less than 24/7 enforcement.

The debate took a turn in August of 2012 when Obama said "a red line for us is we start seeing a whole bunch of chemical weapons moving around or being utilized . . . . That would change my calculus. That would change my equation."[17] Later in the same month Director of the CIA David Petraeus offered Obama a way to respond to the chemical weapons attacks and moved the discussion away from no fly zones by proposing a covert program to arm and train rebel forces. His plan was backed by Secretary of State Hillary Clinton and Secretary of Defense Leon Panetta. (Qatar and Saudi Arabia had already been aiding the rebels, primarily by supplying arms.) That plan lost its major proponent, however, when Petraeus resigned from his post at the CIA in early November 2012. At about that time Obama decisively won a second term, but his strong victory did not appear to make him more ambitious to intervene.

134 *Politics and prospects*

During the course of these debates, which continued through 2013 and beyond, the situation in Syria developed in significant ways. In 2013, the Iranians began arming Assad. In those same months the opposition to Assad grew weaker, more fragmented and more radical and Al Nusra, an al Qaeda affiliate, became a part of the opposition.

General Dempsey continued to fend off calls for a no fly zone. On 30 April 30 2013, he said "We have been the victims of our own success. We have made the very difficult look very manageable for a long time."[18] He went ahead to give a cautious and thorough assessment of the no fly zone option.

> To be effective, a no fly zone would have to have several elements. You would have to knock down some of the integrated air defense system of an adversary. Although stealth technology exists, to have a no fly zone, you simply don't penetrate it, you have to control it. So it means that at some level you would have to degrade the integrated air defense system. Secondly, any time we would put an airman... over potentially hostile territory, you are going to have to have a search and rescue or a personnel recovery plan. So we would have to position resources that, in the event of a pilot going down, either by hostile activity or by mechanical failure, . . . we would have the capability to extract them from that situation. And third, you have to assume, or... *I* have to assume as the military member with responsibility . . . that the potential adversary is not going to sit back and allow us to impose our will on them.... They could in fact act outside of their borders with long-range rockets and missiles and artillery or even asymmetric threats. So yes, you could establish a no fly zone, you have to have personnel recovery, and regionally, in the area that bounds the no fly zone, you better have your readiness condition up in the event that they would take action against the imposition of the no fly zone.[19]

By April of 2013, there was more active discussion of arming rebels. At the same time, Jordan appealed for some US action that would alleviate the pressure of more than 100,000 refugees in their territory. By then more than that number of Syrians had died. Turkey called for a no fly zone over the north of Syria and Jordan offered bases for drone operations against Assad. In mid-2013 Obama authorized the CIA to train rebels covertly in Jordan and a short while later considered asking the Pentagon to take over the program and pursue it overtly.

In July of 2013, when calls for a no fly zone were at their peak, General Dempsey took his strongest stance against the option, declaring that such an operation would cost $1billion per month.[20] By contrast, the no fly zone over Iraq had cost on the order of $1 billion per year.

On 21 August 2013 Assad's military launched gas attacks and killed hundreds of non-combatants. These attacks came two years after Obama said Assad should go and one year after he had said chemical weapons attacks

Politics and prospects 135

would be crossing a red line that would require him to re-evaluate his position.

By the time the situation had reached that point, there was not much reason to believe that a no fly zone, absent sanctuaries and ground forces, would have done much to save lives or to tip the balance against the tyrant. By the end of 2013, the window of opportunity for a no fly zone was probably closed.

What might a no fly zone have accomplished in Syria in 2013, if one had been imposed?

- A no fly zone might have sent a message that the powers that imposed it were not willing to look on passively as Assad abused his people. Admittedly, that message would have been equivocal. It would have said, implicitly, that the policy makers in the US were not willing to sit by and do nothing, but they were not willing to do much more than that either. They are willing to exert force, but it would be in the particular, very limited form represented by a no fly zone – "force lite."
- A no fly zone might have monitored the situation from the air, and typically no fly zones begin as monitoring operations, but monitoring the depredations of a dictator does not save lives or aid his victims, and it may amount to evidence-gathering and case-building for a more substantial intervention which would not be a welcome obligation to those ordering the monitoring. Monitoring operations often turn into sources of pressure for further action, which is one reason why activists recommend them and opponents of deeper engagement resist them.
- A no fly zone might have deprived Assad of his air assets, if it had been an enforced no fly zone and if the rules of engagement had been sufficiently restrictive.
- A no fly zone might have prevented Assad's use of fixed-wing planes, if the no fly zone were designed and enforced in that way, and such a measure would have made movement and supply of Assad's forces more difficult, though in the fairly limited area in which they were operating, movement and supply on the ground was feasible.
- A no fly zone might have deprived Assad of his helicopters, if the no fly zone were designed and enforced to ban helicopters, though that is a much more ambitious project since helicopters can take off and land quickly and are not limited to operating from large and known air strips. Still, depriving Assad of his rotary-wing aircraft would have been both symbolically and practically significant since by early 2012 he was using them to deliver "barrel bombs" that sometimes contained chemical weapons, typically chlorine gases. It was precisely the use of those gas weapons that Obama declared in August 2012 would "change the calculus for me." A no fly zone that curtailed their use would have constituted a response to Assad and a delivery, in some degree, on Obama's implied threat.

- A no fly zone would likely have impeded Assad's killing to some degree. About 10 percent of the killing was done from the air, according to General Dempsey, and that probably could have been abated.[21]
- A no fly zone might also have focused attention and elevated expectations of a more decisive response, a development General Dempsey appeared to have aimed to avoid.

In late April 2013 public opinion was strongly against engagement in Syria. A *New York Times* poll revealed

> sixty-two percent of the public say the United States has no responsibility to do something about the fighting in Syria between government forces and anti-government groups, while just one-quarter disagree. While the public does not support direct military action in those two countries [Syria and North Korea] right now, a broad 70 percent majority favors the use of remotely piloted aircraft, or drones, to carry out bombing attacks against terrorism suspects in foreign countries.[22]

By 2014 the discussion of options had shifted from no fly zones toward covert arming and training of rebels. These options posed difficulties that no fly zones do not present:

- Arming rebels is provocative and is preferably kept covert, or at least plausibly deniable. No fly zones can hardly be covert but do not need to be.
- The rebel groups receiving arms must be carefully vetted, and the arms must be tracked; otherwise, the US may be arming al Qaeda. Even so, it may be impossible to keep weapons out of the hands of radical forces, since they may be sold by intermediaries to any buyer. This problem obviously does not arise with no fly zones.
- Arming rebel groups raises the prospect of mission creep and a possible quagmire.
- Arming and cooperating with rebel groups might also yield casualties. Such outcomes have never followed the establishment of a no fly zone.
- Arming rebel groups might complicate disengagement. In the case of Libya, it was not difficult for the US to terminate its intervention; it just stopped flying missions. Withdrawing from a more complicated engagement could have proven more challenging.
- Arming rebel groups would likely require congressional backing. The riskier an enterprise, the more the White House desires the endorsement of the Congress and the public. Neither were likely to be forthcoming, though there were significant voices in the Senate and in the public calling for such measures. Senator McCain's was the most prominent of these.
- Arming rebel groups was likely to prove controversial. No fly zones have never in practice proven controversial. They have been controversial in

proportion to the degree that they have been dramatic in their effectiveness, which is to say they have not been. There is not much "shock and awe" inflicted on the enemy by a no fly zone, but neither is there much dismay and alarm aroused at home.

By August 2014, President Obama was no longer seriously considering an intervention in Syria. Assad was well dug-in, armed, supplied and resupplied by Russia and Iran. The situation had metastasized as al Nusra and ISIS and Hezbollah were all on the field. Obama, in statements to reporters, treated the idea in retrospect.

Speaking to Thomas Friedman on 8 August 2014, he said:

> With respect to Syria, the notion that arming the rebels would have made a difference has always been a fantasy. This idea that we could provide some light arms or even more sophisticated arms to what was essentially an opposition made up of former doctors, farmers, pharmacists and so forth, and that they were going to be able to battle not only a well-armed state but also a well-armed state backed by Russia, backed by Iran, a battle-hardened Hezbollah, that was never in the cards.[23]

There remained some discussion of no fly zones for Syria. On 1 October 2014 retired Air Force General Charles F. Wald, former deputy commander of the US European Command, made one more call for one, saying that degrading and containing the Islamic State will be a long and difficult mission, possibly requiring a no fly zone in Syria for a decade or more.[24]

In December of 2014, Secretary of Defense Chuck Hagel and Chairman of the Joint Chiefs Martin Dempsey said the Obama administration was still considering establishing a no fly zone over northern Syria to protect Syrian refugees from attacks by their government. Their comments suggested Turkey, which had already absorbed 1.3 million refugees, would collaborate in the creation of a buffer zone and sanctuary for Syrians along the border with Turkey. Hagel and Dempsey made it clear that a no fly zone alone would not be sufficient to create and defend a shelter for refugees.[25]

As late as December 2015, Senator McCain was still pressing for a no fly zone over Syria. Questioning General Selva, USAF, Vice Chairman of the Joint Chiefs of Staff, McCain said it was "embarrassing" for generals to admit "the Pentagon hasn't implemented a no fly zone in Syria out of fear of confronting provocations from the Syrian and Russian militaries."[26]

General Selva explained the military's reluctance to McCain: "If we're asking the question, 'Can we do it?' the answer is 'yes.' Are we willing to engage the potential of a direct conflict with the Syrian integrated air defense system or Syrian forces or, by corollary, a confrontation with the Russians, should they choose to contest the no fly zone? We have not recommended it because the political situation on the ground and the potential for

138 *Politics and prospects*

miscalculation and loss of American life in the air in an attempt to defend the no fly zone don't warrant the no fly zone."[27]

No fly zones in domestic politics

No fly zones played no role in alleviating the suffering in Syria or in responding to Assad's brutalities or in moderation of the creation of refugees. They did, however, play a significant and instructive role in American domestic politics, specifically in the presidential primaries in 2016.

With the exception of Ted Cruz and Donald Trump, every one of the candidates for president of both parties in 2016 called for a no fly zone over Syria. Even though the time for a no fly zone was past, the candidates found calling for one irresistible.

Trump and Cruz blew past talk of no fly zones and promised more extreme measures; Cruz said he would make the desert into glass, an apparent reference to nuclear strikes but perhaps simply nonsense, while Trump said he would kill the wives and children of "terrorists." Given what Cruz and Trump were saying, the chorus of voices calling for a no fly zone seemed reasonable and temperate. Calling for a no fly zone is a good device for a politician who wants to sound concerned, decisive, engaged and forceful, yet sober and moderate.

Hillary Clinton made the most detailed and carefully worded recommendation regarding no fly zones. Speaking to the Council on Foreign Relations in November 2015, one year before the election, she said:

> We should work with the coalition and the neighbors to impose no fly zones that will stop Assad from slaughtering civilians and the opposition from the air. Opposition forces on the ground with material support from the coalition could then help create safe areas where Syrians could remain in the country rather than fleeing toward Europe.[28]

Her statement is worth reviewing phrase by phrase since its careful wording accurately reflects the limitations of no fly zones in Syria and suggests their limitations in any humanitarian situation. It is hard to find a more carefully worded statement anywhere in the literature on no fly zones.

First, she began by saying "We should work with the coalition and the neighbors." This simple assertion is all she has to say on the complex and difficult issue of authorization for the use of force. The clause reflects the lessons of Libya in 2011 where working with the Arab League and the Gulf Cooperation Council provided a kind of multilateral authorization. In contrast to the situation in Syria, the no fly zone and intervention in Libya were backed by a UN Security Council resolution (UNSCR 1973) that went so far as to authorize "all necessary means" to ensure the protection of innocents. That sort of authorization would not likely be forthcoming in relation to Syria or again in any situation in the foreseeable future, both because Security

Council members Russia and China would oppose such a measure and because the sort of blank check represented by the phrase "all necessary means" is unlikely to be issued again since it was quickly and thoroughly taken to its limits as the no fly zone mission developed into an air campaign to oust Qaddafi.

The issue of authorization for use of force from the air without United Nations consent was explored in 1999 when Deputy Secretary of State Strobe Talbott and others made the argument that NATO authorization was no less potent than UN authorization and so was sufficient. A no fly zone in Syria would have to be promoted with arguments like the ones Talbott used, though the coalition in question would be less coherent and long-standing than the NATO coalition.

It is beyond the scope of this book to delve deeper into the phrase "work with the coalition and the neighbors" to explore the many conflicts and tensions that surround the "neighbors" of Syria, including Turkey, Iraq, Iran and Jordan, plus the United Arab Emirates, Qatar and Saudi Arabia. It is enough to note that establishing every no fly zone in the past has always required collaboration with "the neighbors" and that requirement has never been so difficult as in the case of Syria.

Second, she speaks of "no fly zones" in the plural. As was the case in the effort to constrain Saddam from harming the Kurds and the Gulf Arabs between 1991 and 2003, at least two no fly zones would likely be necessary. One to the north might be implemented from Incirlik Air Base in Turkey or Al Asad Air Base in Iraq, and one to the south might be implemented from Jordan, Al Asad or even Saudi Arabia. Geography is always crucial when considering no fly zones. The geography in the Syrian case is on the whole favorable at least so far as the distances aircraft must cover. In another sense it is very unfavorable since the area over which the no fly zone would be enforced includes urban and heavily populated spaces, which is where most of the violence and destruction has taken place in Syria. Enforcing a no fly zone over the deserts of Iraq, where avoiding civilian casualties was not difficult, would not serve as a good model for the difficulties of enforcing a no fly zone over populated areas of Syria.

Third, she leaves unaddressed the issue of what sorts of flights would be banned or controlled. Would both fixed-wing and helicopters be included? Fixed-wing aircraft must operate from airfields while helicopters can originate and terminate their flights quickly at a large variety and number of sites. As a temporary measure, the use of fixed-wing aircraft can be suppressed simply by cratering runways with missile strikes. Would both attack aircraft and transport aircraft be banned? If transport planes are allowed, they may be used to move troops and arms. If they are banned, that may lead to deliveries of food or medicine or innocent civilians being shot down.

Fourth, she says the no fly zones "will stop Assad from slaughtering civilians and the opposition from the air." This leaves unmentioned the fact that Assad has been slaughtering civilians and the opposition, primarily from the ground, using artillery and rockets. A no fly zone does nothing to stop artillery or rocket strikes, unless it morphs into a full offensive air campaign. No fly zones in the past have tended to evolve in that direction.

Her statement also does not address the problem that not only Assad but also the Russians are slaughtering civilians and the opposition from the air. Putin began his unauthorized intervention in September of 2015 but her remarks in November of that year ignored that complication. A no fly zone aimed only at Syrian aircraft would be feasible if "deconfliction" measures were carefully applied and adhered to by both the coalition and the Russian forces. On the other hand, no fly zones aimed at stopping all the strikes on civilians and the opposition to Assad would have to be prepared for many eventualities, including a military confrontation with Russia over their actions in Syria. There might be direct air-to-air confrontations, but far more likely there would be ground-to-air missile attacks where the identity of the forces that fired the missile was disguised. Such developments might carry large strategic implications.

Fifth, her statement assumes that sanctuaries will be created. If they are created, they will need to be protected, and a no fly zone alone does nothing to create or protect sanctuaries or safe zones to which refugees can resort and be secure. Her statement assigns the entire issue of sanctuaries and their protection to "opposition forces on the ground."

When she speaks of "opposition forces on the ground" she highlights the fact that no fly zones in places where there was violence on the ground were not effective unless they were coordinated with ground forces to interdict the ground forces of the targeted regime the way the British and American forces prevented Saddam's military from moving against the Kurds at the time of Operation Provide Comfort.

To allay the inevitable concern that establishing a no fly zone would be the first step onto a slippery slope that would lead to much deeper involvement, she added at once that these forces would have "material support from the coalition," but would not, she implied, include coalition forces. She said that these forces on the ground would "help create safe areas." A no fly zone could of course do no more than help create areas safe from aerial attack. The experience in Bosnia illustrates how difficult it is to deploy peacekeepers and enforce safe areas and the limits of air power to support such operations if there is not a large and capable ground force to truly keep the area safe.

Sixth, it should be noted that she never addressed at all the issue of suppressing the target state's air defenses. In the case of Syria, those might be sophisticated and heavy defenses, strengthened as they no doubt have been by modern Russian surface to air missiles. The no fly zones over Iraq, Bosnia and Libya never faced Russian S-400 missiles, a sophisticated weapon far more capable than any systems encountered in Iraq, the Balkans or Libya. These were brought into use by Russian forces in the last fifteen years. Either the enforcers of the no fly zone would have to fly at some considerable extra risk and fly within the envelopes of the air defense systems, or the systems would have to be suppressed or destroyed, quite possibly at the cost of the lives of Russian missile crews.

Politics and prospects 141

Seventh, she speculates that once one or more no fly zones were in place "Syrians could remain in the country rather than fleeing toward Europe." That is an attractive prospect, but there has never been a no fly zone that offered such protection for safe areas that displaced persons were actually secure in them. Any student of no fly zones remembers that Operation Deny Flight was fully functioning yet could do no more than observe when the Serbians slaughtered 8,000 Bosnian men and boys in Srebrenica in July 1995.

Finally, it is worth noting as well that she does not speak at all of no fly zones as an instrument for defeating ISIS. Neither she nor the other candidates who recommended no fly zones in Syria, including Marco Rubio, Chris Christie, Jeb Bush, John Kasich, Carly Fiorina and Ben Carson, proposed that they would be useful in addressing the roots of the problems there. They implicitly recognized that no fly zones are at most one element of an effort to address some of the threats to innocents in an area.

In the context of American domestic politics, one can add one more item to the list of goals a no fly zone in Syria might have accomplished. Talk of a no fly zone served as a means of temporizing in an essentially static debate. Policy makers who were reluctant to commit resources or forces found the no fly zone debate a never-ending opportunity for discussing a policy option from a near limitless number of angles. After several years of discussions, by 2015, the likelihood of the option ever being applied had dwindled to such a low level that there was little risk of being drawn into action. Then, in 2016, five years into the conflict, the idea of a no fly zone was revived as an armature around which the debate could turn when candidates in the American primary elections needed a posture in relation to the conflict that was at once not too passive nor too violent nor too entangling. Discussion of a no fly zone for Syria performed this function for a span of no less than seven years.

As it entered its seventh year it was clear that the conflict in Syria was not over but that Assad's forces were likely to prevail over the remaining fragments of resistance.

The time for a no fly zone there was past, new actors had intervened and the situation had grown more complicated. Russia had sent what it claimed were volunteers or mercenaries. Iran had sent forces as well as weapons. Hezbollah was contributing fighters. In February 2018 there was a serious clash when Russian forces moved against a position held by Syrian and American forces and were badly bloodied in strikes from the air. In the same month a Russian SU25 jet was shot down and an Israeli F-16 was downed by Syrian ground fire. This led to Israel destroying about a third of Syria's anti-aircraft batteries in the most significant Israeli strikes since 1982.[29] By 2018 the conflict had cost a million lives. Moreover, refugees fleeing Syria had generated or fed nativist pressures in Turkey, Hungary, Austria, Germany, Italy, Poland and even as far away as Norway as populist anti-immigrant parties achieved electoral successes unknown for generations. As this book went to press in the late summer of 2018, Israel appeared to be facing off with Iran, and the two were exchanging blows directly and not through proxies for

142 *Politics and prospects*

the first time. It was idle but still tempting to reflect that at some early point, perhaps in 2011 or 2012, a no fly zone led by the US might have intimidated Assad without overthrowing him and forestalled the downward spiral into a broadened conflict and immeasurable suffering.

As this book was being concluded, a sad coda to Unified Protector in Libya was taking place off Libya's shores. Italy had established a "no-sail zone" between Sicily and Libya. Italian naval vessels patrolled the waters to detect, intercept and turn back boats filled with refugees headed out of West Africa through Libya to Europe.[30] To discourage the traffickers who brought the refugees, the Italian navy was seizing and scuttling their vessels. The traffickers responded by using smaller craft that they could better afford to lose but that were also less seaworthy. They also grew quicker to abandon the boats, and the refugees aboard them, to drift or sink and drown offshore. Amid this setting of rising desperation there have been, in recent months, reliable reports of markets in Libya where refugees have been sold as slaves.[31]

Prospects for no fly zones

The no fly zones focused upon in this book – the multilateral, UN-authorized, country-covering no fly zones in Iraq and Bosnia – emerged from a complex convergence of technological developments, political priorities, humanitarian commitments and changed geopolitical conditions. They emerged from processes as different as the development of precision guided munitions and overwhelming US and allied advantages to the dissolution of the Soviet Union. The outlines of those converging processes, reconstructed in retrospect, are described in the first chapter of this book. This final section will attempt the far more difficult task of predicting the outcomes of similar developments, not in retrospect but as they are occurring. Working from the same sorts of factors that were identified in the first chapter, this final section will attempt to identify some large, converging technological, social, strategic and geopolitical forces and predict their impact on the prospects for no fly zones.

This is speculation as much as it is prediction, but it is speculation that is based on the record of no fly zones, on existing, emerging and foreseeable technological capabilities, on current political circumstances, on perceivable trends in war making and on geopolitical change. It will take into account especially the recent behaviors of the United States and Europe and the observable ambitions of China, Russia and Iran.

Another Operation Deny Flight?

What is the likelihood of another no fly zone on the pattern of Provide Comfort and Deny Flight? How likely is it that there will be another no fly zone authorized by the United Nations, produced under the leadership of the

Politics and prospects 143

United States, established in response to grave human rights violations, covering an expansive area and open-ended in its potential duration?

The chances of that happening are very small. Such no fly zones – declared, authorized, formal and multilateral – will remain an option, but will be an option that will go unexercised. There are many reasons for concluding that such a no fly zone will not occur in the foreseeable future.

First, over the past two decades the US could have exercised the no fly zone option on a number of occasions but did not. Darfur might have been a good situation for a no fly zone any time after 2003; Libya might have been addressed with a no fly zone but a concerted air campaign was chosen instead and Syria could have been the site of a no fly zone, but the option was resisted for seven years and ultimately never exercised.[32]

Second, authorization will be more difficult to obtain than it was in the 1990s when Provide Comfort and Deny Flight were put in place. There was a window of time in the 1990s through 2013 or so when Russia and China were willing to withhold their veto of a UN resolution establishing a no fly zone, but that window has closed. It may prove possible to derive other kinds of authorization via NATO or the Arab League, but the degree and kind of endorsement represented by a vote of the United Nations Security Council will not likely be achievable.

Last time the Security Council authorized a no fly zone, which was UN Security Council Resolution 1973 in March 2011, first France, the United States and Britain, then seven other states of Europe and the Middle East, then all of NATO took the authorization and ran with it. The result was not a no fly zone but an air war waged wholeheartedly on Qaddafi's forces resulting in his death and in regime change. This was not the outcome foreseen when the vote was taken and represented an extremely expansive reading of the authorization to use all necessary means short of a foreign occupation force to protect civilians. With that memory in mind, the UN might not be so open-handed with its no fly zone authorizations in the future.

Third, even if authorization were forthcoming, the US is likely to be disinclined to seek it or to act on it. All past no fly zones were led by the US, organized by the US and enforced by coalitions formed and sustained in large part by the US. That is a pattern that is not likely to be repeated.

Since 2000, American enthusiasm for multilateral operations like no fly zones has been low. Even as the US led multilateral operations in Iraq and Afghanistan, it showed little interest in coordinating national security operations on issues other than counter-terrorism. President George W Bush asserted a right to use force unilaterally and pre-emptively. He invaded Iraq in 2003 without UN authorization and over the protests of other powers. President Obama showed extreme caution and reluctance toward any form of intervention and long resisted acting in Libya, then felt confirmed in his reluctance by the outcome there. President Trump gives no sign of having the kind of strategic patience that a coordinated and multilateral national security policy requires, and even if he did he has not demonstrated the ability or

144 *Politics and prospects*

inclination to lead or cooperate with other countries in a complex and extended effort like the one required to execute Operation Deny Flight. Nor has he built the kind of political capital that he would need to be able to call on other powers to participate in an American-sponsored project.

Fourth, the large gap in capabilities that the US and other no fly zone enforcers enjoyed over the Iraqis and the Serbians has closed substantially. The last no fly zone ended 15 years ago with the invasion of Iraq in 2003. Major changes in technology have occurred in the past decade and a half. There is little reason to expect that a no fly zone over Syria or Iran or North Korea could be enforced without any loss of life as the no fly zones over Iraq or Bosnia were 20 years ago. The fact that the US has a perfect record in enforcing no fly zones has created an expectation of flawless and costless execution, which is highly unlikely. US technological advantages in surveillance, detection and electronic countermeasures, while still great, are not as complete as they were.

Recent events in Syria suggest that the cushion of superiority for the enforcer states has diminished. Russia has upgraded Assad's air defenses and so put any enforcer state's aircraft at greater risk. France, Russia and China all helped Saddam improve his systems prior to the American invasion of 2003.[33] NATO planes met no serious resistance over Libya in 2011, but Qaddafi's systems were far less modern and capable than Assad's. One cannot say how NATO planes would have performed over Syria, but the resistance of two chairmen of the Joint Chiefs, General Dempsey and General Dunford, to deploying them in a no fly zone there may have reflected some degree of concern about their vulnerability.

Much would depend on the way a no fly zone was initiated. If it began with the thorough suppression of anti-aircraft artillery and missile systems, as in Libya, that would require a good deal of destruction at the outset of a no fly zone. If it began with adaptation and careful evasion of such systems, as in Bosnia, this practice would entail taking extra risks, and against far more capable and long-range systems than were faced in Bosnia. The widespread distribution of smaller, man-portable air defense systems must also be taken into account as these are extremely difficult to detect and to suppress, even with good long-term surveillance in advance.

To date integrated air defense systems have proven controllable. The slate for casualties in no fly zones remains clean in the sense that there have been no deaths by enemy fire for the enforcers, but there have been downed aircraft where flight crews were rescued. A downed aircraft puts into motion what can be a risky rescue operation.[34]

Newer surface-to-air missile systems like the Russian S400 have higher ceilings, improved guidance and greater airspeed. The recent record offers evidence of their effectiveness. The Israelis saw an F-16 shot down by Syrian anti-air defenses in February 2018. Israel responded with massive attacks on Syrian and Iranian anti-air systems, but the impression that aircraft could operate with impunity was exploded. At roughly the same time, a Russian pilot ejected and was taken captive in Syria. He died brutally within minutes of contact with the rebels, suggesting the kind of incendiary incident that could arise in the course of no fly zone enforcement. Putin's government controls the media in Russia and downplayed the news of that event, but it would be harder for an American or European leader to exercise such control of the media and to minimize the impact of an incident like the loss of a pilot.

These two recent shoot-downs suggest that the risk of casualties has risen. At some point the risk-to-benefit analysis, which has always been close, will tip into the definitely negative. The risk of casualties in past no fly zones has always proven entirely manageable because it has never been tested, yet the promise of benefit from establishing a no fly zone has only on a few occasions been great enough to make policy makers commit to establishing one. There is evidence that the risks have increased but no evidence that the benefits have risen, suggesting no fly zones may be a less attractive option than before.

In 2002 there was considerable speculation that Northern Watch and Southern Watch had grown too risky and should be discontinued. Those no fly zones were long-established operations in which risks were carefully controlled and air defenses had been thoroughly suppressed. If those no fly zones seemed too risky at that time, a prospective operation in the 2020 timeframe would be hard to justify in a calculation of risk vs return.

The enforcers of no fly zones may simply be willing to accept greater risks in terms of air crews lost or captured and aircraft destroyed. As one person very experienced in enforcing no fly zones put the matter, "The US isn't going to pitch a no-hitter every time it goes to the mound," meaning the perfect records of past years cannot continue indefinitely. This impressive readiness to sacrifice may not be enough to balance against the strong reluctance of those high in the chain of command to risk seeing their people killed or captured, especially if the mission is not of the highest importance. In the air war over Vietnam, American pilots and air crews were sent on repeated, high-risk missions to take out certain crucial and very heavily defended bridges and infrastructure targets. Pilots flew straight into anti-aircraft artillery fire and surface-to-air missile systems. Many died or were captured. Since the days of stand-off precision guided munitions, pilots seldom take those kinds of risks, and the public expectations of casualty-free warfare have escalated. Those expectations are one more factor weighing against another no fly zone.

Fifth, while pre-existing technologies have improved over the last two decades, new technologies have emerged, and these tend not to favor the enforcers of no fly zones. These new technologies include autonomous or remotely piloted vehicles or drones.

Drones may in the future have functions in enforcing no fly zones. They may, for example, make patrolling more persistent, more pervasive and, if a point is reached where patrolling is done only with drones, they may entirely eliminate the risk to aircrews' lives because there will be no aircrews involved. At the same time, however, drone patrol craft of the next decade or two will probably be slow flying, easy to detect and easy to shoot down. When drones are shot down, no lives will be lost but important technology will go over to the enemy to be dissected and reverse-engineered.

Drones may also be used to strike enemy air defense systems and other targets, but these can currently be easily, safely and capably destroyed by manned aircraft using standoff weapons and by missiles. Additionally, the use of drones to provide persistent surveillance of ground activities, be it ground systems such as artillery, tanks or other military equipment (such as was proposed by General Sir Michael Rose during the Bosnian no fly zone operation, termed Operation Antelope).

It is possible that drones will be used to support in-air refueling. Remotely piloted tankers may be able to remain on station longer than piloted ones, performing race-track patterns while manned and un-manned aircraft refuel from them, but the limitation to time on station for a tanker is the fuel load of the tanker, not the fatigue of the pilots. Taken together, it is not clear what new capability drones will add to the enforcement of a no fly zone like Provide Comfort.

Drones will likely offer more promising options to the other side – to those evading or resisting no fly zones. Large numbers of cheap remotely piloted aircraft may be used to challenge, distract and overwhelm the strictly limited numbers of enforcing aircraft and their detection systems. Swarms of small, cheap, expendable drones may be launched in violation of a no fly zone, and though they may prove easy to detect, they may be too numerous to track and destroy or otherwise counter. Experience in Operation Deny Flight showed that helicopters were very challenging to detect and suppress; small, numerous drones linked together to fly in swarms would be exponentially harder.

Sixth, it should be remembered that no fly zones are not easy to execute, as Chairman of the Joint Chiefs Martin Dempsey reminded all in his arguments against one in Syria. General Dempsey continued to fend off calls for a no fly zone, telling journalists on 30 April 2013, that "We have been the victims of own success. We have made the very difficult look very manageable for a long time."[35]

No fly zones are elaborate operations. They depend on close real-time coordination of intelligence and communications, and they involve fleets of 40 aircraft in the air at once. There are many points at which they might be attacked, and no fly zones are made more vulnerable by the fact that they are quite predictable. No fly zone enforcement requires patrols that are repeatedly performed at fairly regular intervals, and the enforcers maintain patterns that are not easy to vary significantly. This factor can be exploited by any opponent aiming to disrupt the operation, although simple mechanical failure can also be a disrupter.

A seventh and final reason why the US and its allies are not likely to impose another no fly zone is that they do not present a very useful or attractive option for fighting the kinds of wars the US has been fighting for the last two decades. No fly zones were useful for the humanitarian interventions of the 1990s, but the US has not engaged in such operations since the terror attacks on 11 September 2001. The operations in Afghanistan, Iraq, Syria, Yemen, Somalia and elsewhere have not featured no fly zones for the obvious reason that the jihadist forces have not used aircraft, except commandeered commercial airliners. Special forces operating from helicopters and in conjunction with surveillance and weaponized drones have been much more successful against that threat. The future shape of US operations against jihadists is delineated in the large and capable drone bases such as the one the US is building in Niger.[36]

No fly zones in the gray zone

Even more than countering terrorists, the United States and its allies must contend with countering hybrid and gray zone warfare. The American National Security Strategy, released in December 2017, focused on China and Russia as greater threats than "terrorist groups with a long reach" to the US and to "the long-standing rules-based international order."[37]

In the third paragraph of its introduction, the statement of national security described China as "a strategic competitor using predatory economics to intimidate its neighbors while militarizing features in the South China Sea." In the next sentence it declares that "Russia has violated the borders of nearby nations and pursues veto power over the economic, diplomatic, and security decisions of its neighbors." The NSS suggests that Russia and China have learned to avoid direct confrontation with the superior military capacity of the United States by resorting to a confusing mix of measures including attacks on currencies, pressures on trade, limits on natural gas flows, bribery and intimidation, misinformation campaigns, interference in elections, cyber operations and the infiltration of ununiformed troops. Russia, for example, has sent "little green men" into eastern Ukraine, and China has dispatched troops disguised as fishermen against the vessels of neighboring countries in the South China Sea. Such measures, collectively referred to as hybrid warfare, have allowed China and Russia to pursue war in "the gray zone," meaning that they have been able to act to achieve military and territorial gains without quite crossing the lines that would lead to outright military conflict with the US.

The essence of gray zone warfare is to leave targets unsure how to respond. By design, there is no moment when a line could be drawn. The contrast between the behavior of Putin and Xi Jinping and that of Saddam, Milosevic, Qaddafi and Assad could not be more dramatic. Saddam, Milosevic and Assad were provocative in the extreme with their inflammatory threats and their flagrant attacks, sometimes with chemical weapons, while Putin and Xi attempt to draw a veil of deniability, no matter how unconvincing, over their aggressions.

There is no *casus belli* that would justify a collective response like a no fly zone, nor would a no fly zone be effective in these circumstances. Nonetheless, their gray zone campaigns must be featured in a book on the topic since those innovative and effective campaigns are pioneering the no fly zones of the future.

Area denial is what no fly zones are for, and Putin and Xi have seen their potential. Russian operations in the Ukraine, for example, created an instant no fly zone of a sort when a Russian Buk missile shot down Malaysia Airlines Flight 17 on July 17, 2014. A de facto no fly zone was established that continues years later. There was no formal declaration; there certainly was no authorization or legitimacy of any kind. In keeping with the methods of hybrid warfare, the same night that the civilian airliner was destroyed, Russia removed the missile system that was used, but they have deployed a number of other mobile air defense units to the Donbas region since then. Two months after the shoot down, Ukraine's government signed a cease-fire agreement that terminated their use of military aircraft for air support or medevac missions. By the time of that cease-fire in September 2014, seven Ukrainian fighter planes, nine helicopters and three transport aircraft had been shot down. Ukraine has been severely limited in its use of its air assets since then.[38]

This represents a significant variation on the no fly zones of the past. It is a no fly zone adapted for gray zone warfare, a stealth no fly zone. It was not announced or imposed openly. If it were raised by a foreign power, it would be entirely denied. It has no declared ROEs, it is not openly patrolled, yet it has been very effective. It lacks most of the traditional elements of a no fly zone, yet it is a no fly zone all the same in the sense that the target is denied the use of its airspace.

China has performed the same trick, but given the marine context it has imposed gray zone variations on a no-sail zone. For almost a decade China has pressed its claims of "indisputable sovereignty" over most of the South China Sea as delineated in its arbitrary "nine-dash line" and done so by deploying ununiformed militiamen in fishing vessels. China has craftily avoided actions that would escalate into a confrontation with US naval vessels while it has intimidated and deterred the vessels of its neighbors. All the while it has quietly created artificial islands on top of fragments of reefs. Those islands now feature missile batteries and landing strips.[39]

The Peoples Liberation Army Navy even innovatively created a short-lived no-sail zone near its coast designed to challenge the freedom of navigation exercises constantly performed by the US Navy, but to did so without creating a possibility for confrontation.

The created no-sail zone that was declared and concluded in such short order that a traverse of the region by US Navy ships could not be organized before the zone went out of existence. It was created to the south east of Hainan Island between 5 July and 11 July of 2016[40] and served as a "test of concept" for a gray zone "pop-up" no-sail zone, much the way its Air Defense Identification Zone, established in November 2013, has served as a test of concept and likely precursor to an eventual no fly zone for the region.[41]

Conclusion

At the time of their inception, no fly zones were an instrument for enforcing the rules that over recent decades have lifted states a short way above the grim floor where existence is a struggle of all against all and life is solitary, poor, nasty, brutish and short.[42] No fly zones played some role in constraining the criminal slaughter committed by Saddam and Milosevic and might have saved some of the half million or more lives lost in Syria. Perhaps a half million lives lost is an understatement. In truth the killing there has gone uninterrupted for so long that even a rough estimate of the dead is impossible.[43]

No fly zones were never more than a single option among the moderate measures that fall between diplomatic protests and various sanctions on the one hand and punitive strikes and air campaigns on the other. They never halted an atrocity or transformed a crisis, though they were important elements in comprehensive processes that did both in Iraq and Bosnia.

No fly zones were modest instruments employed to reinforce a rules-centered order. They were, in fact, very modest, but even the most skeptical student of the record would grant that no fly zones have not proven useless. Since 1968 in Biafra, the US has repeatedly found itself confronted with humanitarian emergencies that seemed to require forceful action but in which use of force was an unattractive option. In some cases, like Rwanda, many Americans have regretted that the US failed to act. In others, like Somalia, many have regretted that the US acted by putting troops on the ground. The humble no fly zone presented something of a third way forward, one which avoided taking action the US would regret, yet avoiding inaction the US would regret as well. No one writes ruefully about the costly American blunder in participating in Provide Comfort, Southern Watch or Deny Flight. No one finds participating in a no fly zone reckless or ruinously costly.

No fly zones were never a way to settle a conflict or force one to an end, but they were a way to put some pressure on bad actors to conform to the rules of a healthy society of nations. They presented an option that always proved constructive and never proved costly.

That is about as far as one can go toward giving no fly zones a ringing endorsement. They have been equivocal devices, always a compromise of sorts between no action at all and some more decisive measure. They have offered a way to avoid putting boots on the ground. They have provided a way to avoid suffering casualties. They have been a means to avoid being drawn into quagmires. They have been a way not to do nothing when something had to be done.

But it is very unlikely that the US will soon again be organizing another no fly zone like the ones in this book. That era appears to be past for the seven reasons explored above. Instead, it appears that the enforcement of the principles of global order that were articulated in the United Nations Charter is a task that the current leaders of great powers are inclined to shun. Figures like

150 *Politics and prospects*

Trump and Putin and British Prime Minister Theresa May appear to be disinterested, disinclined, distracted or in Putin's case outright hostile to the defense of those principles. Xi Jinping has no inclination to enforce an order that he violates as he militarizes reefs and lays claim to the waters far off China's shores. Figures of the nationalist, nativist right like Nigel Farage and Stephen Bannon explicitly celebrate their plans to destroy that order. Heads of state like Erdogan, Orban and Kaczynski could not be recruited into the defense of a rules-based order, even though their predecessors in leading Turkey, Hungary and Poland, all were significant participants in Operation Deny Flight or Operation Provide Comfort.

No fly zones were once useful for undergirding a rules-based order, when the US was the guarantor of one. Now they are used to undermine the rules-based order, to intimidate and to dominate. We will likely see more no fly zones and no-sail zones, but they will be imposed by China and Russia against the smaller nations on their perimeters. Indeed, some are in place, undeclared and denied but nonetheless effective, today.

Notes

1 "A Troubling Victory," *The Economist*, 3 September 2011, www.economist.com/node/21528248. Accessed 3 March 2018.
2 Daalder, Ivo H. and Stavridis, James G., "NATO's Victory in Libya: The Right Way to Run an Intervention." Foreign Affairs, Vol. 91, No. 2, March/April 2012, pp. 2–7. Daalder and Stavridis point out that it was a modest operation, one fifth the size of Operation Allied Force over Kosovo. They cite a total cost to the US of $1.1 billion.
3 Power, Samantha, "Bystanders to Genocide," *The Atlantic*, September 2001, www.theatlantic.com/magazine/archive/2001/09/bystanders-to-genocide/304571/. Accessed 16 March 2018. This article proved influential despite the fact that it appeared in the September 2001 issue of *The Atlantic*.
4 Obama, Barack and Brownback, Sam, "Policy Adrift on Darfur," *Washington Post*, 27 December 2005, www.washingtonpost.com/wp-dyn/content/article/2005/12/26/AR2005122600547.html?tid=a_mcntx. Accessed 1 March 2018.
5 www.washingtonpost.com/wp-dyn/content/article/2009/03/04/AR2009030403022.html. Accessed 1 March 2018.
6 www.washingtonpost.com/wp-dyn/content/article/2009/03/09/AR2009030902475.html. Accessed 1 March 2018.
7 www.washingtonpost.com/wp-dyn/content/article/2009/03/09/AR2009030902475.html. Accessed 1 March 2018.
8 www.nytimes.com/2006/05/31/opinion/31kuperman.html. Accessed 1 March 2018.
9 www.nytimes.com/2006/05/31/opinion/31kuperman.html. Accessed 1 March 2018.
10 www.nytimes.com/2006/05/31/opinion/31kuperman.html. Accessed 1 March 2018.
11 Kuperman, Alan, "Rethinking the Responsibility to Protect," *The Whitehead Journal of Diplomacy and International Relations*, Winter/Spring 2009. http://blogs.shu.edu/diplomacy/files/archives/Kuperman%2520-%2520Rethinking%2520the%2520Responsibility%2520to%2520Protect.pdf
12 www.nytimes.com/2006/05/31/opinion/31kuperman.html. Accessed 1 March 2018.
13 www.nytimes.com/2006/05/31/opinion/31kuperman.html. Accessed 1 March 2018.
14 www.wilsoncenter.org/person/alan-kuperman. Accessed 1 March 2018.

Politics and prospects 151

15 Rudd, Gordon, "*Humanitarian Intervention: Assisting the Iraqi Kurds in Operation Provide Comfort,*"https://history.army.mil/html/books/humanitarian_intervention/CMH_70-78.pdf. Accessed 22 December 2017.
16 Mazzetti, Mark, "Obama's Uncertain Path Amid Syria Bloodshed," *New York Times*, 23 October 2013, www.nytimes.com/2013/10/23/world/middleeast/obamas-uncertain-path-amid-syria-bloodshed.html. Accessed 1 March 2018.
17 Ibid.
18 Dempsey, Martin, 30 April 2013, remarks at breakfast sponsored by the *Christian Science Monitor*, www.youtube.com/watch?v=974DPtfZetQ. Accessed 1 March 2018.
19 Ibid.
20 Dempsey, Martin, 19 July 2013, letter to Senate Armed Services Committee Chairman Carl Levin, http://thehill.com/images/stories/news/2013/07_july/22/dempsey.pdf. Accessed 6 August 2018.
21 In his 23 July 2013 remarks quoted above General Dempsey estimated that 90 percent of the casualties were caused by ground forces and artillery and 10 percent by aerial attacks.
22 *New York Times*, 30 April 2013, www.nytimes.com/2013/05/01/world/Korea-public-opposes-action-in-Korea-and-north-Korea.html?_r=0. Accessed 1 March 2018.
23 Friedman, Thomas, "Obama on the World," *New York Times*, 9 August 2014, www.nytimes.com/2014/08/09/opinion/president-obama-thomas-l-friedman-iraq-and-world-affairs.html. Accessed 1 March 2018.
24 Wald, Charles F., "How to Defeat ISIL from the Air," *Politico*, 1 October 2014, www.politico.com/magazine/story/2014/10/how-to-defeat-isis-from-the-air-111486. Accessed 1 March 2018.
25 Cooper, Helene, "US Considers a No Fly Zone To Protect Civilians from Airstrikes by Syria," *New York Times*, 26 September 2014, www.nytimes.com/2014/09/27/world/middleeast/us-considers-a-no-fly-zone-to-protect-civilians-from-airstrikes-by-syria-.html. Accessed 1 March 2018.
26 Shinkman, Paul, "Pentagon Admits Syrian, Russian Opposition Scuttles Syrian No Fly Zone," *US News and World Report*, 9 December 2015, www.usnews.com/news/articles/2015/12/09/pentagon-admits-syrian-russian-opposition-scuttles-no fly-zone. Accessed 1 March 2018.
27 Ibid.
28 Clinton, Hillary, Speech at Council on Foreign Relations, 15 November 2015, www.cfr.org/event/hillary-clinton-national-security-and-islamic-state. Accessed 16 March 2018.
29 *The Economist*, "Syria's War Heats Up Again," www.economist.com/news/middle-east-and-africa/21737319-islamic-state-routed-assad-regime-pounding-rebel-held-towns-no. Accessed 16 March 2018.
30 Horowitz, Jason, "Italy Plans Naval Mission Off Libya to Stop Migrant Boats," *New York Times*, 27 July 2017, www.nytimes.com/2017/07/27/world/europe/italy-plans-naval-mission-off-libya-to-stop-migrant-boats.html?hp&action=click&pgtype=Homepage&clickSource=story-heading&module=first-column-region&region=top-news&WT.nav=top-news. Accessed 1 March 2018.
31 Peyton, Nellie, "Sale of Migrants in Libyan Slave Markets Sparks Global Outcry," *Reuters*, 20 November 2017, www.reuters.com/article/us-libya-slavery-migrants/sale-of-migrants-in-libya-slave-markets-sparks-global-outcry-idUSKBN1DK2AU. Accessed 16 March 2018.
32 It is interesting to note that the no fly zone option for Syria had a late, brief revival in early July 2017. On 5 July 2017, Reuters reported that Secretary of State Rex Tillerson said the US would be willing to collaborate with Russia in an arrangement that would include no fly zones, ceasefire observers and coordinated aid delivery efforts. Tillerson's statement brought this response from Russian Foreign

152 *Politics and prospects*

   Minister Sergei Lavrov: "We have asked but we haven't got an answer to the question of what no fly zones are envisioned, because there has never been any talk of them." Two days later, on 7 July 2017, Trump and Putin met at the Group of 20 summit in Hamburg. No mention of no fly zones came out of that meeting and the subject appeared to be closed. www.reuters.com/article/us-mideast-crisis-syria-usa/u-s-would-consider-no fly-zone-in-syria-if-russia-agrees-idUSKBN19R00R. Accessed 15 July 2018.
33 Jaffe, Greg, "US Wants China to Answer Allegations it Helped Iraq Upgrade its Air Defense," *Wall Street Journal*, 21 February 2001, A10.
34 The attempt to rescue the SEAL team that included Marcus Luttrell included disastrous loss of life. See Marcus Luttrell, *Lone Survivor: The Eyewitness Account of Operation Redwing and the Lost Heroes of SEAL Team 10*, New York: Little, Brown & Co, 2013.
35 Dempsey, Martin, 30 April 2013, remarks at breakfast sponsored by the *Christian Science Monitor*, www.youtube.com/watch?v=974DPtfZetQ. Accessed 1 March 2018.
36 Schmitt, Eric, "A Shadowy War's Newest Front: A Drone Base Rising From Saharan Dust," *New York Times*, 22 April, www.nytimes.com/2018/04/22/us/politics/drone-base-niger.html?hp&action=click&pgtype=Homepage&clickSource=story-heading&module=second-column-region&region=top-news&WT.nav=top-news. Accessed 25 April 2018.
37 Summary of the 2018 National Security Strategy of the United States, www.defense.gov/Portals/1/Documents/pubs/2018-National-Defense-Strategy-Summary.pdf. Accessed 1 March 2018.
38 Peterson, Nolan, "Putin Has Achieved a No Fly Zone Over Ukraine,"*Newsweek*, 8 October 2016, www.newsweek.com/putin-has-achieved-no-fly-zone-over-ukraine-506433. Accessed 1 March 2018.
39 "Neither War Nor Peace," *The Economist*, 25 January 2018. www.economist.com/special-report/2018/01/25/neither-war-nor-peace. Accessed 1 March 2018.
40 Yinyin, Echo Huang, "China Declares No-Sail Zone in Disputed Waters During War Game," *Defense One*, 5 July 2016, www.defenseone.com/threats/2016/07/china-declares-no-sail-zone-disputed-waters-during-wargame/129607/. Accessed 1 March 2018.
41 Osawa, Jun, "China's ADIZ Over the East China Sea," The Brookings Institution, 17 December 2017, www.brookings.edu/opinions/chinas-adiz-over-the-east-china-sea-a-great-wall-in-the-sky/. Accessed 1 March 2018.
42 The source for these iconic phrases is of course Thomas Hobbes in *Leviathan*.
43 Specia, Megan, "How Syria's Death Toll Has Been Lost in the Fog of War," *New York Times*, 13 April 2018, www.nytimes.com/2018/04/13/world/middleeast/syria-death-toll.html.

Bibliography

Air Force Historical Research Agency, USAF Manned Combat Aircraft Losses 1990–2002, www.dtic.mil/dtic/tr/fulltext/u2/a434084.pdf.
Al Jazeera, "Arab States Seek Libya No Fly Zone," *Al Jazeera*, 12 March 2011.
Associated Press, "Iraqi Military Is Again a Formidable Force," 8 September 1996.
Atkinson, Rick, "The Anatomy of NATO's Decision to Bomb Bosnia," *International Herald Tribune*, 17 November 1995.
Baker, James A. III, *The Politics of Diplomacy: Revolution, War and Peace, 1989–1992*, New York: Putnam, 1995.
Beale, Major Michael O., USAF, *Bombs over Bosnia: The Role of Airpower in Bosnia-Herzegovina*, Maxwell AFB, AL: Air University Press, 1997.
Belasco, Amy, "The Cost of Iraq, Afghanistan, and Other Global War on Terror Operations Since 9/11," *CRS Report RL33110*, 8 December 2014.
Benard, Alexander, "Lessons from Iraq and Bosnia on the Theory and Practice of No-Fly Zones," *Journal of Strategic Studies*, September, 2004, Vol. 27, No. 3, pp. 454–478.
Bethlehem, D. L. and Weller, M., *The 'Yugoslav' Crisis in International Law: General Issues*. Cambridge: Cambridge University Press, 1997.
Bilmes, Linda and Stiglitz, Joe, *The Three Trillion Dollar War*, New York: Norton, 2008.
Boot, Max, "From Saigon to Desert Storm: How the US Military Reinvented Itself after Vietnam," *American Heritage*, November, 2006, Vol. 57, No. 6.
Briquemont, Lt Gen Francis, *Do Something, General!: Chronique de Bosnie-Herzegovine 12 juillet 1993–24 janvier 1994*. Brussels: Editions Labor, 1997.
Brunstetter, Daniel and Braun, Megan, "Recalibrating Our Understanding of the Moral Use of Force," *Ethics and International Affairs*, Vol. 27, No.1, February 2013, www.ethicsandinternationalaffairs.org/2013/from-jus-ad-bellum-to-jus-ad-vim-recalibrating-our-understanding-of-the-moral-use-of-force/.
Bucknam, Mark A., *Responsibility of Command: How UN and NATO Commanders Influenced Airpower over Bosnia*, Maxwell Air Force Base, AL: Air University Press, 2003.
Bush, George H.W., "Address on the End of the Gulf War," White House: Washington, DC Web. 27 February 1991, http://millercenter.org/president/bush/speeches/speech-5530. Accessed 15 October 2015.
Chivvis, Christopher, *Toppling Qaddafi: Libya and the Future of Liberal Intervention*, Cambridge, UK: Cambridge University Press, 2014.
Clary, David E., "The Bekaa Valley: A Case Study," Thesis submitted to the Air War College, www.dtic.mil/dtic/tr/fulltext/u2/a192545.pdf. Accessed 27 June 2017.

Bibliography

Cooper, Helene, "US Considers a No Fly Zone To Protect Civilians from Airstrikes by Syria," *New York Times*, 26 September 2014, www.nytimes.com/2014/09/27/world/middleeast/us-considers-a-no-fly-zone-to-protect-civilians-from-airstrikes-by-syria-.html. Accessed 1 March 2018.

Corum, James S. and Johnson, Wray R., *Airpower in Small Wars*, Lawrence, Kansas: University Press of Kansas, 2003.

Cowell, Alan and Erlanger, Steven, "France Becomes First Country to Recognize Libyan Rebels," *The New York Times*, 10 March 2011, www.nytimes.com/2011/03/11/world/europe/11france.html. Accessed 2 December 2015.

Craven, Wesley F. and Cate, James L. (eds.), *The Army Air Forces in World War II. Vol. I: Prewar Plans and Preparations, January 1939–August 1942*, Chicago, IL: University of Chicago Press, 1948.

Daalder, Ivo H., *Getting to Dayton: The Making of America's Bosnia Policy*, Washington, D.C.: Brookings Institution Press, 2000.

Daalder, Ivo H. and O'Hanlon, Michael E., *Winning Ugly: NATO's War to Save Kosovo*, Washington, D.C.: Brookings Institution Press, 2000.

Daalder, Ivo H. and O'Hanlon, Michael E., "Overextended in Iraq," *Newsday*, 18 February 2001. Accessed 12 October 2015.

Daalder, Ivo H. and Stavridis, James G., "NATO's Victory in Libya: The Right Way to Run an Intervention," *Foreign Affairs*, Vol. 91, No. 2, March/April 2012, pp. 2–7.

Department of State. The Office of Electronic Information, Bureau of Public Affairs. "35. Paper Prepared by the NSC Interdepartmental Group for Africa, Washington, February 10, 1969," https://2001-2009.state.gov/r/pa/ho/frus/nixon/e5/54835.htm. Accessed 19 February 2017.

Devroy, Ann, "'Wait and See' on Iraq," *The Washington Post*, March 29, 1991, pp. A–14.

Economist, "Neither War Nor Peace," *The Economist*, 25 January 2018, www.economist.com/special-report/2018/01/25/neither-war-nor-peace. Accessed 1 March 2018.

Economist, "Syria's War Heats Up Again," *The Economist*, 22 February 2018, www.economist.com/news/middle-east-and-africa/21737319-islamic-state-routed-assad-regime-pounding-rebel-held-towns-no. Accessed 16 March 2018

Economist, "A Troubling Victory," *The Economist*, 3 September 2011, www.economist.com/node/21528248. Accessed 3 March 2018.

Evans, Gareth J., *The Responsibility to Protect: Ending Mass Atrocity Crimes Once and for All*, Washington, D.C.: Brookings Institution Press, 2008.

Finn, Peter and Wilson, Scott, "Gates Says US Military Could Enforce a No Fly Zone in Libya if Obama Ordered One," Washington Post, 14 March 2011, www.washingtonpost.com/wp-dyn/content/article/2011/03/12/AR2011031204978.html. Accessed 13 April 2015.

Foley, Conor, *The Thin Blue Line: How Humanitarianism Went to War*, London; New York: Verso, 2008.

Friedman, Thomas, "Obama on the World," *New York Times*, 9 August 2014, www.nytimes.com/2014/08/09/opinion/president-obama-thomas-l-friedman-iraq-and-world-affairs.html. Accessed 1 March 2018.

Gertler, Jeremiah, "No-Fly Zones: Strategic, Operational, and Legal Considerations for Congress," Washington, D.C.: Congressional Research Service, May 3, 2013.

Gregor, Annelie, "Limited Military Pressure: An Analytical Framework to Assess No-Fly Zones as a Single Instrument in Coercive Diplomacy," Master's thesis, Swedish National Defense College, 4 June 2012.

Halberstam, David, *The Making of a Quagmire: America and Vietnam during the Kennedy Era*, Lanham, MD: Rowman and Littlefield, 2008.

Halloran, Richard, "Many Are Chosen, But Few Get to Wear Stars," *New York Times*, 16 October 1984, www.nytimes.com/1984/10/16/us/pentagon-many-are-chosen-but-few-get-to-wear-stars.html?_r=0. Accessed 15 December 2015.

Hobson, Christopher, *Vietnam Air Losses: USAF, Navy, and Marine Corps Fixed-wing Aircraft Losses in SE Asia 1961–1973*, New York: Specialty Press, 2002.

Hodges, Doyle, "ADIZ'd and Confused: Challenges for the PLAAF, PLAN and PLANAF in Maintaining China's Declared East China Sea Air Defense Identification Zone," unpublished paper, Princeton University, 14 January 2014.

Honig, Jan Willem and Both, Norbert, *Srebrenica: Record of a War Crime*, London: Penguin Books, 1996.

Horowitz, Jason, "Italy Plans Naval Mission Off Libya to Stop Migrant Boats," *New York Times*, 27 July 2017, www.nytimes.com/2017/07/27/world/europe/italy-plans-naval-mission-off-libya-to-stop-migrant-boats.html?hp&action=click&pgtype=Homepage&clickSource=story-heading&module=first-column-region&region=top-news&WT.nav=top-news. Accessed 1 March 2018.

Jaffe, Greg, "US Wants China to Answer Allegations it Helped Iraq Upgrade its Air Defense," *Wall Street Journal*, 21 February 2001, A10.

Joint Publication 3–0, Joint Operations, Washington, DC: NDU Press, 11 August 2011.

Keegan, John, *The Second World War*, New York: Viking, 1989.

Keegan, John, "Please Mr. Blair, Never Take Such A Risk Again," *Daily Telegraph* (London), 6 June 1999.

Kennan, George, "The Sources of Soviet Conduct," *Foreign Affairs*, July 1947, www.foreignaffairs.com/articles/russian-federation/1947-07-01/sources-soviet-conduct.

Kuperman, Alan, "A Model Humanitarian Intervention? Reassessing NATO's Libya Campaign," *International Security*, Vol. 38, No. 1, pp. 105–136.

Kuperman, Alan, "Rethinking the Responsibility to Protect," *The Whitehead Journal of Diplomacy and International Relations*, Winter/Spring 2009, http://blogs.shu.edu/diplomacy/files/archives/Kuperman%2520-%2520Rethinking%2520the%2520Responsibility%2520to%2520Protect.pdf

Kurth, James, "Humanitarian Intervention After Iraq: Legal Ideals versus Military Realities," *Orbis*, Vol. 50, No. 1, pp. 87–101.

Lambeth, Beth, *The Transformation of American Air Power*, New York: Cornell University Press, 2000.

Loeb, Vernon, "No Fly Patrols Praised," *The Washington Post*, 26 July 2002, p. A23.

Luttrell, Marcus, *Lone Survivor: The Eyewitness Account of Operation Redwing and the Lost Heroes of SEAL Team 10*, New York: Little, Brown, 2013.

Luttwak, Edward, *The Pentagon and the Art of War*, New York: Simon & Schuster, 1985.

Mazzetti, Mark, "Obama's Uncertain Path Amid Syria Bloodshed," *New York Times*, 23 October 2013, www.nytimes.com/2013/10/23/world/middleeast/obamas-uncertain-path-amid-syria-bloodshed.html. Accessed 1 March 2018.

McGreal, Chris, "Gaddafi's Army Will Kill Half a Million, Warn Libya's Rebels," *The Guardian*, 12 March 2011, www.theguardian.com/world/2011/mar/12/gaddafi-army-kill-half-million Accessed 16 May 2014.

Mueller, Karl P., "Denying Flight: Strategic Options for Employing No-Fly Zones," Santa Monica, CA: Rand Corporation, 2013, www.rand.org/pubs/research_reports/RR423.html.

156 Bibliography

Mueller, Karl P., "Strategies of Coercion: Denial, Punishment, and the Future Of Air Power," *Security Studies*, Vol. 7, No. 3, pp. 182–228.

Mueller, Karl P., Martini, Jeffrey and Hamilton, Thomas, Airpower Options for Syria: Assessing Objectives and Missions for Aerial Intervention, RR-446-CMEPP, Santa Monica, CA: RAND Corporation, 2013, www.rand.org/pubs/research_reports/RR446.html.

NATO, "Operation Unified Protector Final Mission Stats," North Atlantic Treaty Organization, 2 November 2011, www.nato.int/nato_static/assets/pdf/pdf_2011_11/20111108_111107-factsheet_up_factsfigures_en.pdf. Accessed 30 March 2015.

Obama, Barack and Brownback, Sam, "Policy Adrift on Darfur," *Washington Post*, 27 December 2005, www.washingtonpost.com/wp-dyn/content/article/2005/12/26/AR2005122600547.html?tid=a_mcntx. Accessed 1 March 2018.

O'Hanlon, Michael, *Technological Change and the Future of Warfare*, Washington D.C.: Brookings Institution Press, 2000.

Osawa, Jun, "China's ADIZ Over the East China Sea," The Brookings Institution, 17 December 2017, www.brookings.edu/opinions/chinas-adiz-over-the-east-china-sea-a-great-wall-in-the-sky/. Accessed 1 March 2018.

Owen, Robert C., *Deliberate Force: A Case Study in Effective Air Campaigning*, Maxwell Air Force Base, AL: Air University Press, 2000.

Pape, Robert, *Bombing to Win: Air Power and Coercion in War*, Ithaca, NY: Cornell University Press, 1996.

Pape, Robert, *Dying to Win: The Strategic Logic of Suicide Terrorism*, New York: Random House, 2005.

Peterson, Nolan, "Putin Has Achieved a No Fly Zone Over Ukraine," *Newsweek*, 8 October 2016, www.newsweek.com/putin-has-achieved-no-fly-zone-over-ukraine-506433. Accessed 1 March 2018.

Peyton, Nellie, "Sale of Migrants in Libyan Slave Markets Sparks Global Outcry," *Reuters*, 20 November 2017, www.reuters.com/article/us-libya-slavery-migrants/sale-of-migrants-in-libya-slave-markets-sparks-global-outcry-idUSKBN1DK2AU. Accessed 16 March 2018.

Philipps, Dave, "Special Operations Troops Top Casualty List as US Relies More on Elite Forces," *New York Times*, 4 February 2017, www.nytimes.com/2017/02/04/us/navy-seal-william-ryan-owens-dead-yemen.html.

Post, Lori Ann, Raile, Amber N.W. and Raile, Eric D., "Defining Political Will," *Politics & Policy*, Vol. 38, No. 4, pp. 653–676.

Power, Samantha, "Bystanders to Genocide," *The Atlantic*, September 2001, www.theatlantic.com/magazine/archive/2001/09/bystanders-to-genocide/304571/.

Power, Samantha, *A Problem from Hell: America and the Age of Genocide*, New York: Perennial, 2003.

Price, Alfred, *The History of U.S. Electronic Warfare, Vol. III*, United States: Association of Old Crows, 2000.

Priest, Dana, "The Battle Inside Headquarters: Tension Grew With Divide Over Strategy Series: The Commanders' War: 3/3," *The Washington Post*, p. A1, 21 September 1999.

Prunier, Gérard, *The Rwanda Crisis: History of a Genocide*, New York: Columbia University Press, 1995.

Public Papers of the Presidents of the United States: George Bush, Washington, DC: National Archives, 1991.

Rose, General Sir Michael, *Fighting for Peace*, London: Harvill Press, 1998.

Bibliography 157

Ricks, Thomas E., *Fiasco: The American Military Adventure in Iraq*, New York: Penguin, 2006.

Rudd, Gordon W., *Humanitarian Intervention: Assisting the Iraqi Kurds in Operation Provide Comfort, 1991*, Washington, D.C.: Department of the Army, 2004.

Sanger, David E. and Shanker, Thom, *Confront and Conceal*, New York: Crown, 2012.

Schelling, Thomas C. *Arms and Influence*, New Haven, CT: Yale University Press, 1966.

Schmitt, Eric, "A Shadowy War's Newest Front: A Drone Base Rising From Saharan Dust," *New York Times*, 22 April, www.nytimes.com/2018/04/22/us/politics/drone-base-niger.html?hp&action=click&pgtype=Homepage&clickSource=story-heading&module=second-column-region&region=top-news&WT.nav=top-news. Accessed 25 April 2018.

Schmitt, Michael N., "Clipped Wings: Effective and Legal No-Fly Zone Rules of Engagement," *Loyola of Los Angeles International and Comparative Law Review*, Vol. 20, 1998, pp. 727–789.

Schwarzkopf, Norman H. and Petre, Peter, *It Doesn't Take a Hero: General H. Norman Schwarzkopf, the Autobiography*, New York: Bantam, 1992.

Serafino, Nina, "Peacekeeping and Related Stability Operations: Issues of U.S. Military Involvement," *Congressional Research Service Report RL33557*, 24 January 2007, p. 21, www.dtic.mil/dtic/tr/fulltext/u2/a479080.pdf.

Seybolt, Taylor, *Humanitarian Intervention: The Conditions for Success and Failure*, New York: Oxford University Press, 2007.

Shacochis, Bob, *The Immaculate Invasion*, New York: Viking, 1999.

Shinkman, Paul, "Pentagon Admits Syrian, Russian Opposition Scuttles Syrian No Fly Zone," *US News and World Report*, 9 December 2015, www.usnews.com/news/articles/2015/12/09/pentagon-admits-syrian-russian-opposition-scuttles-no-fly-zone. Accessed 1 March 2018.

Smith, Graeme, "Rebel Military Chief Rebukes NATO," Globe and Mail, 16 April 2011, p. A14.

Specia, Megan, "How Syria's Death Toll Has Been Lost in the Fog of War," *New York Times*, 13 April 2018, www.nytimes.com/2018/04/13/world/middleeast/syria-death-toll.html.

Telegraph, "Libya's UN Ambassador Denounces Gaddafi," *The Telegraph*, 25 February 2011, www.telegraph.co.uk/news/worldnews/africaandindianocean/libya/8349048/Libyas-UN-ambassador-denounces-Gaddafi.html. Accessed 30 March 2015.

Thomas, Ward, *The Ethics of Destruction: Norms and Force in International Relations*, New York: Cornell University Press, 2001.

United Nations, "Former Yugoslavia UNPROFOR Profile," Department of Public Information, 31 August 1996, https://peacekeeping.un.org/en. Accessed 2 December 2017.

United Nations General Assembly, 60/1, 2005 World Summit Outcome, New York: United Nations, 24 October 2005, www.un.org/womenwatch/ods/A-RES-60-1-E.pdf. Accessed 2 December 2015.

UN Security Council, "Resolution 686," 3 March 1991, http://daccess-dds-ny.un.org/doc/RESOLUTION/GEN/NR0/596/22/IMG/NR059622.pdf?OpenElement. Accessed 17 October 2015.

UN Security Council, "Resolution 687," 3 April 1991, http://daccess-dds-ny.un.org/doc/RESOLUTION/GEN/NR0/596/23/IMG/NR059623.pdf?OpenElement. Accessed 17 October 2015.

UN Security Council, "Resolution 781," 9 October 1992, www.ohr.int/other-doc/un-res-bih/pdf/s92r781e.pdf. Accessed 27 May 2014.

UN Security Council, "Resolution 836," 4 June 1993, UN DocS/RES/836.
UN Security Council, "Resolution 1441," 9 October 1992, http://daccess-dds-ny.un.org/doc/UNDOC/GEN/N02/682/26/PDF/N0268226.pdf?OpenElement. Accessed 11 October 2015.
United States Strategic Bombing Surveys, Maxwell AFB, AL: Air University Press, reprinted 1987, https://web.archive.org/web/20080528051903/http://aupress.au.af.mil/Books/USSBS/USSBS.pdf. Accessed 27 June 2017.
Wald, Charles F., "How to Defeat ISIL from the Air," *Politico*, 1 October 2014, www.politico.com/magazine/story/2014/10/how-to-defeat-isis-from-the-air-111486. Accessed 1 March 2018.
Walt, Vivienne, "Gaddafi's Son: Last Gasp of Libya's Dying Regime," *Time*, 21 February 2011, www.time.com/time/world/article/0.8599.2052842.00.html. Accessed 30 March 2015.
Yinyin, Echo Huang, "China Declares No-Sail Zone in Disputed Waters During War Game," *Defense One*, 5 July 2016, www.defenseone.com/threats/2016/07/china-declares-no-sail-zone-disputed-waters-during-wargame/129607/. Accessed 1 March 2018.
Wheeler, Nicholas J., *Saving Strangers: Humanitarian Intervention in International Society*, Oxford: Oxford University Press, 2000.

Index

10th Special Forces (SF) Group 44
24th Marine Expeditionary Unit 44
86th Tactical Fighter Wing 44

A-10 Warthog 43
Abdullah, King 100
Abizaid, John 44, 62
about no fly zones: air defense systems evaded, suppressed or destroyed 8–10; ethics of no fly zones 28–32; how no fly zones works 14–17; instances of no fly zones 4–8; matters of definition 1–2, 32n1, 32n3, 33n6; no fly zones and the maturation of air power 17–20; no fly zones compared to ground occupations 3–4; no fly zones compared to naval blockades 2–3, 33n7; requirements for no fly zones 10–14; varieties of 8; what a no fly zone can do – strategy 22–28; what a no fly zone can do – tactics 20–22
Abu Salim prison 101, 103
Afghanistan 27, 131, 143
Ahmad, Hashim, Sultan 38
Ahtisaari, Martii 95
Aidid, Mohamed Farrah 25
Air Defense Identification Zone 1, 148
air defense systems: evaded, suppressed for destroyed 8–10, 33n7, 140
Air Force (US) 19–20
air policing 17–18
air superiority 35n32
air supremacy 20, 35n32
aircraft identification 16–17
Akashi, Yasushi 69
al-Bashir, Omar 127
al-Essawi, Ali 102–103
al-Islam, Saif 102
Al Nusra 134, 137

al Qaeda 136
Albright, Madeleine 92, 93, 128
Annan, Kofi 92
Arab League 7, 11, 29, 102, 105, 138, 143
Arab Spring 100, 132
Aristide, Jean-Bertrand 26
Assad, Bashaar 8, 132, 133, 134–136, 138, 139, 141, 142, 144, 147
authorization 10–11, 29–30, 60, 139
AWACS *see* E-3 Sentry/AWACS

B-2 bombers 108
B-12 stealth bomber 12
B-52 bombers 47
Bab al-Azizia (Qaddafi's HQ) 118–119
Baker, James 41–42, 43
Banja Luka 70; shoot-down incident 73, 76, 80, 82–83
Bannon, Stephen 150
Barzani, Massoud 41, 46–47
Battle of Mogadishu 22, 25, 101–102
Bedminster, New Jersey 33n5
Beirut 25
Ben Ali, Zine el-Abidine 100
Benghazi 7, 30, 101–106, 113, 115, 117, 121, 125, 126, 131
Berlin airlift 24
Berlin declaration 116
Biafra 24–25, 35n38, 149
Bihac 70–71, 72, 79–80, 81, 85
Bilmes, Linda 16
Black Hawk Down incident 25, 45–47; helicopters 48–49
Black September Movement 103
Blair, Tony 95
Boehner, John 120
Boeing 707 48–49

Index

Bosnia xi, xii, 6–7, 8–9, 31, 45, 60, 126, 131, 140, 142, 144, 146, 149; on the conflict in the former Yugoslavia 65–67; lessons learned from the Bosnia no fly zone 96–97; NATO 65, 66, 67, 68, 69, 70, 72–73, 76, 80, 83, 87, 88, 96; Operation Antelope 78–79, 146; Operation Decisive Edge 88; Operation Deliberate Force 7, 83–89, 126; Operation Deliberate Guard 88; Operation Mistral (Bosnia/Croatia) 85; UN responses before the no fly zone 67–68; *see also* Operation Deny Flight
Bosnia Herzegovina, establishment of 88
Bouchard, Charles 115
Boutros-Ghali, Boutros 67, 76, 81, 106
Brennan, counter-terrorism chief 102
Briquemont, Francis 73, 75, 77, 89
Bush administration 40, 42, 45, 59–60, 127
Bush, George H. W. 4, 35n36, 38, 40, 43, 50, 51, 67
Bush, George W. 143
Bush, Jeb 141
Butler, Richard 6

C-130 helicopters 48–49
Cameron, David 104
Carson, Ben 141
casualties, risk of 119, 144–145
Chernomyrdin, Viktor 95
China 1, 103, 142, 148, 150
Christie, Chris 141
Churchill, Winston 18
Churkin, Vitaly 76
circular error probability 19, 34n27
Clark, Wesley 23, 94
Clarke, Richard 26
Clinton administration 86, 91, 92, 127
Clinton, Bill 47, 51, 53, 92–93, 95
Clinton, Hillary 102, 105, 107, 113, 133, 138–141
collateral damage estimate (CDE) 119
combat-air-patrol-based no fly zone 10, 34n15
combat identification 16
Combined Air Operations Center 17
Congressional Research Service xi, 16
Cot, Jean 73
Cox, Christopher (R-CA) 53
Cruz, Ted 138
CSAR (combat search and rescue planes) 13

Daalder, Ivo 87, 88–89, 113
Dabbashi, Ibrahim O. 103
Darfur xi, 126–128, 143; moral hazard and Responsibility to Protect 128–132; non-intervention policy 128–131
Dayton Peace Accords 7, 86–89, 90, 91–92
de Lapresle, General 79, 80, 81
Defense Writers Group 53
Dempsey, Martin 133, 134, 136, 137, 144, 146
diplomatic resources 11
Donilon, Tom 102, 106
drones 145–146, 147
Dunford, General 144

E-3 Sentry/AWACS 13, 14, 16, 17, 19, 34n17, 34n18, 34n29, 43, 45–47, 48–49
EA-6B Prowler 19, 48–49, 82
Erdogan, President 150
Étendard aircraft 76
ethics 28–32
exclusion zones 32n2

F-15 43; and the Black Hawk incident 45–47
F-15C 48–49
F-15E Strike Eagle 48–49, 114
F-16 17, 43, 48–49
F-16C 72
F-16CJ 82
F117A prototype 19
Farage, Nigel 150
Federal Aviation Authority 33n5
Fiorina, Carly 141
Fitzwater, Marlin 40
fixed-wing aircraft 139
Friedman, Thomas 137

Garner, Jay 44, 62
Gates, Robert, Secretary of Defense 102, 104, 105, 106, 122
geography and terrain 12–13, 39, 50, 60, 103, 113, 115, 125, 127, 139
Gilman, Benjamin (R-NY) 53
Goldwater-Nichols Act (1986) 20
Gorazde 76, 77–78, 85
Gortney, William 113
gray zone 147–148
Grenada 25
ground occupations 3–4
Gulf Cooperation Council 7, 138

Hagel, Chuck 137
Hainan Island 148

Haiti 26–27, 102
Ham, Carter 108
HARM (high-speed anti-radiation) missiles 49, 82
helicopters 139, 146; in attack role 72; flying protocol for 71; rules of engagement 71–72
Hercules C-130J 26
HJ Resolution 68 120
Holbrooke, Richard 86, 87, 91
Hungary 11
Hutu Power 26, 102
hybrid zones 147–148

IFF (identification friend or foe) 16, 17, 45–47
Implementation Force (IFOR) 87
in-air refueling 146
Incirlik Air Base, Turkey 5, 9, 12, 14, 15, 43, 47, 48–49
International Criminal Court 104, 125
International Federation for Human Rights 101
Iran 141–142
Iran Air Flight 655 16
Iraq xi, xii, 4–6, 8, 9, 27, 29, 31, 126, 131, 142, 143, 149; assessing no fly zones 56–61; cost of land war 16; cost of no fly zones: financial 58, *59*; cost of no fly zones: lives 57, *58*, *59*; establishing the first no fly zone 38–40; geography and terrain 39, 50; lessons learned from 61–62; northern no fly zone 40–49; NATO 22; Operation Desert Fox 49, 53–54, 59–60; Operation Desert Strike 47, *58*; Operation Hammer 47; Operation Haven 4, 22–23, 33n13; Operation Intrinsic Action *58*; Operation Iraqi Freedom 21, 27, 47, 52, *58*; post Desert Fox no fly zone enforcement 54–56 ; southern no fly zone 49–54; US troops extracted 22; *see also* individual operations
Iraq Liberation Act (1988) 53
Iraq Survey Group 52
ISIS 27, 137, 141
Islamic State 126, 137
Israel 20, 141–142
Italy 12, 142

J-21 Jastreb 17
J-22 Oraos 17
Jaguar aircraft 48, 49

Jalil, Mustafa Abdel 103, 104
Jamerson, James 43, 44
Janvier, Bernard 81, 83, 85, 86–87
Jibril, Mahmud 102–103
jihadist forces 147
Jodice, Ralph 115–118
Joint Publications 3–0, *Joint Operations: Exclusions Zones* 32n2
Joint Task Force Odyssey Dawn (Libya) *see* Operation Odyssey Dawn (Libya)
Joint Task Force-Southwest Asia 51
Jones, Jim 44, 62
JTF Alpha 44
JTF Bravo 44
jus ad bellum 36n46
jus ad vim 29, 36n46
Just and Unjust Wars 28–29
just war theory 30–32

Kaczynski, Lech 150
Karadzic, Radovan 76, 87
Karremans, Lieutenant Colonel 84
Kasich, John 141
KC-97 Stratofighters 24
Keegan, John 18, 96
Kennan, George 57
Khobar Towers, Saudi Arabia 12, 52
Kosovo 23, 89–96
Kosovo Force (KFOR) 95
Kosovo Liberation Army (KLA) 90, 91, 92
Kosovo Verification Mission (KVM) 91
Kuperman, Alan 31, 128–131
Kurdistan Patriotic Union (KDP) 41, 46–47, 52
Kurdistan Worker's Party (PKK) 47
Kurds 4–6, 22–23, 40, 133, 139, 140; autonomy 46–47; infighting 52; refugees 33n13; Saddam's attacks on 41–42, 48, 59–60
Kurth, James 29
Kuwait 22, 60

"La Belle" nightclub, West Berlin 103
Lake, Anthony 128
laser-guided bombs 19, 34n27
Libya 7–8, 8, 9, 13, 27, 31, 60, 131, 132, 136, 138, 142, 143; air defenses 112; aircraft carriers 108; aircraft used 108, 117; "all necessary measures" 100, 113, 115, 122, 138–139; assessing the Libya no fly zone 121–122; and China 103; combat search and rescue (CSAR) 114; downed pilots 114;

executing Odyssey Dawn 108–114; executing Unified Protector 114–121; geography and terrain 103, 113, 115, 125; lessons learned 122; NATO 94, 105–108, 113, 115, 118, 121, 125, 131, 139; no fly zone enforcement 112; protection of civilians 116; summary of coalitions forces *109–111*; surface-to-air missiles 112; target approval 114, 117; United Nations' response 101–105; uprising in 100–101; *see also* individual operations
Libya Contact Group 119–120
Lockerbie, Scotland 103
Locklear, Samuel 108, 116, 119
logistics 12

MacArthur, General 104
Major, John 42
Malaysian Airlines Flight 17 8, 147, 148
Marine Corps (US) 19–20, 44
Markale marketplace 66, 76, 86
May, Theresa 150
MC-130E 43
McCain, John 136, 137
McPeak, Merrill 128
Mesopotamia 17–18
message sending xii
Mi-24 Hind 72
military resources 11
Milosevic, Slobodan 7, 23, 25, 28, 30, 60, 86, 87, 90–96, 147, 149
Mirage 2000 87
Mirage 2000D 72
Misrata, Libya 119
Mladic, Ratko 76, 79, 85, 86–87
moral hazard 128–132
Mount Igman 73, 75
MQ-1 Predator 78
MQ-9 Reaper 78
Mubarak, Hosni 100
Mueller, Karl 10, 32n1
Mullen, Mike 106

nation-building 132
National Conference for the Libyan Opposition 101
National Security Strategy (NSS) 147
NATO xi, 6, 11, 14, 21, 29, 143; Bosnia 65, 66, 67, 68, 69, 70, 72–73, 76, 80, 83, 87, 88, 96; Iraq 22; Joint Task Force Odyssey Dawn 108; Kosovo 89–96, 92; legitimate targets 118–119; Libya 94, 105–108, 113, 115, 118, 121, 125, 131, 139
naval blockades 2–3, 33n7
navigation 18–19
Navy (US) 19–20
NCTR (non-cooperative target recognition) 16–17
New York Times 136
no fly zones: combat air patrol vs offensive counter air no fly zones 10; compared to ground occupations 3–4; compared to naval blockades 2–3, 33n7; costs: financial and lives 57–59; difficult to execute 146; in domestic politics 138–142; effectiveness xii, 57, 60–61; enforced constantly or intermittently 9; equipment and personnel 14–15; ethics 28–32; flexibility 54; formal or informal 8; hybrid and gray zones 147–148; instances of 4–8; and jihadist forces 147; last resort 31; length of 3; lessons learned from Bosnia 96–97; lessons learned from Iraq 61–62; lessons learned from Libya 122; limitations to 61, 89, 131, 138; and the maturation of air power 17–20; method of initiation 144; in new light 126–142; operation 14–17; politics of 125–126; probability of success 30–31; "proof of concept" 20; proper intent 30; proportionality 32; pros and cons xii–xiii; prospects for 142–148; punitive measures immediate or delayed 9; requirements for 10–14; and sanctuaries 9; strategy 22–28; tactics 20–22; utility of 55; weaknesses 53
no sail zones 142, 148
Norden bombsight 18, 34n24
North Atlantic Council 73, 115, 116
Nuclear Non-Proliferation Treaty 48

Obama administration 102, 105, 128, 137
Obama, Barack 27, 104, 105, 106, 107, 132, 133, 134–135, 137, 143
Obey, David 26
offensive counter air (OCA) model 10
O'Grady, Scott 82–83, 84
O'Hanlon, Michael 33n8
Operation Allied Force (Kosovo) 23, 89–96
Operation Antelope (Bosnia) 78–79, 146
Operation Decisive Edge (Bosnia) 88

Operation Deliberate Force (Bosnia) 7, 83–89, 126
Operation Deliberate Guard (Bosnia) 88
Operation Deny Flight (Bosnia) xii, 6–7, 9, 12, 21, 24, 31, 32n2, 69–83, 88, 89, 96, 102, 141, 146, 149, 150; after Gorazde 77–78; aircraft used 70, *74–75*; attacks on air defense systems 33n7; and Bosnian Serb air defenses 29; Bosnian Serbs challenge no fly zone 79–82; the Captain Scott O'Grady shoot-down 82–83; enforcement and patrolling 14, 17; experimentation with enforcement 73–77; geographical conditions 12, 13; Operation Antelope 78–79; operational requirements 72–73; proper intent 30; repeat of 142–147; success of 72; and UNPROFOR 73, 75–78, 79
Operation Desert Fox (Iraq) 49, 53–54, 59–60; costs of *58*
Operation Desert Storm (Iraq) xi, 3, 4, 5, 8, 20, 29, 35n36, 38, 60, 81, 133; attacks on air defense systems 34n19; costs of *58*; proper intent 30
Operation Desert Strike (Iraq) 47; costs of *58*
Operation Ellamy *see* Operation Odyssey Dawn (Libya)
Operation Enduring Freedom (Afghanistan) 27
Operation Hammer (Iraq) 47
Operation Harmattan *see* Operation Odyssey Dawn (Libya)
Operation Haven (Iraq) 4, 22–23; personnel 33n13
Operation Horseshoe (Kosovo) 91, 93
Operation Inherent Resolve (ISIS) 27
Operation Intrinsic Action (Iraq) *58*
Operation Iraqi Freedom (Iraq) 21, 27, 47, 52, *58*
Operation Krivaja (Bosnian Serb Army) 84–89
Operation Mistral (Bosnia/Croatia) 85
Operation Mistral 2 (Bosnia/Croatia) 87
Operation Mobile *see* Operation Odyssey Dawn (Libya)
Operation Mole Cricket 19 (Syria) 20, 34n31
Operation Northern Watch (Iraq) xii, 4–6, 9, 12, 21, 23, 24, 33n12, 47–49, 102, 126, 145; aircraft used, standard package *15*; attacks on air defense systems 33n7; challenges in imposing 16–17; costs 15–16, *58*; enforcement and patrolling 13–14, 48–49; equipment and personnel 14–15, 34n15; geographical conditions 12; proper intent 30
Operation Odyssey Dawn (Libya) 7–8, 9, 10, 12, 24, 27, 29, 108–114, 131; attacks on air defense systems 33n7; geographical conditions 12; proper intent 30
Operation Provide Comfort (Iraq) 4–6, 23, 24, 33n13, 40–49, 126, 132–133, 140, 149, 150; aircraft used 43; costs of *58*; proper intent 30
Operation Sky Monitor (Yugoslavia) 11, 13, 21, 68
Operation Southern Watch (Iraq) xii, 4–6, 12, 21, 32n2, 49–54, 102, 126, 145, 149; attacks on air defense systems 33n7; costs 15–16; costs of *58*; geographical conditions 12; proper intent 30
Operation Storm (Croatian government) 85
Operation Unified Protector (Libya) 7, 10, 24, 114–121, 125, 126, 142; geographical conditions 12; proper intent 30
Operation Uphold Democracy (Haiti) 26–27
Operation Vigilant Warrior (Iraq) 51–53; costs of *58*
Orban, Viktor 150
Organization of the Islamic Conference 102

Pale bombing 78–79, 81, 83, 84, 87
Pan Am Flight 103 103
Panetta, Leon 133
Pape, Robert 3
Patriotic Union of Kurdistan (PUK) 41, 46–47
peacekeeping 77, 140
Peoples Liberation Army Navy 148
permissive entry 27
"perpetual petrol problem" 10
Petraeus, David 133
pilot loss 57, *58*
PLO 34n31
politics 125–126; domestic 138–142
Potter, Richard 44
Powell, Colin 88
Power, Samantha 102

PPLI (precise participant location and identification) 16
Presidential Decision Directive 25 26
Prince Sultan Air Base 12
prohibited zones 2, 33n5
proportionality 32
Putin, Vladimir 140, 145, 147, 150

Qaddafi, Muammar 7–8, 9, 29, 30, 96, 100, 131, 143, 144; atrocities 102, 103, 104; and Black September Movement 103; defense network 112; executed 121, 125; family assets frozen 104; flees to Sirte 121; headquarters at Bab al-Azizia 118–119; lost legitimacy 118; uprising against 100–101, 105

Racak 91
radar 16, 17, 19, 55, 82
radio 26
RAND Corporation xi, 27–28; report (2013) 32n1
Rasmussen, Anders Fogh 115
RC-135 Rivet Joint aircraft 18–19, 48–49
rebels, arming and training of 136–137
reconnaissance 18–19
refugees 142
regime change 53, 59, 131, 132, 143
Republican Guard (Saddam) 6, 41, 50, 51, 54
Republican National Convention 2
Responsibility to Protect (R2P) 30, 100, 101, 104, 127, 128–132
"retrospective SEAD" (suppression of enemy air defenses) 80
Rice, Susan 102, 106
Ricks, Tom 56–57
risk-to-benefit analysis 144–145
Robin, Linda 27–28
Rome Statute of the International Criminal Court 101
Rose, Michael 75, 76, 77–79, 80, 81, 146
Rubio, Marco 141
rules of engagement 2–3, 13, 17; helicopters 71–72; Operation Sky Monitor 68; permissive 106, 107
Russia 140, 144, 150; and Kosovo 91, 92; and Ukraine 8, 148; US relations with 95
Rwanda 26, 102, 126, 127–128, 149
Ryan, Michael 83, 86

S-400 missile 140, 144
SA-6 surface-to-air missile 34n31
SA-8 mobile surface-to-air missile 119
Saddam Hussein 4, 6, 21, 22, 23, 29, 31, 35n36, 38, 48, 133, 139, 140, 147, 149; attacks on Kurds 41–42, 48, 59–60; attacks on Shia 41–42; containing 39–40, 56–57, 60–61; defiance 45, 55, 56; despised 60; KDP requests assistance 46–47; Operation Desert Fox and 53–54; Operation Northern Watch and 40; Operation Southern Watch and 49–54; Operation Vigilant Warrior and 51–53; weapons of mass destruction 52–53
safe zones 9, 21–22, 85, 140, 141
sanctuaries 9, 140
Sarkozy, Nicholas 102–103, 104, 107
Save Darfur movement 127, 129
Schelling, Thomas 93
Schmitt, Michael N. 32n3
Schwarzkopf, Norman 4, 5, 22, 38–39
Sea Harrier 72, 76
SEAD (suppression of enemy air defenses) missions 82
seizures of airspace 8
Selva, General 137–138
September 11, 2001 27, 40
Shalgam, Abdurrahman 103
Shalikashvili, John 43, 44, 62
Shelton, Hugh 54
Shia 40; Operation Southern Watch and 49–51; Saddam's attack on 41–42
Shi'ites 4, 5, 6
Short, Michael 94
Silkworm missiles 45
skills, improved 19–20
sky monitors 8
Smith, Leighton "Snuffy" 77–80, 83, 85, 87
Smith, Rupert 81, 82, 83, 86
Somalia 22, 25, 35n40, 127
Soubirou, André 78
sovereignty 28
Srebrenica xii, 31, 83–89
Stabilization Force (SFOR) 88
Staglitz, Joe 16
stand-off warfare 3, 33n8
Stavridis, James 115
Suleiman, Omar 100
Supreme Council of Armed Forces (SCAF) 100
surface-to-air missiles 34n31
Syria xi, 60, 128, 132–138, 137, 141, 143, 144

Index 165

Tahrir Square, Cairo 100
Talabani, Jalal 41, 46–47
Talbott, Strobe 95, 139
targeteers 117
targeting 18–19
technologies, improved 145–146
temporizing 141
Terbil, Fathi 101
TFR (temporary flight restriction) 33n5
Tornado aircraft 48, 49
training, improved 19–20
Transportation Security Administration 33n5
Trump, Donald J. 33n5, 138, 143–144, 150
Turkey 5, 9, 12, 33n12, 42, 137; limits imposed by 47, 48, 54, 60

Udbina air base 79–82
Ukraine 8, 148
United Nations xi, 6, 11, 13, 14, 29, 32n2, 50, 65, 126–127
United Nations Charter 149
United Nations Declaration of a Responsibility to Protect (2005) 30, 100, 101, 104, 127, 128–132
United Nations General Assembly 21
United Nations Inspectors 52–54, 56
United Nations Interim Administration in Kosovo (UNMIK) 96
United Nations Iraq-Kuwait Observation Mission 39
United Nations Monitoring Verification and Inspection Commission (UNMOVIC) 56
United Nations Protection Force (UNPROFOR) 6–7, 67–68, 85, 86, 88, 89; Dutch peacekeepers 84–85; French soldiers 82; hostages 67–77, 68, 80, 81, 82, 83, 89; and Operation Deny Flight 69–70, 73, 75–77, 76, 77–78, 79
United Nations Security Council 11, 21, 29, 53, 104, 125, 143
United Nations Security Council Resolution 678 5
United Nations Security Council Resolution 686 38
United Nations Security Council Resolution 687 39, 48, 52
United Nations Security Council Resolution 688 42, 50
United Nations Security Council Resolution 713 67
United Nations Security Council Resolution 743 67
United Nations Security Council Resolution 757 67
United Nations Security Council Resolution 781 6
United Nations Security Council Resolution 816 6, 69
United Nations Security Council Resolution 836 69, 73
United Nations Security Council Resolution 844 69
United Nations Security Council Resolution 949 51
United Nations Security Council Resolution 1160 90
United Nations Security Council Resolution 1199 90
United Nations Security Council Resolution 1203 91
United Nations Security Council Resolution 1244 96
United Nations Security Council Resolution 1284 56
United Nations Security Council Resolution 1441 56
United Nations Security Council Resolution 1970 104, 116
United Nations Security Council Resolution 1973 7, 106–107, 113, 115, 116, 122, 138, 143
United Nations Special Commission on Iraq (UNSCOM) 21, 52–53, 56
United States: implementation of no fly zones 1; no fly zones as exclusion zones 32n2; Russia, relations with 95
USS Princeton 3

Vietnam Syndrome 22, 23, 24
Vietnam War 18, 59, 83, 145
Vincennes incident 16
Voorhoeve, Defense Minister 84
Vrbanja Bridge 82

Wahlgren, Lars Eric 69
Wald, Charles 43
Wald, Charles F. 137
Walzer, Michael 28–29
weapons inspections/inspections 6
weapons of mass destruction (WMD) 52–53
Weinberger principles 25
White House, flight restrictions surrounding 2, 33n5
Woodward, Margaret "Maggie" 104, 108, 113, 117

World War II 18
Wright, Gordon 70

Xi Jinping 147, 150

Yeltsin, Boris 95
Yom Kippur War (1974) 34n30

Younes, Abdel Fattah 117, 121
Yugoslavia 27, 31, 65–67; Operation Sky Monitor (Yugoslavia) 11, 13, 21, 68

Zawiya, Libya 104
Zepa safe area 85
Zinni, Anthony 6, 21, 23, 53, 54, 56–57